PRAY SILENCE FOR 'JOCK' WHITTINGTON

PRAY SILENCE FOR
'JOCK' WHITTINGTON

From Building Sewers
to Suing Builders

❧❧

Sir Francis McWilliams GBE

Malu Publications

2002

First published in England by
Malu Publications
PO Box 3415, Brighton BN2 1WZ

JAK cartoon
by kind permission of *Evening Standard*, London

ISBN 0-9543332-0-9

Typeset from the author's disk by Scriptmate Editions
Garamond True Type 12/13pt

Manufacture coordinated in UK by Book-in-Hand Ltd
20 Shepherds Hill, London N6 5AH

To Wyn

'Wit and grace and love and beauty in ae constellation shine,
To adore thee is my duty goddess o' this soul o' mine'

Robert Burns

Acknowledgement

Throughout my life I have been most fortunate that many people too numerous to mention individually have helped and supported me.

First of all were my parents and my brother, sisters, teachers, priests and nuns, and many friends.

Finally and importantly were Wyn to whom this book is dedicated, my sons Douglas and Michael and their wives Ianthe and Rowena. Nor must we forget Christopher my grandson.

I owe a great debt to them all.

Contents

Prologue

'My Lord Mayor, you are probably a target for the IRA.'

This dramatic announcement came from Douglas Woodward the Chief Commoner, leader of the Common Council of the City of London.

We were in a hotel room in Warsaw on an official visit to Poland. An urgent message had come through from the Commissioner of the City of London Police Owen Kelly that I should be warned of the danger. Later my wife Wyn and I were told that we should vary the route to and from our home in St Albans to avoid the possibility of ambush.

At first I was slightly shocked, but then I realized that after the explosion of the huge bomb in Bishopsgate in the City of London two months earlier on 24th April 1993, my profile as Lord Mayor could not have been higher. I had assured the world that, whatever the IRA or anyone else could do to try to disrupt the business of the City, we were tough enough and had a robust enough infrastructure to deal with it. We believed that since the objective of the terrorists was to cause maximum disruption to that business, it was our task to ensure that the disruption was kept to a minimum. Otherwise they had won. The City and the staff of the City Corporation had responded magnificently to the demands made on them.

I told the world on television and by radio that the City would be back in action by Monday morning!

The bomb had gone off just after 10.20 am on the Saturday.

My statement was usually made against the backdrop of the City Nat West Tower with gaping windows and curtains blowing in the breeze. The pictures flashed around the world. My sister Jean phoned from Australia to say that she had seen me on the news. It was all a bit theatrical, but it got the message across. The message was simple. Unquestionably we had had a major incident. We were not denying it. But we wanted the world to know that we had the resilience and the robustness to cope.

Never, never in my life, have I felt so proud as when City workers streamed through Liverpool Street Station on that Monday after the bomb. The stationmaster said that it was just like any other Monday. London, which had survived plagues, fires and the devastation of the blitz, was not about to be cowed by an IRA bomb.

So I should not really have been surprised that I might be a target. I suppose that if you stick your head above the parapet you can expect to be shot at. Despite the scale of the damage, the bomb attack had not been the propaganda coup that the IRA had expected. I imagine that to some extent they blamed me.

My next reaction to the chief commoner's news was, 'Should I tell Wyn my wife? How would she react? Would it be fair to burden her with the knowledge?' I decided to tell her as, if she was about to lose her husband, she had a right to know. As I returned to our room I rehearsed what I would say to break the news gently. After over forty years of marriage I should have known better than to have misgivings about Wyn's courage and strength of character. She put her arms round me and said, 'If anything happens to you, I hope that it will happen to me at the same time.' She then smiled and continued brightly, 'If they do get us we can't really complain. We've had a wonderfully exciting life and have enjoyed ourselves all the way.' What a woman!

She was undoubtedly right. Our life together has been improbable, exciting and enormously enjoyable. I had journeyed from a very modest terrace house in Edinburgh to the medieval splendour of the Guildhall in the City of London. I was the holder of one of the best-known and most prestigious offices in the land. There was sufficient parallel to the legend of the most famous holder of the office of Lord Mayor of London for one of the Scottish newspapers (I think that it was the *Daily Record*) to dub me 'Jock Whittington'.

An Edinburgh childhood

Every year near Christmas in theatres around the country panto-mimes are staged. These are fantasy stories such as Cinderella, Jack and the Beanstalk, Aladdin and others. One of the most popular is 'Dick Whittington'. This tells the story of a boy from humble origins who comes into the City of London and through good fortune rises to become The Lord Mayor. Although Sir Richard Whittington was a real person the pantomimes are a fantasy and fantasies do not happen in real life. Or do they?

This is the story of a Scottish boy from a very modest family—a family of six children that had known unemployment and hardship. He was brought up in Portobello, a seaside suburb of Edinburgh.

Through the sacrifices of his parents and the determination of his mother to see that her children were educated the boy, the fifth of the six children, is sent to university to study civil engineering. By a stroke of good fortune he meets and marries a wonderful girl.

Their sense of adventure takes them to the tropical paradise of Malaya. They produce two brilliant sons. An act of kindness results in a friendship with a man who becomes the Ruler of the State of Selangor and eventually the King of Malaysia. They become friends also of many of the leading figures in the new Malaysia.

At the age of fifty the pair return to England. Purely by chance they come to live in the City of London. The Scottish boy is elected first to the Court of Common Council, then Alderman for the ward of Aldersgate, then Sheriff of the City of London and finally becomes Lord Mayor.

Fantasies do happen in real life and this is how it all happened.

My father, Sergeant John McWilliams MM of the 8th Battalion Royal Scots was undoubtedly a war hero. He was proud of his war service but like many of his contemporaries the horror of it all never really left him. He was reluctant to speak about why he had been decorated with the Military Medal, for 'bravery in the field'.

Like many young men of the time he had been a member of the Territorial Army. He was called to active service at the very beginning of the war and served throughout the conflict. He was one of those who called themselves the 'old contemptibles', after the Kaiser's reference to 'a contemptible little army', who served from the start of the war.

According to those who had served with him from 1914 to 1918 he inspired calm confidence in the most dangerous situations. Often under heavy shellfire, he led the horse-drawn wagons taking supplies to the front lines during the major battles of the war like Mons, Ypres and the Somme. He came through the dreadful carnage unharmed. My mother said that she had spoken with some of my father's comrades in arms and they regarded my father as lucky to be with.

The only thing I can remember him telling us about the war was about the first Christmas when he was in the trenches in the front lines. It was Christmas Eve. Just about midnight the British soldiers heard, quietly at first but gradually increasing in volume, the Germans in the trenches opposite singing the carol 'Stille Nacht' (Silent Night). When it was finished the British soldiers sang. So it went on through the night, each side taking it in turn to sing. Next morning they exchanged gifts and there was a football match. I gathered that neither the British nor the German authorities were pleased with this fraternisation.

My father had, apparently, been offered a field commission but had been dissuaded from accepting by my mother. The casualty rate among 2nd Lieutenants was enormous. German snipers easily picked them out, because they were the ones carrying revolvers while the others carried rifles. My mother preferred to have a live sergeant rather than a dead officer.

Lloyd George had promised 'a land fit for heroes', but the returning sergeant found great difficulty in settling down to civilian life. I was born on the 8th February 1926 at 2 Carlyle Place, Edinburgh. This is a very modest terrace house halfway between the city centre and Portobello. Later we moved to Portobello. My birth certificate gives my father's occupation as a spirit dealer's assistant. I understand that he was working for a cousin of his who owned a public house.

My first memory of my father was when he was working for McVities, a well-known Edinburgh bakery, delivering bread. He had a horse-drawn van. I think that it must have been one of the happiest times of his life, being in charge of a horse and travelling around meeting people. I believe that he lost this job when they decided to change over to motor-vans. Although he could drive, he loved the horse and argued (too strongly as it turned out) to retain the horses. This would have been around 1929. The middle of a world recession is not a good time to argue yourself out of a job.

At that time horse-drawn vehicles made most major deliveries. Milk, coal and bread vehicles used single horses. Pairs of horses pulled the vehicles delivering heavier loads such as beer. Keen gardeners watched out for the horses passing, with bucket and shovel at the ready to dash out to pick up the horse-dung. There was great competition and you had to be quick. After a period of unemployment my father had a variety of jobs. Some of them he lost because he felt that he knew more than those in charge. He probably did, but he was not always very tactful in the way that he said it. For a while he was working on the erection of power lines and the construction of the power station at Portobello where we lived. He was on the roof of the power station on the day shortly after war broke out in 1939 when a lone German fighter plane flew over spraying bullets at him and his fellow workers. I thought that this was very exciting. It was probably because of my father's connection with building works that I eventually decided to study Civil Engineering.

He had a wide variety of friends and considerable sensitivity. He seemed to have friends everywhere. My brother John and I got involved in impromptu football games on the beach on Sunday afternoons. I think I was involved because the ball was mine. As choirboys we had already been to not one, but two church services. We were due to go to two more later in the day. On the principle that we had already followed the Commandment to keep holy the Sabbath day, we saw nothing wrong with enjoying ourselves between services. Someone spoke to my father about the football. He took the view that although he was personally quite happy with what we were doing, we had to respect the feelings of our Presbyterian neighbours who did not think that it was proper to take part in football games on the Sabbath. We gave up Sunday football. We played table tennis and snooker instead.

This respect for other people's feelings is one of the memories of my childhood. If someone in the street died the curtains of the neighbouring houses would be closed as a sign of sympathy. If a funeral passed along the road people would stop and men would remove their hats as a mark of respect for the deceased. Nowadays we all seem to be much too concerned with our own rights to worry about respect for the feelings of others.

On another occasion my father heard from one of his friends that I had been playing cards for money at the Home Guard. He pointed out that I could not afford to lose money that way. I answered that I had in fact won, not lost. He took the view that, as a matter of principle, if you can't afford to lose you should not gamble. He was right, of course. That was the end of my card playing for money. Probably because of him I hate seeing people who look as though they cannot afford it buying tickets in the National Lottery. I am deeply sceptical about gambling of any sort and in particular about the value of the Lottery.

My father had been caught in one of the German gas attacks during the 1914/18 war. In later life his lungs started to cause him problems. He decided that, although he liked working outside, doing so in all sorts of weather was not good for his health so he took a job as a process worker in a factory owned by Unilever. He remained there until ill health eventually forced him to retire early. For as long as I can remember he had great faith in an ointment called 'Snowfire'. It came in the form of a green block, which softened with body heat. He used it for rubbing his chest if he had a cold; for strains; for skin infections and any other form of illness. When we lived in Longridge he came to stay with us on a visit. We had a leaking valley gutter and as it was raining heavily we could not get anyone out to repair it. My father's solution was 'Snowfire'. He softened it in his hand and I applied it to the damaged gutter where it hardened. It worked.

Going to auction sales gave my father great enjoyment. He was an avid reader and would return from them with large quantities of books. I think that he bought them by the yard. This made him a very useful source of information when it came to essay writing or history. He also bought golf clubs at the sales. There were always plenty of the hickory-shafted clubs and old golf-bags in the house.

Golf in Scotland was very cheap. We all played golf at one time or another and to this day I play when I can find the time. The course that we played on was at one time in the Guinness Book of Records as the cheapest golf course in the world. When we played we could buy a season ticket for three old pence and then it cost only a penny a round. It now costs about £5.00 a round.

In all the years that I have played I have never had a hole-in-one. The only time that I might have claimed one was when I was about twelve. I had hit my tee-shot over a mound in front of the green and when my partner, Tom Lynch, and I reached the green we found the ball in the hole. There were two little urchins running hell for leather away from the green. Being Scotland, if the ball had gone into the hole of its own accord, I was sure that they would have stayed to make some remark. I had to conclude from their flight that they had put the ball in the hole. So sixty years on I am still trying.

My father was a very sociable man. In Edinburgh there is a custom of presenting wooden benches in memory of deceased persons. These are placed at strategic locations. In my father's retirement years he was often to be found sitting on one of these seats meeting friends and exchanging local gossip. When I was Lord Mayor on one of my visits to Edinburgh I presented and unveiled a bench in memory of my parents. It is located on a corner near where my father enjoyed his frequent gossips. My brother-in-law Bill Hunter was sitting on the bench one day waiting for a bus. Two local worthies sat down beside him. They were discussing the fact that a Portobello 'laddie' who had become Lord Mayor of London had presented it. 'He is my brother-in-law' Bill said. 'Ask him when he is going to put some cushions on it', commented one of them.

In retrospect I think that my father knew that he should have achieved more than he did. Later I believe that he came to terms with it and he was content to see the achievements of his children as the justification of his life. He was a great storyteller. In his retirement he could often be found with his grandchildren grouped around him, as he regaled them with some fantasy tale that he made up as he went along.

I was playing golf with my elder son Douglas one day. I remarked that my father would have been pleased that one of his sons was a member of The Honourable Company of Edinburgh Golfers, one of Scotland's most prestigious golf clubs. At the time I was rising up the ladder in the Court of Aldermen in the City of London. Douglas replied, 'I imagine that he would also have been happy to know that his son was well on the way to becoming the Lord Mayor of London.' He would have been bursting with pride.

My mother was born in Kilty Clogher, a village in the West of Ireland. Wyn and I have visited it. It is an attractive place set in some lovely countryside. The soil is very poor and it is easy to see why many generations found it necessary to emigrate. The people are very friendly. We were introduced to a number of people named McSherry, my mother's maiden name, and Gallacher, my grandmother's maiden name.

My mother was brought to Scotland when she was six weeks old. Her parents settled in a mining village called Fauldhouse about halfway between Edinburgh and Glasgow. There she grew up. After she left school, she was for a while a trainee teacher in a local school. Eventually however she became housekeeper to a brother and sister who owned a large house in Edinburgh. The experience widened her horizons considerably. The brother George Robb, a lawyer, lived with us for a number of years after his sister died. I think that my mother had promised the sister when she was dying that she would provide a home for her brother. Mr. Robb died when I was quite young.

My parents married in 1915. It must have been on my father's leave from France. Pictures of them, my father in his army uniform, show them to be a handsome couple. Like most children however I remember my parents as being old, my father balding and slightly plump and my mother's hair streaked with grey. Over the ten years between 1919 and 1929 my mother produced six strong healthy children, four daughters and two sons Isobel, Helen, John, Jean, Francis and Patricia. She was formidably ambitious for them.

She was a good manager. Somehow through all the difficult periods she was able to feed and clothe her growing brood. Even in the periods, during and after the Second World War, when food was rationed, she managed to provide nourishing fare for us all. Both her scotch broth and her potato soup were legendary. Her mainstay was stew. This contained a small amount of meat, lots of gravy, suet dumplings called doughboys and mountains of potatoes. The stock for her soup was derived from marrowbones which butchers were happy to get rid of. How would we have survived in this age of BSE? Chicken was a luxury sometimes served for Christmas dinner. But that depended on the state of family finances.

I was talking to my sister Helen recently about the occasion that my mother sold a beautiful oval-shaped rosewood table. I think that she had inherited it from the Robbs, her former employers. I was in the house when the second-hand furniture dealer came. He looked at the table, sucked his teeth, and said that it was awfu' heavy, and that nobody would want it. He would however as a friendly gesture take it off her hands and give her 10 shillings. Lord knows what such a table would be worth today.

Helen remembered the sale of the table and the reason for it. It was a typical example of my mother juggling with her resources. My eldest sister Isobel and Helen had joined the Girl Guides. They needed uniforms. The table was sold but the proceeds would only buy one new and one second-hand uniform. Because she was the elder Isobel got the new uniform. Helen to her chagrin had to be content with the other, with the hat several sizes too large resting on her ears. My school friends and my friends from university enjoyed visiting our house. If they were there at a mealtime my mother seemed to adopt the 'put another potato in the pot' principle. My father could generally be relied upon to take part in any debate that was going on with my friends. One of them said to me one day that he wished that his own father, who seemed to be very stern and lacking in humour, was like mine. We lived in Portobello, which lies two and a half miles to the east of Edinburgh. In the 1930s before holidays in Spain became the norm, Portobello was a popular seaside resort beloved by Glaswegians. They used to spend their annual holidays on the beaches. Portobello has a main High Street with a series of streets, which run off it towards the beach.

My memories start when we lived in Wellington Street. This was a very pleasant street running towards the beach. I liked the house and was disappointed when we moved to a flat in Bath Street a short distance to the west. Bath Street also runs towards the beach but it was a much busier street. The flat was up a staircase where there were three other flats. I think that we moved for two reasons: the rent was five shillings per week cheaper and one of my mother's friends, a very domineering lady called Mrs. McCusker, lived in one of the other flats on the staircase. The flat that we occupied had once been the first convent in Portobello. The nuns of the Ursuline Order who taught at St. John's school had lived there. Later when my mother's legs were giving her a lot of trouble we moved to a ground floor flat further up Bath Street so that she would not have to climb the stairs. In Britain because the prevailing wind is from the southwest the industry and poorer class housing is usually located on the eastern side of towns. In Portobello the reverse is true. The better class housing was to the east. We had moved west.

During the Summer school holidays my mother would send some of us to her mother in Fauldhouse. She used the rooms that we vacated to take in what she called, paying guests. Between that and my father taking part-time work in the evenings in a local hotel we children never realised that we were actually quite poor. For my part I have to confess that it was only when I went to University that I realised the kind of sacrifices that my parents must have made to ensure that their children had the best education possible.

My sisters hated going to Fauldhouse but John and I enjoyed it enormously. We had lots of cousins and there were all sorts of exciting things to do. We played on railway lines, climbed up huge coal tips and indulged in other such dangerous occupations which would certainly have incurred my mother's wrath had she known. For us Fauldhouse was another world. It was populated by miners who earned their living by going down into the bowels of the earth in cages, lowered from giant wheels. Miners had faces blackened by coal-dust and walked through the streets wearing hard helmets with little lamps on the front. The lamps contained carbide which, when wetted, gave off a gas which provided a flame. Miners coughed a lot, smoked cigarettes that they rolled themselves, or smoked foul-smelling tobacco in clay pipes. They also had scars that were blue in colour. Apparently if they got a cut when they were down in the mine they rubbed it with coal-dust. Coal-dust was supposed to be a disinfectant but I understand that it also helped provide evidence of an injury that enabled the miners to apply for compensation. When the cut healed it took on a blue colour.

At weekends groups of men would gather in secluded places and play pitch and toss. They would bet on whether the two pennies, which were flipped up in the air by one of the players, would come down as heads or tails. If they were not flipping coins they were playing card games such as pontoon or brag. They did not object to us as we watched fascinated by it all. However, gambling was at that time illegal. If the crowd of watching children became so large that it might attract the attention of the police the players would chase us away.

Miners also had strange hobbies. One of these was a game of quoits, pronounced 'kites', which was played with heavy steel rings. The rings were thrown from one end of the pitch to land in a clay pit about 15 yards away. In the centre of the pit a steel spike was embedded. The object of the game was to try to ring the spike. From what we could see the game was an excuse for gambling and a lot of money changed hands. Greyhounds and their smaller cousins, whippets, were another hobby. These were apparently raced at tracks, which existed all around Fauldhouse. I picked up such useful pieces of information as, how to slow your dog down so that no one would notice. This was done by coating the inside of the dogs groin with soap solution. After the soap had hardened, a dog racing would shorten its stride because if it stretched fully it would pull the hairs. Thus it would appear to be racing at full speed but was losing two or three inches on every stride. Over a quarter of a mile this would amount to several yards. The soap could be sponged off quickly after the race.

The miners also kept pigeons. Periodically they sent them off in cages. The cages were loaded on to lorries and sent to distant places. The owner then waited anxiously for the birds to return. Before they were sent off the birds, which were male, were put in a cage with a female bird for a short time and then removed. This was to remind them of the sexual delights that awaited them on their return. It was supposed to make them return home quicker. Each bird in the race had a ring put on its leg. When the bird returned the ring was removed and put into a special clock to determine the winner. My grandmother in Fauldhouse was a tall woman. When she was dressed to go shopping on a Friday, she wore a large hat and looked very formidable. She had a strong Irish accent. She employed a boy to carry the large amount of groceries that she purchased. After her shopping expedition she used to bake on her open coal fire. She baked mainly girdle scones and potato scones and her sons, my uncles, who all lived nearby, came in one after another to sample her baking which they had known since childhood. We children waited our turn to taste the delicious warm scones spread with butter and strawberry jam.

It never ceases to amuse me that Catholics are usually referred to as 'devout', whilst Presbyterians are referred to as 'staunch'. Be that as it may, my mother was indeed a devout Catholic and was a frequent attender at morning Mass. Sometimes she must have been weary with her household duties and in pain because of varicose veins, which afflicted her for as long as I can remember, but she hardly ever went on a holiday. Apart from the odd visit to the cinema or the Women's Guild she had few outside interests. When she had the chance to sit down she was a reader of romantic fiction.

She was dedicated to the task of seeing that her children, especially her sons, were successful. My mother wept when the Conservative Party was defeated at the General Election in 1945, believing that the country should have shown its gratitude to Winston Churchill by re-electing his party into power. She said that she would never vote again.

My mother never owned a modern household appliance and only very late in her life had electricity in the house. Until then she had gas for lighting and cooking. Hot water was provided by a back-boiler in the coal-fired grate. Her cooking utensils were large cast-iron pots and kettles, which were extremely heavy to lift. She lived in a rented house throughout her married life, never owning her own home. But in her declining years she lived like a duchess with my youngest sister Patricia and her husband Bill in a beautiful Georgian house in Portobello.

She outlived most of her contemporaries, which gave her great satisfaction. In the end life had its compensations.

My memories of my childhood seem to be of golden summer days, spent either on the beach at Portobello, catching crabs or eels at the rocks at Joppa, or running wild in Fauldhouse. I had bright red, spiky, hair. Red hair is supposed to signify a bad temper. I think that I might have been proof of that. I was somewhat temperamental and could be a real nuisance. If I wanted something I would go on and on about it until either I got it, or, just as likely, I got a clip on the ear. At one stage I had the notion that I wanted to play a banjo. I cannot now think why. I went on and on about it for a long time. The whole family got tired of my constant refrain that I wanted to play a banjo. Thank goodness it was one of the occasions that I did not get my own way. Imagine a George Formby with a Scottish accent.

When not wearing my school clothes I would be wearing a woollen jumper and old trousers. I enjoyed sliding down a concrete parapet on the sea wall, and the seat of my trousers was constantly in need of patching. But my mother, although good at many things, was no great needlewoman.

It was during one summer holidays when I was twelve years old that I first tried smoking. A friend, Jackie McGowan, and I bought a packet of five Woodbine cigarettes. They cost twopence. We smoked two each and halved the fifth one. Afterwards I thought that we were stupid. By halving the fifth cigarette we had two wasted ends left. If we had smoked the fifth cigarette between us we would only have had one. I did not like smoking very much as it made me feel sick. I did not feel that it was worth feeling sick just to pretend that we were grown up and I have never smoked since.

Many years later Wyn and I were at a party at the palace of the Ruler of the State of Negri Sembilan, in Malaysia. I said to her, 'You know how you don't believe me when I say that I gave up smoking when I was twelve years old. Why don't you ask that fellow standing over there?'

'What has he got to do with it?'

'That is Jackie McGowan, the lad that I smoked with.' He was a rubber planter on an estate in Negri Sembilan and was a close friend of the Ruler. I had not seen him for about eighteen years.

Some years after that Wyn was talking to our younger son Michael about smoking at boarding school. Michael said, 'I tell the other boys that in our family we give up smoking when we reach the age of twelve.' We are a family of non-smokers.

When I see those old black and white films of children playing in the streets they remind me of the games that we used to play: Marbles in the gutter on the way to school, Cockie-dunty, played from one side of the street to the other, Kick-the-can where one side captured members of the other side, and the can had to be kicked before they could be freed. There were endless games of Hide and Seek. When we were not on the beach or playing in the street, we would wander further afield to climb Arthur's Seat, which is, I believe, an extinct volcano.

There are a number of these isolated hills around Edinburgh but Arthur's Seat is the largest of them. It rises up in the middle of Holyrood Park in the heart of Edinburgh. When you reach the top the view of the whole of Edinburgh and the Firth of Forth is magnificent. On a clear day the coast of Fife and the hills to the North seem very close. They say that, like Rome Edinburgh is built on seven hills. I think that that is an exaggeration but there certainly are some superb spots from which to view the City. The golf course on the Braid Hills is quite distracting to play as there are fantastic views in all directions. That is on the days that you can see anything at all.

We looked forward to the Saturday visit to the local cinema. Cowboys and Indians, Bing Crosby musicals, Laurel and Hardy and the Three Stooges was the normal diet, together with a serial of Tarzan. There were also the horror films with Boris Karloff as Frankenstein or Bela Lugosi as the vampire. It cost tuppence and we used to get a halfpenny for sweets. In today's money that was in total the equivalent of 1p. For the halfpenny the shopkeeper would give you a half of a bar of Highland Cream Toffee. The films were all very moral and the goodies always came out on top. It was a bit hard on the Indians, however, as apart from the Lone Ranger's buddy Tonto, they were almost always baddies. Our sporting heroes were varied according to the season. Depending on what we were playing we would adopt the name of our particular favourite. When two people wanted to be the same person this could cause serious disputes. In the winter we played football in one of the many parks. We used our jackets for goalposts. As Catholics our heroes could only be from either Celtic or Hibernian. Nobody would have dreamt of being a player from Rangers or Heart of Midlothian. So we were Jimmy McGrory who was a prodigious header of the ball or Jimmy Delaney, a flying winger. As I was neither a prodigious header of the ball (indeed, I hated trying to head the heavy leather ball) nor a flying winger (although I had aspirations), I usually finished up as Joe Kennaway, the Celtic goalkeeper. In summer we aspired to be Jack Hobbs, Don Bradman, Denis Compton or Len Hutton. The more ambitious of us sought to hurl the ball as fast as Harold Larwood. If we were running, we would choose to be Sydney Wooderson breaking the world record for a mile. My father was once prompted to say that we used the house as a hotel, only coming home to eat and sleep. It never seems to have rained. Was this the start of global warming?

Listening to sporting events on the wireless (it wasn't called radio at that time) was nothing like seeing them on television. For soccer matches the pitch was notionally divided into squares and whilst the commentator was describing what was going on a voice in the background called out the number of the square in which play was taking place. Cricket commentators were usually quite good. Len Hutton's magnificent innings of 364 against the Australians in August 1938 was fascinating to hear. Every time that we had to leave the house we switched on as soon as we returned to see how he was doing. As we did not have electricity in the house our wireless was powered by a lead/acid battery. We had two of these. One was in use while the other was being recharged at a local shop.

We all walked to school. There was usually a friendly policeman, to see the children across the busier roads, either Sergeant Bob Grant or PC Jock Hardy, both of them friends of my father. In those days if you misbehaved on the street and a policeman saw you he would threaten to box your ear and he was quite likely to carry out the threat. If you complained at home about it you would be told that you must have deserved it. You would then have had your ears boxed again by one or other of your parents.

Education

As Catholics we followed each other at regular intervals into the local Catholic school St John's Portobello. For a number of years there were always three or four of us attending St John's at one time. The remainder were at Holy Cross. The logistics of getting everyone ready was a considerable exercise. Ensuring that boys washed behind their ears, sorting out who was most desperate to go to the toilet and seeing that everyone had some breakfast were my mother's main tasks. Most of the time we got on quite well as a family but the one thing that we all hated was my sister Jean's hair. She had very thick wavy hair that had to be subjected to severe combing and brushing. This was carried out by my mother to the accompaniment of howls of anguish. It was a tremendous relief when Jean took on the task of combing her own hair.

By any standards St. John's was an excellent school. The teachers were dedicated and aimed to ensure that their pupils reached their full potential. The school catchment area included some of the mining villages to the east of Edinburgh. Some of the children who attended came from families who were on very low incomes and were entitled to free school meals. It seemed to me to be very exciting to have your lunch in the large school hall. I kept asking my mother to let me try it. I imagine that there were times when we too would have been entitled to free meals but she would never allow it. However one time she was unwell and I was given the money to buy my lunch. I was hugely excited. It was ghastly! Never again!

Some of these children were given free boots from a police charity. The soles of the boots were covered with metal studs to make them last longer. We boys envied them because the studs made them ideal for striking sparks on the granite pavements and for making slides in frosty weather.

Among the teachers at St. John's were nuns from the local convent. My memories of them are of thoughtful and caring women dedicated to their vocation and the children that they taught. It was the same with the priests that I came into contact with as a choirboy in the church. I find it difficult to relate to the recent accusations of cruelty and sexual abuse that have been made against some priests and nuns. Clearly, as has been proved, there were bad apples in the barrel but fortunately I never came across them. I believe too that there is a considerable amount of judging what was acceptable in the past by what would be acceptable in the present day.

The education that we received was broadly based. As well as the three Rs, there was a generous helping of PE. We had singing and folk dancing, Scottish, English and Irish. Occasionally there were great concerts for Edinburgh schools in the Usher Hall. We sang and once we gave an exhibition of Morris Dancing. History, both Scottish and English, was a major subject. Memorising the names of both Scottish and English kings was quite a feat. I have recently been reading an updated version of Scottish history. It is clear that what we got was a very sanitised version of the story of our great Scottish heroes. Another problem was that history stopped in 1914. Nothing later than that seemed to be considered as part of our education. Geography was mainly about that large part of the map of the world that was coloured pink, the British Empire, on which the sun never set.

I bought my first bicycle by doing a paper round. But after I had been doing it for about six months my mother said that I should stop. She thought that getting up so early in the morning was making me tired and interfering with my schoolwork. She was probably right but I think that the real reason was that she thought that it was bad for the family image. The family image was all-important.

One thing that my mother insisted upon was that we spoke properly. She realised that no matter how well educated you are, if people cannot understand what you are saying they will not take you seriously. In school it was the same. We had to read to the class in turn. We also recited poetry. Woe betide anyone who mispronounced the words. We learned the Lowland Scots language of Robert Burns but this was balanced by Sir Walter Scott and Robert Louis Stevenson. Later it was Wordsworth, Tennyson, Coleridge and lots of Shakespeare. I can still quote reams of Shakespeare. One of my favourite quotations to engineers who complain about the status of the profession is from Shakespeare's Julius Caesar, 'The fault, dear Brutus, lies, not in our stars, but in ourselves, that we are underlings'.

Outside it was a different story. Glottal stops and vernacular words were used in abundance. Even so our cousins in Fauldhouse still thought that we were a bit posh. We used what were virtually two different languages. Unlike many of today's children, for us swearing and obscenities were seldom heard except among the miners in Fauldhouse. When I went to university I found that I spoke in very much the same accents as the other students who had attended some of the great Edinburgh schools. I suppose that it can be called an educated Edinburgh accent. There is a difference between having a Scottish accent and speaking one of the Scottish dialects. These can be very difficult to understand. I have seen a television programme where young people from Edinburgh were being interviewed about drugs. There were sub-titles so that the viewers could understand what was being said. I was one of the viewers who needed the sub-titles.

Today one of the difficulties of call-centres set up in places like Liverpool and Newcastle is that it is often almost impossible to understand what is being said because of the ways in which many of the inhabitants speak. Many organisations are locating their call-centres in places like India. People there are taught to speak English in a way that can be understood by anyone in the English-speaking world. For companies engaged in competitive international markets this is essential. Teachers in Britain should take note of this; otherwise the children are disadvantaged by not being able to seek employment outside their own area. All too often their own area is an area of high unemployment.

I have never found it a disadvantage to speak with a Scottish accent. Certainly in Malaysia Scotsmen had a high reputation for integrity, education and capacity for hard work. If anyone ever had to ask where I came from it was time for me to return to Edinburgh to refurbish my Scottish accent. In the City of London, being a Scottish Lord Mayor seemed to be an advantage. At least it was different. When I was Lord Mayor I visited my old primary school,

St. John's. I was delighted to find that the atmosphere in the school was as I remembered it, happy and caring. It is the kind of state school that today people buy houses near so as to be within the catchment area. The children of today are being given the same kind of start that I had. Perhaps among the children I met there is a future Lord Mayor. Interestingly the first question that I was asked by the children at both St John's and at a primary school in St Albans that I visited was 'Has the Lord Mayor got any friends?' I think that they remembered the story of Dick Whittington and wondered whether I had a cat.

John and I enjoyed being in the church choir. As choirboys we actually attended four services on a Sunday. We were quite happy to spend a large part of Sunday in church provided the remainder was spent in enjoyment. I loved the simplicity of Plain Chant, the smell of the incense and the ceremonies for the Feast Days throughout the year. The problem was of course that being in Latin, a language not heard very often on Portobello High Street, most of the services were unintelligible to the great majority of the congregation. It could all be very boring for both adults and children. This was a pity, for some of the language was very beautiful. Ostensibly the reason for using Latin was to preserve the integrity of the services, since Latin was the language of the early church in Rome. I rather suspect that the reason was to maintain a separate priestly class away from the common herd. However I was very sad when later changes to the liturgy meant that the Latin versions are seldom heard nowadays. I think that they threw out the baby with the bath water. I much prefer to have English interspersed with a bit of Latin, and one great advantage of the Latin mass was that it was the same wherever you went. Being choirboys meant that by assisting at weddings and christenings we sometimes received tips, a useful source of income. There used to be a Scottish custom that male guests at a wedding would have a pocket-full of coins. So after a wedding it was necessary to get out of the church fast. It was fun scrambling for the coins thrown for the urchins and if you were lucky it could be profitable.

It was at the great Feast Days of Easter and Christmas that the choir could really shine. Normally we were singing Gregorian chant, which is designed for choir singing and is not too demanding on voices. For the Feast days there were variations and we sang much more demanding pieces by Palestrina, Bach and other composers which I know that professional choirs at the great cathedrals take as everyday events but we were a part-time choir with Canon Franklin alone to teach us. That we were able to sing these much more difficult compositions was a considerable achievement.

Canon Franklin was a most interesting man. For one thing he was English. At that time we did not meet many English people. He is the only person that I have ever known whose eyes were different colours. One was brown and the other blue. He had been a Church of England clergyman and in his forties he had converted to Catholicism. He was a genuinely holy man and was known and admired by the people of Portobello, Catholic and non-Catholic alike. Later he was upset when he heard that I had lied about my age to join the Home Guard. He did not believe that the end justified the means. I imagine that he had a considerable influence on my own attitudes to life.

In due course Wyn and I were married by his curate who at that time was Father McCullough but the Canon although of considerable age, and suffering from severe arthritis, insisted on coming to bless us. Some time later, not long before he died, we went to see him when he was in hospital. He told us that we were going to Borneo. At the time we were living in Lancashire and had no intention of going anywhere in the Far East. Borneo eventually became part of Malaysia and years later we did visit it. We often wondered why he insisted that we were going to Borneo.

My brother John and I had quite good voices and quickly learned to read music. At one time, there was talk that we should have proper voice training. Unfortunately when I reached the age of thirteen my voice did not so much break as crack. In addition I had great difficulty in finding the right key. So much so that when I was Lord Mayor and the Guildhall School of Music and Drama made me an Honorary Member the family was highly amused.

Every year there was what was called a 'Mission'. The purpose of the Mission was to try to bring back to the Church those Catholics who had left it, and to increase the faith of those who remained. Every evening for a week, there were services for different groups. One evening it would be men only. Another evening it was women only and so on. As members of the choir, we were expected to attend each evening. The preachers were usually from an order called the Passionist Fathers. We called them 'The Passionate Fathers'. They all appeared to be ten foot tall. They had booming Irish voices that echoed round the church and were inclined to invite the congregation to 'Come down to the gates of Hell with me'.

Hell appeared to contain a vast number of the souls of those who had indulged in 'fornication'. Being too shy to ask anyone what the word meant it was not until I started singing Rugby songs that I found out. In later life I wondered whether this preoccupation of the clergy with sex was because they were not supposed to indulge in it and were jealous of those who could do so legitimately. It certainly appeared to be a major preoccupation.

Throughout my sunny childhood, I had one problem. I used to get sick with excitement. It took the form of my face becoming gradually paler and paler and at a certain stage, I would deposit the contents of my stomach where I was. At parties, the older members of the family would tend to keep an eye out, and rush me off before disaster struck. When I was about eight years old I was given the task of carrying the rather heavy brocade train worn by the Archbishop of St Andrews and Edinburgh who was paying a visit to St John's church. There I was, spiky hair slicked down with water, dressed in immaculate white starched surplice and black cassock, proceeding down the aisle of the church clutching the ends of the train. With every step that I took my face changed colour. First it became deathly pale, and then it gradually took on a greenish tinge. My poor mother watched in horror. As she prayed fervently she had a vision of the remains of my breakfast being deposited in the beautifully embroidered garment. Her prayers were answered. Shaky but still upright and my breakfast still in its correct place I completed the long walk.

My sisters and brother were all reasonably bright. From St John's, we followed each other to Holy Cross Academy. It was the Scottish equivalent of a grammar school. If you were clever enough, you could get a place, if not, you could get one by paying. My parents only had to pay for one of my sisters; the rest of us won 'bursaries', as they are known in Scotland. John was a very difficult act to follow—one of those annoying people who could top his class with the minimum effort and good at most sports. I had to try hard to keep up the standard, but though John was three years older, in my teens I rapidly grew taller than him, so at least I was spared from wearing his 'hand me downs'. My sisters all disliked having to wear clothes that their elders had outgrown.

Because Holy Cross was a Catholic school many of the pupils were of either Irish or Italian extraction. Edinburgh has a flourishing Italian community, including the ice cream makers, Luca's, with their famous shop in Musselburgh which for many years has been considered to make the best ice cream in Britain. Some of the Italian boys used to go off to summer camp in Italy as members of la Vangardista, the young Fascist organisation. As far as I know, they seemed to enjoy it but when they returned they stood out because they had had their heads shaved all over. Today the hairstyle would be the height of fashion.

One of the Italian pupils at Holy Cross was a boy we called Eddie Paolozzi. He was good at art and as he sat next to me I often benefited from his help in doing my drawings for me. Unfortunately the teacher realised that these drawings were far too good to be mine and she used to throw us out of the class to sit next door. I think she realised that she couldn't teach either of us anything, him because he is now the world famous artist Sir Eduardo Paolozzi and me because art has never been one of my greatest skills. Little did she know that both the naughty boys that she threw out of the class would end up with knighthoods! I wish I had kept some of Eduardo's drawings—they would now be worth a fortune...

It was at Holy Cross that I started to play rugby football. I loved it. I found it most useful later on, when I moved around in making my way up the ladder in local government. When I arrived in any town to take up a position, I immediately took myself to the local Rugby

Club. It was the quickest way of meeting people and enjoying a social life.

1938 was a year of growing tension. Hitler was making threats. We were being told about air raid precautions. We were measured for gas masks. Then the Prime Minister, Neville Chamberlain went to Berlin to talk to Hitler. The film news showed him stepping off a plane, waving a piece of paper, saying 'Peace for our time'. The building of air raid shelters continued.

The Pope died in 1939. A new pope, Pius XII, was elected. He has in recent years been criticised for not doing more to condemn the treatment of Jews in Germany but at the time he seemed to be the only person in Continental Europe who was making any sort of criticism of both Hitler and Mussolini.

The evacuation of children from the cities was started. Thousands of evacuees were dispersed to country areas. Some children were sent to Canada and America. At one stage, there was talk of my sister Patricia and me being sent to relatives in Canada.

In 1939, Germany invaded Poland from the West. Russia invaded Poland from the East. War was declared on Germany. Chamberlain announced that we were already at war on the radio at 11.15 in the morning on Sunday 3rd September. The ultimatum to the Germans that they must withdraw from Poland by 11am had expired. After hearing the announcement on the wireless, John and I went off to the 11.30 Mass. During mass the air-raid sirens sounded but nobody paid any attention. It turned out to be a false alarm.

When war had been declared in 1914 it is said that people were dancing in the streets. In 1939 there was no such celebration. There was, however, some feeling that the humiliating appeasement of the previous twelve months was ended. Nobody was looking for a quick end to the conflict. It was thought that air power would eventually decide it. However I do not believe that anyone imagined the ferocity of the bombing that would take place.

As well as invading Poland the Russians invaded Finland. The Finns put up a brave fight but eventually were overwhelmed by vastly superior numbers. When I was Sheriff we visited Helsinki with the Lord Mayor. We were shown a Coventry Climax mobile fire-fighting pump, maintained in complete working order. A group of British firemen had taken it to help the Finns to fight the fires when the Russians were bombing Helsinki. During 1940 some of us from school were called upon to act as stretcher-bearers for casualties arriving by train in Edinburgh after the evacuation from Dunkirk. Like most youngsters at that time I could not wait to be involved in some way. Patriotism seems to be a dirty word nowadays, equated to that form of xenophobia that is exhibited by the thuggish element of football supporters. For us it was a question of doing what we believed to be our duty to our country in the face of the aggression of an ambitious dictator who seemed to be intent on subjugating Britain and the whole of Europe.

Fire-watching was one of the duties that senior boys undertook. Two or three of us would spend the night in the school in case there was an air raid. We learned to use what was called a 'stirrup-pump', a hand pump that produced a jet of water, which was sufficient to put out an incendiary bomb. They say that St. Paul's Cathedral owed its survival to this simple device. Sometime towards the end of 1940 I met one of my former school friends. He was older than I was and, although he was not old enough, he had joined the Home Guard—'Dad's Army'. I decided to do likewise. I was tall for my age, and I think that they were desperate for numbers. I had no difficulty in persuading them that I was seventeen years old. My father had also joined a Company of the Home Guard near where he worked.

I was probably one of the youngest members of the Home Guard in the country. I suppose I could be likened to the gawky Private Pike in the television series. It was said that the Home Guard uniforms came in two sizes: Too Big and Too Small. I was long and thin, entirely the wrong shape for the standard uniform sizes. Fortunately at that time photographic material was in short supply and there is no photographic record of me in my Home Guard uniform. Such a record would indeed have been an embarrassment. As is well known Hitler was preparing to invade Britain at that time. I am not saying that he abandoned the idea because of my induction into the Home Guard but the two events were almost contemporaneous. The whole of the armed forces were short of weapons since most of the arms and ammunition had been left on the beaches of Europe. So we were issued with pikes. These consisted of a bayonet stuck in the end of a length of galvanised iron tubing that had been painted green. Someone had unearthed a drill manual from the fifteenth or sixteenth century and we carried out that drill. The Lord Mayor's bodyguard is the pikemen of the Honourable Artillery Company who parade carrying huge long pikes. I used to tell them that I had actually done pike drill in earnest!

When the German Panzer Divisions, which had rolled irresistibly across Europe, arrived, we would be ready for them! God help us!

Much later we learned to make 'Molotov cocktails'. These were bottles filled with petrol with a rag stuffed in the top. The idea was that you lit the rag and jumped up on to the tank. You then thrust the bottle through the air vent. It then burst into flames inside the tank. It all sounded highly dangerous, but we were assured that the Russians had used the tactic very successfully. Fortunately, I was never called upon to try it out. I felt very grown up. Staying up all night on guard duty, learning to play poker and having the odd glass of beer. Once or twice I fell asleep in class.

When Germany invaded Russia, Stalin, who until then had been a hated friend of Hitler, suddenly became the loveable 'Uncle Joe'.

It is probably difficult for present generations to recognise fully the contribution to the survival of Britain that was made by Winston Churchill. We have all become so used to the spin doctoring of politicians that we have become very cynical about their utterances. In 1940 the Germans had overrun Europe. The Americans were still only selling arms to us. They had not yet decided to get involved. Britain stood alone. We were the last bastion against the seemingly unstoppable might of the Third Reich. The radio broadcasts of Winston, roaring defiance across the Channel, was the platform on which the morale of the British people was built. It was, I suppose, spin doctoring of a kind but it was for the benefit of the nation, not narrow political interest. We who heard his speeches can never forget them. The hairs on the back of my neck still rise when I hear recordings of the famous 'We will fight on the beaches' speech with its closing line 'We will never surrender!' What these speeches meant to the people who were seeing their neighbours and relatives blown up and their homes and places of work flattened can only be imagined by future generations.

In these modern times it has become fashionable to decry the role of the Royal Family. Those who lived through the war can remember how they were the focus of loyalty to the nation. It is so much better to have as head of state someone who regards the role as a sacred trust rather than some elected politician who is there for what he can get out of it. We can all quote examples of the latter type from America, Europe and around the world. The great celebration of Her Majesty's Golden Jubilee showed that the majority of the British people appreciate her dedication and sense of duty.

I listened to a woman on the radio recently decrying the annual Remembrance Day commemoration. She said that it was a glorification of war. What a fool! Anyone who has experienced war knows that it is a cause of suffering and death. It is usually the weakest and most vulnerable who suffer most. There is precious little glory in modern war. The real purpose of Remembrance Services is to remind people of the horror of war and to persuade them that it should only be a last resort. Of course, old soldiers are proud that they served their country when they were needed. Of course, many of them enjoyed the comradeship of like-minded people brought together in a common cause. Just as my father had been reluctant to speak of his wartime experiences, so too my brother never spoke of the four years that he served in the army. Being intelligent and sensitive I believe that he was horrified by the futility of it all.

The education at Holy Cross was of a very good standard. Discipline was strong, and the use of the leather strap, called a 'tawse' was not discouraged. It was a co-educational school. The way some of the girls had crushes on some of the masters was a great source of amusement to us macho males. When we were at school, in the senior classes we used to have dances. I had two left feet and I was hopeless at ballroom dancing. My eldest sister, Isobel, decided that if I was going to university I should have some social graces. On her days off from the hospital where she was a nurse she taught me to dance. Not long after I started at university I met one of the girls from school at a dance. She was mightily surprised at the vast improvement in my dancing.

To get to Holy Cross from Portobello we took the tram. The City Corporation gave us a free season ticket. The journey lasted about half an hour. This was enough time to do most of your homework. The teachers were not generally impressed with the standard of writing as the ride could be bumpy in certain places.

In 1942 I passed my Scottish Highers. I took six subjects at Higher level, which at that time was regarded as pretty good. Nowadays some young people take nine or ten.

I had been quite good at Latin. The Latin teacher wanted me to become a Latin teacher. I had other ideas. I gave up Latin when it came to choosing the subjects to study for my Highers. After I had finished my Higher Examinations, I was asked to help out the senior master in the junior school. For certain periods, I was looking after a class of eleven year olds. After a week I was convinced that the majority of them were juvenile delinquents, destined, if not for the gallows, certainly for prolonged sojourns in prison. At any rate it confirmed my view that I was not suited to teaching.

With a friend, Alex Wilson, who had achieved similar grades to me, I was sent by the school to see a careers adviser. Alex, an only child, was advised to apply to go to university. The adviser did not think that my parents would be able to afford to send me to university. He advised me to look for a job and suggested a job as a surveyor. I was prepared to accept his advice. When I returned home I told my mother what he had said. She was furious. 'How dare anyone say that we could not afford to send our son to university?' It was decided that if I was accepted, I would go to Edinburgh University. My father was quite happy to go along with it if my mother thought that we could manage.

When I later worked on a building site I saw that most of the men, when they were paid, would open their pay packets and take out some of the money to go to the pub on the way home. My father always handed over his pay packet to my mother unopened. Managing finances was her department.

I enjoyed my schooldays. By most measures I did well and eventually won a bursary to Edinburgh University.

The minimum qualification for acceptance at university was three subjects at higher level and two at lower level. With my six at the higher level there was little doubt that I would be accepted. I was granted a bursary by the City of Edinburgh. At the tender age of sixteen I prepared to take up a place in the University of Edinburgh Engineering Department to read Civil Engineering. To me it was almost unbelievable. I imagine that I was the first member of my family ever to have a university education. I am sure that my brother could have achieved that distinction if he had so desired. My mother would have made it happen.

During the period between leaving school and starting at university Alex and I found work on a building site. We were employed as bricklayer's labourers at a wage of one shilling and twopence per hour. For us it was fun. We were fit, we were doing something new, and we were actually earning money. With a couple of young Irishmen we started to have races wheeling barrow loads of sand, gravel or concrete. Although a large number of Irishmen served in the British forces, in Ireland, a neutral country, there was no conscription. Some Irishmen came across and worked on the building sites for six months and returned home before they became liable for income tax. Whilst our racing did a great deal to improve productivity, it apparently did not meet with the approval of some of the older men on the site some of whom had been drafted after working as clerks, bus conductors or other non-manual occupations. There was no way that they could keep up with us. I heard from my father, who had heard from a friend, that their output was being compared unfavourably with ours. They were not very happy. The foreman was very happy with us but he was a bit of a diplomat. After I spoke to him he started to give us jobs where we could compete between ourselves without upsetting the others.

One of the interesting things that I learned at this time was how to dig trenches properly. On the site there was a man whose sole job was to dig by hand trenches for drains. This task he performed with meticulous care and precision. It was also done at considerable

speed and with minimum effort. It was a joy to watch a real professional at work. Alex and I also learned a bit about bricklaying. The
foreman was not impressed when he came round the site and caught
us doing the bricklaying while the tradesmen sat having a cigarette. It
was also fun to hear some of the men arguing with the foreman
about discrepancies in their wage packets. Some of them were practically illiterate but they could calculate how much they were due to
the last halfpenny. This may not sound much of an achievement, but
since we were working overtime, it involved calculating so many
hours at ordinary time, so many at time and one eighth, so many at
time and a quarter, and some at time and a half—Impressive mental
arithmetic. There were Alex and I, who had both just successfully
completed not only Higher Mathematics but also Advanced Mathematics, seeking the assistance of our fellow workers in calculating
our wages.

We then did a spell on a forestry operation in the Scottish borders
near the river Tweed. We did felling, crosscut sawing and sawmill
work. Again, we treated it as fun and enjoyed it enormously. Some
of the men with whom we worked did a spot of salmon poaching in
their spare time. They used to take the fish that they caught into
Edinburgh to sell to the hotels. One night they took Alex and me
with them to show us how they fished. They had a torch and a gaff
(a long-handled hook). The idea was to play the light from the torch
on the surface of the water to attract a fish. Gradually it was brought
closer and closer to the bank until it was close enough to hook it.
Unfortunately, before the light had time to attract a fish it attracted a
bailiff. We had to scarper pretty quickly. When any of my City
friends asked me if I fished in Scotland, I used to reply, 'only with a
torch and a gaff.' Some of them were horrified.

I had to leave the Home Guard when at university I joined the
Senior Training Corps. It was expected that after we graduated we
would become officers in the Royal Engineers. Accordingly we wore
collars and ties with our uniform like officers in the army. We had a
shoulder flash that read 'STC RE'. When we went to camp we used to
tell people (usually the local girls) that it stood for Specially Trained
Commandos Royal Engineers. They were duly impressed. On one

occasion we had to gather together as a group to deter a local lad from starting a punch-up with one of our friends, Alan Moodie. The lad's girlfriend had been too impressed by Alan.

At the same time I was invited to help to run a company of the Army Cadet Force. I was duly commissioned as a 2nd Lieutenant. I was not much older than some of the lads but they seemed quite happy to take orders from me. This was especially so after one of the Saturday dances which we ran for them. I was attacked by a youth whom I had ejected from the hall for being a nuisance and he was waiting for me when I came out with my sister Patricia and my cousin May. I had no desire to get involved but he rushed at me. I had no alternative but to clobber him. Next morning, at the Sunday parade, the story flashed round, gaining momentum with every telling. I had inflicted all sorts of grievous damage on the poor lad. I am sure that the main damage had been to his pride but my reputation soared and discipline was never a problem thereafter.

We had a pipe-band and I was responsible for seeing that they practised. It wasn't a difficult task as they were extremely keen. They were also very good. When we went to camp it was difficult to get them to take part in other activities. All that they wanted to do was practise piping and drumming. It was wonderful to see the swagger and self-confidence of the boys. When they were marching along playing the stirring tunes they were transformed. They were no longer messenger-boys, tea-boys, apprentice bricklayers and carpenters. They were musicians absorbed by what they were achieving. I am sure that some of them would have been regarded as thick at school. In the band they were doing something that they enjoyed, and doing it well. It was a great boost to their confidence and self-esteem. I still believe that our education system should be geared towards finding out what people are good at. We should then enable them to become qualified in that discipline. In short, I believe in the NVQ system of starting off at a basic level and taking students higher step by step.

It was also about this time that my rugby career took off. I was invited to play for the Dunfermline Club, which is in Fife. I played at wing-forward. The previous wing-forward Maurice Henderson, who had come from Holy Cross Academy to Dunfermline, had later been capped for Scotland. I am afraid that I was not in that class. Although I had to pay the normal weekly subscription of two shillings and sixpence they agreed to pay my fare from Edinburgh to Dunfermline. I thought that I was close to being a professional rugby player. When I see the size of present day players, I think that I would be fortunate to get into the extra-extra fourth fifteen. I am pretty sure that no one would agree to pay my fare to play for them.

Life at University was fairly low key. Because of restrictions such as the blackout, social life was fairly limited. It was pointed out to us early on that we were very privileged to be allowed to continue our education at a time when many of our contemporaries were giving their lives for our country. We still had Rag Days in aid of the Edinburgh Royal Infirmary but apart from Saturday night dances at the Union or at King's Buildings, where the engineering department was located, extra curricular activities were minimal. In any case, what with academic work and my other duties I was kept pretty busy. One of my friends at University was Gregor Clark. He like my brother John could get the highest marks with the least effort. He loved to play bridge and all too often he would persuade some of us lesser mortals to play when we should have been working. We would then have to struggle to make up for lost time while he seemed completely unaware that not everyone could perform the way that he did. The night before the start of the Final Examinations he took himself off to the cinema. He got the highest marks that anyone had achieved for many years.

Around Christmas, we students used to get temporary work in the Post Office. We sorted and delivered mail. One year I was sent to deliver mail in Leith Walk. Although just around the corner from Edinburgh's most famous and fashionable street, Princes Street, the contrast could not have been starker. The dwellings were flats, approached by dark narrow staircases. Empty beer-bottles clattered down the stone steps if you happened to kick them. The rank smell of urine pervaded the air. Because the letters were usually addressed to the number of the staircase it was often necessary to knock on doors to ask which floor the addressee inhabited. The reactions varied. 'Are you the Polis? (Police)', from behind a closed door was quite common. In other cases the tired-looking young woman, wearing nothing but a flimsy dressing gown, obviously was disappointed that you were not a customer. My education in human existence took a huge leap forward.

I did not get involved in student politics but on one occasion I was invited to go to a meeting of young Unionists as the Conservatives were called. A scion of one of Scotland's aristocratic families whose name I have forgotten addressed us. The gist of his talk was that the Conservatives were the natural ruling party of this country because they had been bred for it. His analogy was racehorses bred to win the Derby. As can be readily imagined, with my background, it was not a concept that commended itself to me. I expressed my disagreement, no doubt in forceful terms. Apparently the speaker returned to headquarters and said that there had been a crowd of left-wingers at the meeting. I have never belonged to any political party!

By now my parents were beginning to see the fruits of their years of struggle paying off. My eldest sister, Isobel, was a highly successful nurse in a prestigious hospital. She was, and still is, although in her eighties, hyperactive. She runs everywhere and never stops. The second eldest, Helen was an officer in the ATS. We always thought that she would take up writing as she had a gift for words. She still writes beautiful letters. My brother John, who sadly died recently, eventually became the Managing Director of a rubber company. While in the army he suffered from the fact that he was much cleverer than those above him and, like my father, did not mind showing it. Jean, my next sister before enjoying life in the WAAF had worked in the office at the Unilever factory where my father worked. She spent some time in Northern Rhodesia, now Zambia, and now lives in Australia. My youngest sister Patricia was still at Holy Cross Academy taking her Highers prior to becoming a nurse. She was always regarded as the baby of the family. Now in her seventies, she is still treated as such by her elder sisters. She should have been a doctor as she is a brilliant diagnostician. If any of the family is suffering from an ailment, Patricia is the first port of call. Even over the telephone, her diagnosis is invariably correct. Her eldest son, Gordon, not long ago, suggested that she go to university to study medicine.

My father's fellow workers could not understand how he had managed to educate his children so successfully on his wage. They seemed to think that he was some sort of 'remittance man' in receipt of a private income. It really was due mainly to the determination of my mother to see that her children 'got on' as they say in Scotland.

Starting work, and marriage

During the war years food rationing and the blackout were of course inconveniences but Edinburgh did not suffer much from German attacks. It was difficult to realise that other cities in Britain were suffering great devastation. While London, Coventry, Liverpool and Clydeside were being blitzed the beautiful Georgian squares and terraces of Edinburgh remained undisturbed. The war had largely passed them by.

Because the authorities wished to get us through the university course as quickly as possible the long summer vacations were eliminated. The result was that I graduated in December 1945 at the age of nineteen. Nowadays most young people do not start their university education until they reach that age. There is not much of what I learned at university that I have used in my engineering career. In fact I thought that quite a lot of what we were learning was out of date. However I proved that I was capable of learning.

At this stage, with all my military training, I should have proceeded to take up a commission in the army. After all, I had been trained in the use most types of gun from .38 revolvers to 25 pounder field guns. I had used most types of automatic weapon from Browning automatic rifles to Thompson sub-machine guns—the 'Tommy gun' that was the favourite weapon of the Chicago gangsters in the 1930s. I knew how to use various types of explosive in order to blow up a variety of bridges and buildings. I knew how to erect Bailey bridges and pontoon bridges and could perform all sorts of complicated drill movements. In addition, I had already held a commission in the Cadet Force. I pictured myself as starting off well up the ladder. The high command would be trembling in their boots for fear for their jobs. However, fate decreed otherwise. Because of an ear infection I'd had when I was younger, my medical category was downgraded. At the same time the office of the City Engineer of Edinburgh applied to have me directed to work for them. I had worked for the City Engineer for work-experience during some of the holiday periods and when he heard that I had graduated he thought that I would be of more use in his office than elsewhere. Apparently the authorities agreed. Many of my friends from University also found themselves directed to civilian work instead of going into the forces.

The war was now over and the Government wanted people to begin the task of bringing the country back to normality. So it was that instead of becoming a member of His Majesty's forces I was directed to perform my National Service in the City Engineer's Office in Edinburgh. Previously I had worked without pay. Now they started to pay me. Even for those days my pay, less than three pounds a week, was not very much but it was the start of my career in Local Government.

It has been said that before, and immediately after the war, there was religious discrimination against Catholics in Scotland with regard to employment. It was certainly so in some of the Clydeside shipyards. There, as at Harland and Wolff's in Belfast at the time, if you had attended a Catholic school you had no chance of a job. To the best of my knowledge I have never suffered any such discrimination in my life. Interestingly enough however when I worked in the City Engineer's office I was asked whether it was because my father was high up in the Freemasons that I had managed to get employment there. My brother John had been asked the same question when he was employed in the North British Rubber Company. There, the Freemasons were called 'the knuckle-crushers union'. In the Edinburgh Royal Infirmary my sister Patricia was also asked if she had Masonic connections because it was difficult to get into the Infirmary for training. It does seem that there was a perception that such connections were required. My father was not even a member of the Catenians, which is supposed to be the Catholic equivalent of the Freemasons.

Perhaps it was just as well that I did not go into the army. I was terribly disappointed with the results of the Yalta conference. We had gone into the war ostensibly to save the Polish people from the Nazis. After six years of war and at a cost of millions of lives the Poles were then put under the control of a system that was as bad, if not worse, the Communists. I would have wanted to take on the Russians.

Edinburgh is a beautiful city and I felt very privileged to be employed there. When I was Lord Mayor, I said that I had been fortunate in that, I was born in the most beautiful city in the world, Edinburgh, had lived most of my working life in the friendliest city in the world, Kuala Lumpur, and had become the first citizen of the greatest city in the world, London. How lucky can you be?

Among the people who I worked with in the City Engineer's office was an old man whose name was Kermack. He had been called back from retirement. His hands had a terrible shake, but once he had his hand on the drawing board, he could produce the most beautiful copperplate printing. His drawings took a long time to produce, but they were masterpieces. When he reminisced about 'the old days', he was talking about the late nineteenth century. He could remember the Scottish doggerel poet, William Topaz McGonagall, author of 'The Tay Bridge Disaster', which is widely claimed to be the worst poem in the English language. McGonagall, who died in 1902, used to travel around selling his books of poems in the City offices.

The President of the Institution of Civil Engineers at this time was the City Engineer of the City of Liverpool, Sir Pierson Frank. I met him when he paid a presidential visit to the Edinburgh branch of the Institution, of which I was a member. He told me that to progress in Local Government you had to be prepared to move around. So, after two years in the City Engineer's office, which was the period for National Service, I applied for a post in Staffordshire. I was successful, and prepared to leave home for the first time. I was sorry to leave Edinburgh but I wished to further my career.

Until recently I was on the Board of the East of Scotland Water Authority. When there was talk of carrying out work at this or that sewage works, I could say 'I remember when that was built'. It is interesting also to go back now and see some of the areas that I can remember as green fields. They are now completely covered either by houses or factories. The buildings look as though they had been there forever.

The day before I was due to leave Edinburgh I went to the local branch of the Trustee Savings Bank to close my account. I don't think that there was very much in the account, but my visit to the bank eventually changed my life. When I returned home I told my mother that there was a beautiful girl working in the bank. I left for Stafford the following day. I did not expect to be back in Edinburgh for some time and I thought that I would never see her again.

I enjoyed working in Stafford. For one thing, I was being paid about three times the salary that I had been paid in Edinburgh. Motorways were being planned and we had a section of the M6. I was given my first bridge to design.

I found my work very interesting and, at times, exciting. On one occasion, I was carrying out a road survey with one of my colleagues, David Morris which entailed going up an outside staircase on to the roof of a roadside garage. The roof was quite large and on two levels. Between the two levels was a flight of four or five steps. On the upper level, restrained by what appeared to me to be a totally inadequate piece of string, sat an enormous Great Dane. It looked like a lioness, sitting there playing with its 'bone'. The 'bone' was a horse's skull. I had to go past this monster to stick a coloured ranging pole in the grass bank beyond the roof. While I had the pole I did not feel too vulnerable. On the way back it was a different story. Gingerly I sidled past the animal, trying not to attract its attention. I had reached the top of the steps when I heard a roar. I felt the dog's teeth sinking into my bottom. Thinking of the film 'The Hound of the Baskervilles' I managed to remain upright with the fierce beast firmly attached to my rear end. The owner immediately came to my rescue. He was very apologetic. Of course, he said it had never done anything like that before. I found this hard to believe, as I had done nothing to provoke the animal. He also said that he would pay for a new pair of trousers for me.

David decided that there could be no more surveying that day. He had seen the horror on my face as I felt the dog's teeth sinking in. He decided that no matter what I said, I had had a serious shock. He was also worried about infection from the bite. We repaired to the nearest pub. David explained what had happened and asked the owner if he had any Iodine. The owner produced a bottle and some cotton wool directing us into one of the rooms beside the bar. There I was lying on one of the benches with my bottom bared with David standing over me with the bottle of Iodine. The door opened and a head popped round. A very surprised customer called 'Sorry!' and beat a hasty retreat. The Lord only knows what he thought we were up to. I was too embarrassed to go out into the bar after David had completed his ministrations. I later bought a pair of expensive trousers and sent the dog-owner the bill.

I lived in digs. My landlady was a widow called Mrs Horton. She had a huge tomcat called Peter that she allowed to sit on the dining table. I quite like cats but I was not fond of Peter. When Mrs Horton wasn't around, the other lodgers and I would shoo him off the table. She knew this, because every time one of us came into the room the cat's ears would flatten and it would jump down off the table. She went on holiday once and we pledged to look after the cat. We did our best, but on the Saturday evening one of the other lads, Jimmy McLellan, and I were going off to The Swan when we remembered that we had not fed the beast. We hunted for it everywhere, and eventually, found it up a tree. We managed to get it down and Jimmy carried it into the house. He dropped it on the floor but before we could shut the door the cat had scarpered. He did not return until Mrs Horton came back from her holiday. Apparently, he had gone to the house next door to get fed. Jimmy and I were not flavour of the month.

The standard of rugby was good and after-match Saturday evenings at The Swan Hotel were fun. The best beer, Worthington E, was the equivalent of 4p a pint. At closing time, we descended en masse on the Town Hall to bestow our company on the local maidenry at the weekly dance. The band was not too bad, but the male singer always sang flat. I could sympathise as I have a tendency to do the same.

What more could a young man want?

When I wasn't playing rugby, I would sometimes go for the weekend to Manchester. Gregor Clark, my friend from University, was working there. Sometimes he came to stay in my lodgings in

Stafford. We decided to go home to Edinburgh for Christmas and New Year. One Saturday evening Gregor and I decided to go to The Plaza where there was a dance on. It was a place where we were likely to meet some of our friends who were on leave from the Forces or back from English exile as we were. I had only been in the hall a few minutes when I saw her. I couldn't believe it. It was the girl from the bank! She looked gorgeous. Slim and not very tall (she wore quite high heels to make up for it), she wore a white dress that set off her long, thick, dark, wavy hair. She was talking to one of her friends and she had a lovely smile, with perfect teeth. I did not even know her name.

I told Gregor that I had to get her to dance with me. We sidled up to near where she was standing. When the music started I immediately presented myself in front of her and asked her to dance. I think that she was too surprised to refuse, and we had our first dance together. She told me that her name was Wyn.

Was it love at first sight? I do not know, but that was in December 1947. We were both twenty one years old. We have been dancing together ever since.

Although Wyn did not recognise me, I tell her that it was only because she had seen my bank account that she agreed to dance with me. We laughed and joked together. She says that, when the dance ended I told her that she could step off my feet as the music had stopped. I took her to meet Gregor. Afterwards, he opined that we were attracted to each other because we had the same sense of humour. I imagine that laughing at the same things is a good start for any relationship. We do indeed have a similar sense of humour. I can honestly say that we are 'best friends'. Most mornings we have a discussion about what we have read in the newspapers or heard on the radio. Most days we have a laugh about something. In modern parlance 'We can communicate with each other'. The standard chat up line of married men used to be that their wives did not understand them. I have been heard to say that my problem is that my wife understands me only too well. Not a good chat up line. Recently when we celebrated our Golden Wedding, Wyn in her speech said that she was reminded of the lady of mature years who was celebrating a similar occasion and was asked if during all the years of marriage she had ever thought of divorce. She replied 'Divorce never, murder dozens of times.'

Wyn had left the bank shortly after I had seen her there. Our chance meeting was the most fortunate of the lucky coincidences that have been a feature of my life. We saw each other every day until I returned to Stafford. I wrote to her immediately I arrived back there. Wyn still has the letter. It turned out that I knew her uncle Jack who was employed by the City of Edinburgh Engineer's Department.

Wyn's father was not very keen on his daughter having anything to do with Catholics. Whenever Wyn received a letter from me he would say 'Another Epistle from the Romans'. He would not attend his own daughter's wedding to me, but he later became very friendly with my father and he attended my sister Patricia's wedding. I think that, by that time, he had discovered that Catholics did not all have cloven hooves and long tails. When we visited him with our elder son Douglas, and Wyn said, 'Go to your grandpa', his joy at picking up his first grandson was something to behold.

I returned to Edinburgh as often as I could to see her. Eventually, nearly three years later, on 30th September 1950, we were married. We went to Dublin on our honeymoon. There I took Wyn to watch a rugby match at Lansdowne Road. Food was still rationed in Britain but not in Ireland. In recognition of the fact that we were on our honeymoon I was given two eggs at breakfast while Wyn only got one. This was recognition indeed that a new husband had to keep his strength up. On the way back, we were almost completely broke. When we stopped for a meal we had only enough money to buy one fish and chips between the two of us.

We took up residence in a house supplied by my employer, which by this time was the Tyldesley Urban District Council. Tyldesley lies about ten miles to the West of Manchester. I had previously, in order to gain practical experience, spent a year with a civil engineering contractor. The pier at Bowness-upon-Windermere is a monument to my construction skills. The work was interesting and Bowness is a lovely place. Because the demolition of the old pier and the construction of the new one could only take place in the off-season between October and April we had to carry out the work during that period. If it had not been for playing rugby for Kendal, a winter in Bowness would have driven me mad. Some years ago I took the family to Bowness to see the pier. The boys jumped up and down on it to show that it was still safe.

I had however decided that my future lay in local government. After Bowness I had obtained a post as an Assistant Engineer in Tyldesley Urban District Council. I had subsequently been promoted to Deputy Engineer to the Council. When I had applied for the post of Deputy, the Engineer, Bill Barber told me not to be disappointed if I was not appointed, as I was very young for the post.

When I had been interviewed for the post of Assistant Engineer that I first held, it had been great fun. The whole Council were seated in a horseshoe pattern looking towards a dais where the Chairman and the Council officers sat. The candidate being interviewed sat at the apex of the horseshoe so he had members of the Council on either side of him. On these occasions it was customary for the Chairman to start off by asking a few general questions about you. The Engineer would then ask about the type of work that you had done. After this, the Chairman would ask if any of the members would like to ask a question. Usually nothing further was asked. But on this occasion the member who was sitting on my right said in a broad Lancashire accent 'Dost tha play roogby?' I replied that I did. He continued, 'What position dost tha play?' I replied that I played wing forward. He called to the Chairman, 'We need one o' them.' The man on the other side was a typical collier. His head was shaved for easy washing at the pithead—I suppose that nowadays, it would be called a Grant Mitchell haircut. He said, 'If you came to Tyldesley where would you live?'

I replied that I would have to look for digs.

'You're not a bad looking lad, you should have no trouble at all in Tyldesley.'

The other members laughed uproariously. I blushed furiously and the Chairman banged his gavel loudly.

Later, the Engineer told me that there was no doubt that I was going to be appointed. The councillors liked me on sight and they were unanimous in offering me the post. The two councillors who had spoken were both right. When I arrived in Tyldesley to take up my appointment, I found digs with a retired miner, Joe Kelly, and his wife. Between them they took it as their aim in life to see that I should be as comfortable as possible, and should be fed as well as possible. In those days, food was still severely rationed but in the summer, when I was not playing rugby, I put on quite a bit of weight and had to train hard to get it off again.

When I first arrived to take up residence in Tyldesley it was a wet Sunday evening. It looked very depressing and I wondered whether I had made a mistake. On the Monday I went down to the rugby club. I had written to say that I was coming and would like to play. The selectors were picking the team for the following Saturday and it actually turned out that one of the regular wing forwards was injured. On the strength of the reputations of the clubs that I had played for, Dunfermline, Stafford and Kendal, they decided to put me in. From then on I was a regular. Eventually, after a couple of years, I became captain.

The rugby in Tyldesley was of an excellent standard. We were a Rugby Union club in the heart of a Rugby League area. We had to play attractive rugby if we wanted anyone to watch. They had a saying that if the ball was for kicking it would be round. Even the full back was expected to run with the ball when he caught it. In modern rugby, because of changes in the rules, that is no longer unusual but at that time in Rugby Union the fullback was always expected to kick. As a wing forward, it meant that I had a lot of running to do to cover him which made me much fitter than I had been When I went back to Edinburgh I would turn out for the Holy Cross Academy Former Pupils. As I seemed to pop up everywhere, one of my friends said, 'Do you play everywhere for this club in Lancashire?' Tyldesley was a typical Lancastrian industrial town. With its coalmines and cotton mills and row upon row of terrace houses it was like a painting by LS Lowry. Many of the houses did not have a proper toilet and still had a night-soil collection from outside bucket lavatories. When we lived there, in the early morning, you could still hear the sound of people going to the mills wearing wooden-soled clogs. They have a saying in Lancashire 'From clogs to clogs in three generations'. Strangely enough, the Chinese have a similar saying, which says that fortunes are made and lost in three generations. The American version is, 'from shirt-sleeve to shirt-sleeve in three generations'.

King George V visited the town of Tyldesley in 1936. The *Manchester Guardian* (as it then was) described it as being 'unblushingly ugly'. I suppose that that was not an unfair description of it. Years later, a friend of ours Joan Hassall, who was born in Tyldesley, was on a visit to Edinburgh. She said, 'I can't believe it. Today, I have met two people who actually came to Tyldesley on holiday!' The two people were Wyn and my sister Patricia. Because there had been mining disasters over the years, people in such areas as Tyldesley find that helping each other comes naturally. One old miner told me that there were families in Tyldesley who had been in debt to shopkeepers from the General Strike in 1926 until the start of the war in 1939. Nobody pressed for payment.

The barber who cut my hair was a rabid Bolton Wanderers fan. We used to have bets—the price of a haircut. He would bet on Bolton and I would bet on Tyldesley Rugby Club. As Bolton lost more than they won, and Tyldesley won much more than they lost, I could built up a tranche of free haircuts to last through the summer till the season started again.

Parenthood and emigration

My next target was to become a full member of the Institution of Civil Engineers. I was already a student member and had to sit the final examination which you could not sit until you had reached the age of twenty three. In April 1949, two months after I had reached the minimum age, I was due to go to London to appear before the examiners. I thought that I should make myself look more mature so I grew a moustache. Wyn liked it. Over fifty years on, quite white, it is still there.

I satisfied the examiners that I knew enough engineering to be a corporate member but I had to wait until I reached the age of twenty five before I could use the designatory letters after my name to show that status. Engineers love designatory letters after their names. Nowadays, if I were to put all those letters to which I am entitled on my notepaper there would be precious little room for the correspondence.

When we arrived in Tyldesley together after our marriage Wyn charmed everyone. She found as I had that she was welcomed into the community with great warmth. The butcher's wife, whose son played rugby, made sure that her first attempt at cooking a Sunday joint was a great success. When I met the son at rugby training on the following Tuesday he said that his mother had given her the tenderest piece of meat in the shop. She had apparently commented that if Wyn made a mess of that she had to be a terrible cook.

My employers had given us the house but then we had to furnish it. Before we could move in our next-door neighbour had made sure that it was spotless from top to bottom. A Mr Griffiths ran the main furniture shop in Tyldesley. A tubby, Pickwickian character who had moved from Scotland many years before, he supplied us with all our needs. Mrs Griffiths showed Wyn how to make curtains. We were to pay for it all as and when we had sufficient money. I think that we managed it in about a year. In the month that we finally paid the debt off we survived on eggs and cheese. Wyn had learned to make a cheese soufflé and our luxury was shortbread, which Wyn had also learned to make. Years later we met Mr Griffiths' son Dick in Malaysia. He was a rubber planter.

Wyn was known as the rugby player's wife. She joined the Dramatic Society and played the leading role in a play called 'The Lady From Edinburgh'. She was a great success. From then on I was 'the actress's husband'. The people in Tyldesley were marvellous, full of warmth and always ready to help. They were, I suppose, 'nosey', but not in a nasty way. They genuinely wanted to know all about you. Lace curtains twitched all the time. When we had left Edinburgh Wyn had borrowed a couple of suitcases from her mother. After we had been in Tyldesley for about six weeks she decided to send them back to Edinburgh by rail. One morning, after I had gone off to work, she was leaving the house carrying the suitcases. A window of the house next door shot open and a voice, full of concern, called out 'You're not leaving us so soon, are you, love?' Our neighbour thought that she was running home to mother.

When you work in an area where there is mining subsidence you learn all sorts of interesting things. Sewers apparently run uphill. Water mains suddenly split and houses have to be abandoned, as they are about to collapse. As Deputy Engineer I had charge of the water distribution system. I would get messages saying 'Could you ensure that the water pressure in the mains is kept up on Sunday, as the Methodist Church is having a special service?' They had an organ that depended on water pressure for it to work. In November 1951, our elder son, Douglas was born in the Firs nursing home in Leigh. We were overjoyed. Wyn's great pride was to take him out in the magnificent pram that we bought. Unfortunately, the beautiful covers on it got very dirty from the grit and dust in the air. One day, when he was working for the CBI Douglas was at a lunch, sitting next to Sir William Barlow, who at the time was Chairman of BICC. During their discussion, Sir William said that he had just returned from 'the north'. When Douglas asked where he had visited, he replied that it was a place called Leigh in Lancashire that Douglas had probably never heard of. Douglas replied that not only had he heard of it but that he was actually born there.

Not long after Douglas was born, I was appointed to the post of Engineer and Surveyor to the Urban District Council of Longridge, a lovely area to the North-east of Preston. I had really made a tremendous start in local government and I was a Chief Officer at the age of twenty six. I always seemed to be doing things at a very young age.

We should have been content. We had a nice house in a nice area. I was soon playing rugby for Preston Grasshoppers. I had an excellent job and our future looked very bright indeed. However Wyn and I both felt that there was a whole wide world that we would never see if we carried on climbing up a small ladder.

In areas such as Longridge the people can become astonishingly parochial in outlook. This was brought home to me very vividly at a meeting of the housing committee to decide on the allocation of houses being built by the council. They were discussing one couple. A member said, 'He's not a local lad.' Someone else said, 'But he's married to a local lass and they've lived in Longridge for fifteen years.' By this time, I thought that the man must have come from outer space. He actually came from Ribchester three miles along the road.

After considerable discussion Wyn and I came up with the idea was that we would go abroad for three or four years to see what it was like. We could always come home again if we did not like it. I did not think that a spell overseas would harm my career prospects so we took the decision that I should look for a post overseas. In this as in most of the important decisions throughout our life together Wyn and I have found that we tend to come to the same decisions. We may arrive at the decision by different routes but the result is the same. I went to a lecture on lateral thinking once. At the end of it I said to the person sitting next to me, 'My wife thinks like that all the time.' Feminine intuition may be an example of lateral thinking.

Purely by chance I saw an advertisement for an engineer in Malacca in Malaya (as it then was). I applied. The man who interviewed me told me that I was a surprise applicant. Apparently nearly all the advertisements that they put in the technical press attracted replies from the same people. I told him that this was the first time that we had thought of seeking employment overseas and was delighted when my application was successful. Actually when I eventually took up my post in Malacca I discovered to my surprise that I was being employed at a salary higher than the salary that had been advertised.

It was all very exciting for Wyn and me. Apart from our honeymoon in Ireland neither of us had been outside the United Kingdom before and here we were contemplating moving to start a new life in a country on the other side of the world. For all that we knew about it we might have been going off into outer space. I think that some of our relatives thought that we were mad. We thought that it would be fun.

What an adventure! We started to read about Malaya. We learned that it lay between three and seven degrees north of the equator. That the capital was Kuala Lumpur and the average temperature was in the nineties. It was also said to have very high humidity. The population was given as being around 10 million. We had to sell all the furniture that we had bought new not so long before. There were injections to get and clothes to buy. We were given a book, which recommended that we take with us solar topees, and spine pads. Most people had stopped wearing such things long before the war. There was still the threat of the Communist insurrection and our relatives were fearful for our safety. One of our neighbours in Longridge promised that she would keep an eye on the newspapers to see if we had been shot.

When I arrived in London on 26th March 1953 to catch a flight to Singapore the streets were already being decorated for the celebration of the Queen's Coronation. The BOAC flight left at one minute to midnight. It was the first time that I had been on an aeroplane and of all planes I found myself on a Comet. I looked out of the window at the jet engines with flames shooting out of them. I was sure that we were in for trouble. This was in the middle of the problems with metal fatigue and eventually after several crashes the Government decided that all Comets should be grounded until the cause of the problem could be discovered. But this had not happened yet.

The plane stopped in India. When we took off again a passenger who came on board told me that he had been at the airport three weeks earlier and had watched a Comet crash after take-off, just the thing to inspire confidence. This particular Comet arrived safely in Singapore but a month later it crashed in the Mediterranean. This was the plane that was salvaged and subjected to the tests that showed that the crashes were caused by metal-fatigue. Fortunately the metal had not been sufficiently fatigued when I flew on it.

When you step off the plane in Singapore you are immediately hit by the heat and the humidity. You sweat profusely. My new boss from Malacca Paddy McDowell had come to meet me. The first thing that he did was to take me to buy some white drill shorts and Aertex shirts. Once I was wearing these I found that I very quickly became acclimatised. We stayed overnight at the famous Raffle's Hotel, renowned for its Gin Sling, before proceeding to Malacca.

Malacca

The day after I arrived in Singapore I was walking along the street and quite literally bumped into a friend that I had played rugby against at school. He had also been at university at the same time as I had.

It has been said that for many years Scotland's two biggest exports were whisky and people and Malaya had its fair share of both. It did not surprise me that from time to time I met school and university friends who were also living there. I played rugby against a lad called Jimmie Meikle, who was a former pupil of Trinity Academy just down the road from Holy Cross, and who I had played against at school. As he was a scrumhalf and I was a wing forward we were old rivals. Niall McLeod who had been a fellow student at Edinburgh University came to live in the house behind ours. There was another amazing coincidence when I served in the office of Sheriff of the City of London in 1988. Simon Block, my brother Sheriff, and I discovered that we had played in the same State rugby team in Malaya in 1953.

Wyn was coming out by sea with Douglas who was now sixteen months old. I had to get things organised before she arrived just over a month after I arrived in Malacca and was booked into the Government Rest House, a sort of hotel owned by the Government. The idea was that government officers who were transferred around the country could find accommodation there until they obtained permanent accommodation. Non-government employees could stay there for a limited period if there were vacancies. Staying at the Rest House when I arrived was Dr. McMahon who was taking up the post of Chief Medical Officer of the Settlement of Malacca. He was one of the most senior doctors in the Government Service. He had been a prisoner of the Japanese during the war in the notorious Changi Jail, but he was very reluctant to speak about his experiences. Dr. McMahon was so senior that he was able to choose where he wanted to work. Rather than work in one of the larger states or the headquarters in Kuala Lumpur he chose Malacca because he liked the atmosphere. He was a devout Irish Catholic whose wife had remained in Ireland to see to the education of their six children. He was about to move into the Chief Medical Officer's house, a large building in the grounds of the General Hospital and he offered to take me in as a paying-guest until Wyn arrived.

When he heard that I was staying with the Chief Medical Officer, one of my overseers told me that there was some cheating going on at the Hospital. It was with regard to the bread deliveries and patients were going hungry because of a shortage of bread. I passed the message on to Dr. McMahon one evening. The next morning he was off very early. At lunchtime he told me that he had arrived at the hospital as the bread was being delivered. There was indeed a scam being worked. Those who were receiving the bread were signing for large quantities that were not being delivered. McMahon warned me that this was the sort of corrupt practice, which could occur if checking systems were allowed to fall into disuse. In Britain Wyn and I had had our name on a register for a car for a year or two and there was no telling whether we would have been able to afford it when our name came up. Wyn had driven an ambulance when she was sixteen and had a driving licence. She had learned to drive on a vehicle where she had to double-declutch in order to change gear. This was a difficult technique to master but she had passed her test and had driven the large ambulance in the blackout with headlights masked so that there was only about one square-inch of light. It must have been very scary. I did not have a licence, so I had to take a driving test before I bought a new Ford Consul so that I could make the 250-mile journey from Malacca to Singapore to meet Wyn and Douglas off the ship.

The Emergency was at its height with the area between Malacca and Singapore particularly dangerous because of Communist terrorist activity. Before I started my journey I was warned that, under no circumstances, should I stop between the villages along the route. In Malaya along the main roads there were villages every twelve miles because in the days when government officials travelled by bullock-cart twelve miles was a day's journey. During the

Emergency most of the villages had barbed wire fences round them and gates which were closed at night. Curfews were strictly enforced.

So just over a month after my arrival in the country I drove south to Singapore, expecting to be ambushed at any moment by machine-gun-toting communist terrorists. Much of the way the road was bordered by rows of rubber trees. As I had started out on my journey early in the morning I could see the rubber tappers making the cuts in the bark of the trees to abstract the milky latex which is chemically treated to make the rubber that we see in our car tyres. There was not much traffic and everything seemed quite peaceful. Occasionally a convoy of military vehicles with armoured cars and Malay or British troops in them would pass, a reminder that there was a nasty, vicious war on, with British rubber-planters and tin mine managers often prized targets. At that time the economy of Malaya was heavily dependent on the export of tin and rubber and one of the aims of the terrorists was to try to upset the economy of the country. Because of the war in Korea the prices of both commodities had been pushed up to very high levels enabling the owners of the mines and the rubber estates to make it financially rewarding for managers to put up with the risks of remaining in their posts. Many of them however sent their families home to Britain for safety.

In those days the *Straits Times* used to publish the names of the passengers who were on the ships that were due to arrive the next day. Among those listed as arriving on the s.s. *Corfu* were 'Mrs McWilliams and two children'. When I had left about a month before there had only been one. Thankfully it turned out to be a misunderstanding.

My employers, the Municipal Council of Malacca, had sent a lorry to escort us back to Malacca and to carry our luggage. After spending a night in Singapore we started our journey North. We had been going for an hour or so when Douglas started to get restless. Wyn suggested that we stop the car and put him down to sleep in the back. Without thinking I stopped at the side of the road and we settled him on the back seat. Our escort lorry had disappeared ahead of us. It was not until we reached a village about ten miles further on that we caught up with it. It was parked beside the police station and the driver was explaining to a policeman that we had been following him and had disappeared. Apparently we had chosen one of the most dangerous sections of the road to stop. Ignorance is bliss.

The house we were given in Malacca by the Municipality was a lovely colonial style bungalow raised off the ground on wooden columns, set among mature trees and bushes. There were huge angsanas, colourful red and yellow flame and graceful casurina trees besides all shades of bougainvillaeas, oleanders, ixoras and caesalpineas. It was a most pleasant introduction to life as a 'colonial'.

The grounds round our house were maintained by the Municipality and our part of the grounds had a tennis-court, the surface made of ant-hill earth, was rolled and swept to give quite a true playing surface.

One evening, about a week after we had taken up residence in this very pleasant house I heard a scream coming from the bathroom. I dashed in half-expecting to see Wyn being mauled by a tiger, or at least being squeezed by a large python. I found her standing fully clothed quivering. She pointed at the bath. The tap was running and scuttling hither and thither in the bath was a spider, probably it was about the size of a 50p coin. In addition it had a large white sac under its belly. I quickly got hold of a newspaper, rolled it up and hit the spider. The white sac burst and hundreds of tiny spiders ran out. I washed the whole lot down the plughole. I hope that some of them survived to frighten some other 'Mem' (the term used by Malayans for expatriate ladies)—I hadn't the heart to be a mass murderer of infant spiders. The usual occupant of the bungalow was the Municipal Secretary who was away on leave. When he returned we moved into a house nearby which was huge and, apart from everything else, had rooms for six servants! It had a large sitting area upstairs with over fifty pairs of louvered shutters. The house had been designed and built by the Municipal Engineer in the 1930s. All the timber had been picked in the jungle by the Engineer himself and floated down the Malacca River. It had then been left to season before being used in the construction.

In Malacca there are occasional storms that come from Sumatra, which lies across the Malacca Straits to the West, and are therefore called Sumatras. Driven by a strong wind Sumatras do not last long but heavy rain came horizontally through the louvers on the shutters, hit the ceiling and so gave the effect of an internal waterfall. Considerable mopping up was required.

Tropical thunderstorms can be awesome. The sky turns black then the great flashes of lightning are followed almost immediately by loud cracks of thunder that seem to shake the building that you are in. Rain pours down in solid sheets. Umbrellas are practically useless but the local umbrellas called payongs made from varnished paper on a wooden frame are widely used to try to keep the rain off as you make a quick dash to your car. In the car, windscreen wipers have difficulty in removing the large volume of water so that you can drive. Keen to experience a tropical storm the King of Saudi Arabia paid a visit to Malaya. He had timed his visit to coincide with what should have been a rainy season but although he remained for a week, he left without seeing one.

We settled down well. Some people found it difficult to come to terms with the high temperature and humidity but we quickly got used to it. The mosquitoes however took a particular liking to Wyn and she was very quickly covered in little blisters from their bites. She recovered from these and seemed to acquire immunity from them except that some time later she was infected with Dengue fever, a malaria-like fever. Fortunately unlike malaria it does not recur. Thereafter we both found Malaya to be a very healthy place to live.

One problem with the house was that there was a colony of rats in the roof. You could hear them cavorting about above the ceiling when you lay in bed. We were told that they were a harmless species and that they did not carry the deadly diseases normally associated with rats. That was fine until one day we saw one. It was huge. It was running up the bathroom wall with a whole bar of soap in its mouth. We had heard of people on oil palm estates who had a python in their roof to keep down the rat population. We were not that brave so we got the rat exterminator from the Municipal Health

Left: Sgt John McWilliams
and Mary Ann McWilliams
1915

Below left: Wyn McWilliams
aged twenty one

Below: Francis McWilliams
Graduation 1945

The Staff of Petaling Jaya Development Corporation.
Sir Francis McWilliams is front row fourth from the right

The Municipal Councillors and Executive Officers of the
Town and Fort of Malacca, 1954
Sir Francis McWilliams, standing second left

Sir Francis and Lady McWilliams supervising the construction of the Petaling Jaya stall at a trade exhibition in Singapore, 1954

Golf Match at HRH the Sultan of Selangor's Palace. Seated l to r: Tom Critchley Australian High Commissioner, The Yang Dipertuan Agong (the Raja of Perlis), HRH the Sultan of Selangor, Tengku Abdul Rahman (the first Prime Minister of Malaya), the Thai Ambassador, Dato' Bill McLeod. Sir Francis McWilliams is standing third from the right

House with Kindergarten next door. 1965

Our cook Ah Zoon

The McWilliams family 1958

Two amahs,
Theresa and Tangachee
(Both later had arranged
marriages and were
happy)

Staff of Assunta Primary School.
Lady McWilliams third from left in front row

One of the classes at St Anne's Kindergarten.
Teacher on left,
Mrs Murad.
Lady McWilliams
on right

Sports Day at St Anne's, 1966
Douglas is the starter. Michael is the marshal

Department to do the job. We had two house servants, one called Mary and the other called Theresa. They were both of Chinese extraction and coincidentally Catholics. Mary was paid 120 Malayan dollars (about £15.00) per month and Theresa 60 (£7.50) per month. We had a part-time gardener at 20 Malayan dollars per month, and a part-time driver who drove a night-soil lorry at night who was paid 30 Malayan dollars. I was paid about 1600 Malayan dollars (about £200.00) per month. Considering that in England I had been earning around £55.00 per month we thought that we were quite well off. Government and quasi-government salaries included a High Cost of Living allowance. This was sometimes referred to as a, 'Cost of High Living allowance'.

Theresa was about eighteen. She had been an orphan brought up by the nuns in a local convent. At that time it was still quite common for Chinese girl babies to be abandoned at the door of a convent. Boys were valued but girls were looked on as another mouth to feed. Convent girls were looked on as good wives, being obedient, and hard working and appreciated having a home of their own. They were also very frugal. When the nuns deemed that Theresa was old enough they found a husband for her and she married very happily. A young Tamil girl called Tangachee who was the gardener's daughter replaced Theresa.

Shortly after he returned from his leave the Municipal Secretary had gone to Kuala Lumpur. He was to represent the Resident Commissioner in his role as President of the Municipality at a meeting. The next morning, there were lurid headlines in some of the newspapers. 'Municipal Secretary caught with his pants down', was one of the less obscene headlines. Apparently, he was a homosexual. To provide a cover he had married a local Eurasian girl. On his trips away from Malacca he was in the habit of picking up partners. On this occasion he had picked up a young man and they were caught by the police in his car. I think that he was fined. It caused a great scandal. The Resident Commissioner was especially angry because it had happened when the Municipal Secretary had been representing him. Shortly afterwards the Municipal Secretary left Malaya for New Zealand.

Malacca was known as 'Sleepy Hollow'. It had once been the centre of a powerful Sultanate. Subsequently it had been under the control of the Portuguese and then the Dutch. Eventually, there was an exchange between the Dutch and the British. The British took over Malacca and the Dutch took over Batavia. Each nation in turn left its mark. Together with Singapore and Penang, Malacca formed what were called the Straits Settlements. The Straits Settlements were governed by the Colonial Office, each of the Settlements having a Resident Commissioner who was Her Majesty's representative. The Resident Commissioner in Malacca was also President of the Municipal Council. He was a well-known bottom-pincher. All the ladies knew to keep out of his reach.

The heads of the various departments were all expatriates as were many of the senior staff. In the Municipality I was to all intents the Deputy to the Municipal Engineer Paddy McDowell who was from Northern Ireland.

When Wyn and I arrived there Malacca was a town of about 60,000 people of many different colours and ethnic origins. The original Malays lived mainly in the rural areas around the town. They were rice and vegetable farmers and fishermen.

The Portuguese had left their mark with a community, which had settled in Malacca and had intermarried with the local people. They were a closely-knit community and had names redolent of the romantic period of sea exploration such as Rodrigues, DaCosta and DaSilva. They spoke a form of the Portuguese language, called Cristang. It would have been fully understood in the sixteenth century but was almost unintelligible to a modern Portuguese. They were all Catholics and since they had all attended the Catholic Mission schools they also spoke English. Because of this many of them tended to obtain junior supervisory jobs like the Eurasians in India. But some of the Portuguese had fallen on hard times. The government had set aside a piece of land and built houses on it for them. It was called the Portuguese Settlement. Those who could, moved out of the Settlement as soon as they could afford to do so. Those who remained eked out a living by fishing. On the Feast of Saints Peter and Paul they decorated their boats and on one occasion I was asked to help to judge the decorated boats.

The Portuguese had a great devotion to St Francis Xavier, a Portuguese Jesuit missionary. His body lies in Goa on the east coast of India. While it was being carried there from the Far East it had come to Malacca on its journey. A church had been built in Malacca, in his honour. The original church is now a ruin. A new church was built and for nearly four hundred years the Portuguese government has paid to keep a Portuguese priest in Malacca. Even when there was a Communist government in Portugal they still paid for the priest.

For hundreds of years people from China have travelled all over the Far East as traders and migrants. Many of them settled in Malacca, their descendants retaining their ancient culture, rather in the same fashion as the Portuguese. The Malacca Chinese cemetery is reputed to be the largest Chinese cemetery outside China. They have Chinese names but they generally speak none of the Chinese dialects, although they speak the Malay language fluently. They are known as the Straits Chinese or colloquially as 'Babas' (I never found out why). Their ladies are called 'nonyas' and have a distinctive form of dress which is recognised throughout Malaysia. Their gold brooches and earrings have been handed down in families for many generations and are valuable antiques. When they marry they dress in old Manchu style costume. Malacca was indeed a very good place to buy Chinese antiques. Unfortunately at the time when they were very reasonably priced we did not have the money to purchase many.

Shortly after our arrival in Malacca Wyn and I were invited to a Chinese wedding. At the dinner we were enjoying our first experience of proper Chinese food with, among the delicacies Abalone. Someone asked what it was. Told that it was sea slug there was a clatter of chopsticks on plates. Wyn and I were assured that it was quite edible and ate it quite happily. Seated at the same table was a British rubber-planter. He said that he did not eat Chinese food as he had tried it when he had arrived in Malaya before the war and did not like it. He had not tried it again.

Most of the Indians in Malaya came from South India. They spoke Tamil, which must be the most quarrelsome sounding language in the world. The Malays say that when God was giving out languages He took up a tin and half filled it with stones and shook it, and that is the Tamil language. There were also Malayalees from around Trivandrum in India. They were mainly employed in the steel-erection and pipe-laying business. There were Indian Muslims and Pakistanis. There were people of mixed race of various hues. Some of them had come from India, some were Portuguese, and some were the progeny of liaisons between rubber-planters and their workers.

Since young planters were not allowed to marry until they had reached a certain level of seniority it was not uncommon for a bachelor to have a Tamil 'maid' in his house to look after his needs. On some rubber estates there was a sort of 'Droit de Seigneur' and it was regarded as a mark of favour on the family of a girl so chosen. Most of these planters were moved from estate to estate. The plantation companies deducted a fixed maintenance allowance from their salaries for any children left behind.

When we first arrived Wyn and I found it difficult to distinguish between the different races. True their complexions varied in colour from very pale to very dark but the thing that we noticed most was that everyone smiled a lot. They say that when you arrive in a new place to live you should take photographs of the things that strike you as strange. At the beginning you see things more clearly. You usually adjust to them very quickly and they no longer seem strange. We did not do this and very quickly became used to the sight of old ladies with their feet bound in accordance with the old Chinese custom, painfully thin opium-smoking rickshaw pullers and other such unusual sights which have long since disappeared. Some of the first Tamils that I saw I thought were bleeding from their mouths. It turned out that they were chewing betel nut.

Formerly, the Straits Settlements were administered by the East India Company under a charter granted by the British Government. The administrators brought many of the Indian colonial attitudes with them to Malaya. Not least of these was that the administrators were 'The Heaven Born'. As such they were vastly superior to anyone else. Each civil service post was equated to a military rank. I presume that the Governor was a general, the Settlement Secretary a colonel and so on down to the humblest second lieutenant. At dinners among government staff people had to be seated according their rank. Woe betide a hostess who got it wrong. Since we were not in government service we were to some extent excused strict compliance. If you needed to know and had experienced servants they could set you on the right path. They knew who was who. Their own status was determined by the status of their employer.

Once, some time after we had moved from Malacca Wyn and I were at a party where it was announced that 'colonels and above' would lunch in one room and others in another. As we were trying to decide whether or not I held the rank of colonel a friend who was the third wife of the first Yang Di Pertuan Agong (The King) of Malaysia told us that as we were friends of hers I had to rank at least as a colonel.

Most of our social life in Malacca centred on The Club. It had a hall with a bar, for dances, a 'padang' (sports field) for rugby, hockey, soccer and cricket. A swimming pool and a nine-hole golf course were located near the sea, just outside the Municipal boundary. Although soccer, cricket and hockey matches were played against local teams, membership of the Club itself was restricted to Europeans. There was a proposal to open the membership to non-Europeans, with the debate at a meeting called to discuss the matter very heated and emotional. Most of the argument was spurious but the proposal was heavily defeated.

Our social life was among fellow expatriates, many of whom had lived for years in the country and apart from shopkeepers, their servants and people at work, never met any local people, nor sadly met any of them socially. Being an expatriate Briton gave you a status that you never had in UK. I suppose that you became part of some kind of superior class. It could at times be embarrassing. If I was driving along the road and one of the road gang supervisors, called a 'mandore' was coming in the opposite direction on his bicycle he would dismount and practically get down on his knees until I had passed.

Wyn and I played badminton, tennis, golf, and swam. According to the season I also played rugby or hockey. The hockey was terrifying. Malaya was Olympic class and some of the local police whom we played against were in the Malayan team. I never really got used to the ball flying around at the speed of a bullet. Sometimes, after a game of golf we would go to the swimming club and watch the magnificent tropical sunsets. The sun like a huge flaming red ball dropped spectacularly into the sea.

We were sitting there one evening under the gently swaying coconut palms, watching the sun go down in a glorious display of reds and golds, drinking a cold Tiger beer (one of the best beers that I know). Harry Mathieson, one of our friends, remarked, 'People spend hundreds of pounds to go to exotic places to do this, and here we are actually being paid to do it.' He was right. Life was indeed very pleasant as an expatriate in Malaya unless you were a planter on a lonely rubber estate with terrorists on your doorstep. Harry, the State Agricultural Officer, was born in St Andrews and had played golf almost as soon as he could walk. He was one of the best golfers in Malaya, and also a very good speaker of the Malay language.

Working in a quasi-government organisation, I was expected to learn the Malay language. The Municipality paid for me to have a 'munshi' (Malay teacher) come twice a week to teach me. He was much more interested in improving his English than teaching me his language, and as a result, I did not learn as much as I had hoped. I did, however, pass the examination set by the Government and was paid extra for doing so. One day I heard an engineer, who had been in the country for many years speaking the language with a Cockney accent. It sounded dreadful. I determined that I would learn to speak it properly.

Colonialism is often portrayed as having been exploitative. In many ways, it was. Certainly, the Commonwealth was used by the British as a source of vital commodities and as a captive market for goods produced. Preferential tariffs enabled British manufacturers to corner markets. It may seem unbelievable now, in these days of the ubiquitous Nissans and Hondas, but at one time 40% of all cars purchased in Malaya were Austins. In return, however, the British set up systems of local and central administration and of education, which were designed to lead the Commonwealth country towards independence. The same cannot, however, be said of the Dutch and the Belgians. Of the Dutch it was said that they gave too little, and took too much. Some of the Belgian colonies were the private property of the King. The French operated a system geared towards colonisation and settlement by citizens of the mother country. The British system led to the joke that after independence, usually the first president had been educated at the London School of Economics and the second president, at Sandhurst. This was not so much a fault in the system but rather in the people who were operating it.

My first job at work was to complete a land reclamation scheme and lay out a park and garden. This had to be completed in time for an opening ceremony as part of the celebration of the Queen's Coronation. I had only just over two months to do it. Fortunately the weather stayed dry until I had filled in the land with lorry-load after lorry-load of earth. After it was levelled and lightly rolled, black soil was brought in from the jungle and spread. Turf was laid and trees and shrubs planted and then we had a mini-monsoon. I was fortunate to have the excellent advice of my friend Harry as to what to plant and how to plant it. By the beginning of June I had to get grass cut and the bushes trimmed. Such are the joys of gardening in the tropics.

The Coronation was celebrated with a floodlit pageant with all communities taking part. There were also many sporting events. There are still trophies being played for called 'The Coronation Cup' whose origins have long been forgotten. One of the Municipal Councillors in Malacca, Mr Mahindasa, was a former teacher. He was Singhalese, having come from Ceylon. He was certainly more British than the British. During the occupation of Malaya by the Japanese he had been in the habit of declaring openly his allegiance to the British. He was a teacher and a very popular man. The Japanese were loath to arrest him. However, he would call out to his friends in the street 'Did you hear the BBC last night?' He would then relate loudly the latest defeat that had befallen the Japanese. Eventually they decided that he was going too far and they put him in jail. They had already killed his brother called Pamindasa. Fortunately before they could do Mr Mahindasa any harm the Japanese had to leave. He was very friendly and spoke the most impeccable English.

One of the great advantages of taking a post overseas is the chance to assume greater responsibility at a relatively young age. In Malacca I found this to be the case. However some of the problems were of a type that had nothing to do with engineering. Not long after I arrived, one afternoon a group of our road workers were ushered into my office. They were Tamils. Many Tamils had been brought to Malaya from South India to work on the roads and on the rubber plantations. In the Municipality when they retired they went back to India. The money that they had saved in the Municipal Provident Fund enabled them to buy a piece of land and live in relative comfort.

The group consisted of two couples aged about forty and a small girl who looked about twelve years old. The girl was carrying a tiny baby. The overseer who was in charge of the group explained that one couple were the parents of a young man who had worked for us. He sadly had died recently. The other couple were the parents of the girl. There was a dispute about who was entitled to the deceased man's Provident Fund. One couple claimed that the young man had married their daughter and that the baby was the child of that marriage. They claimed that the girl was entitled to the money. The other couple did not deny that their dead son was father of the child. However they denied that there had been any marriage. Because none of the group spoke any English the overseer had to interpret for me. I heard the story at great length. Then I asked the overseer what he recommended that I should do. He said that he thought that both parties would be satisfied if I decreed that the money should be shared equally between the young man's parents and the young girl. So I made a judgement after the fashion of King Solomon. I ordered that the money should be split down the middle. Both parties went off seemingly happy with the decision.

Because Malaya was promoting the use of rubber in road surfacing I conducted an experiment with rubber in a road surface. It was on a bridge that had quite steep approaches. I did one side with rubber and the other without. Any time I returned to Malacca in later years I would go to have a look. All I can say is that the result was inconclusive. Neither side showed signs of wear.

We had been in Malacca for about six months when the Settlement Water Engineer Ken Buchanan was due to go on long leave for six months and I was asked to take on the job while he was away. There was a large programme of work being completed and one of my responsibilities was testing the large cast iron pipes that had come from England. The pipes had apparently crossed the Indian Ocean in the middle of a monsoon. As a result of the rough seas many of them had cracks. In those days, the fine cracks could not be detected until the pipes had been laid, filled with water, and put under pressure. Once the pressure was applied there would suddenly be an almighty crack and the water would gush out. It was most frustrating work. Nowadays, the pipes could be tested before they were laid. Wyn said I became so immersed in the failures of the pipelines that I hardly spoke to her for about three months.

Before he had left for his leave Ken had told me that every week I had to visit the site of one of the dams at Asahan in the North of the State of Johore. As this was a dangerous bandit area, if I wanted, the police would give me a Smith and Wesson .38 revolver. Although I had learned to use one in my Home Guard days I did not take advantage of the offer. If you are going to use such a weapon properly you have to practise with it. In a fight with a terrorist using an automatic weapon a revolver would have been pretty useless in my hands. I also believed that carrying a weapon I would be a target for the weapon rather than for myself. The waterworks foreman told me that when Ken went to visit the dam he had carried the revolver slung low clearly visible in a holster like a cowboy in a film.

When Ken returned from his leave we discussed the matter. He decided to take my advice and forget about asking for a revolver. Not long afterwards the police rang him up and invited him round to the police station. They wanted to show him something. It appeared that they had shot and killed a Communist terrorist. He was carrying the camp diary in his pack. One entry of a few days before stated, 'The European engineer came to the dam. He was unarmed so we did not open fire.'

On one of my visits to the dam I had called in to a rubber estate where the manager was an old planter named Shepherd. He had been on the estate since 1926 and often came into Malacca to play golf, at weekends. He had asked me to call in when I was passing. During the war when the Japanese had come to the estate he was away in the volunteers. His house servants had taken all his personal effects and hidden them. When he returned after the war was over everything had been brought back and put in its place. He was a nice old man and highly respected by his workers. When he had accused one of the estate contractors of cheating and had sacked him, the staff warned him that the contractor had links with the terrorists and could be dangerous. Not long afterwards terrorists ambushed Shepherd on the estate and shot him dead.

It was events like this that brought home to you the fact that, although in Malacca itself you were quite safe, outside the town you could be in danger. Driving back from rugby matches on your own you were half-expecting your headlights to pick out a tree that had been felled across the road as an ambush. Wyn always worried when I was playing in places like Johore that were known for serious terrorist activity. Because of the heat and the high humidity I found it difficult to get fully fit for playing rugby. I think that others found the same. The result was that the standard was not as high as I had been used to. Even Wyn said that it was not the same game that she had enjoyed watching. After a couple of seasons I gave it up.

There are none so Scottish as the Scots abroad. The further they are from Scotland the more Scottish they become. We were eight thousand miles away and the St Andrew's Night Ball was the great event in the social calendar. Preparations started many months in advance. Practices of Scottish dances were held. You brought along the guests that you were going to invite to the ball so that they too could learn the complicated reels, Strathspeys and Schottisches that were to be performed on the night. The Ball was held in the Malacca

Club on the nearest Saturday to the 30th November, the Feast of St Andrew, patron saint of Scotland. This occurred in 1954, when Wyn was just recovering from her bout of Dengue fever, but she was determined to attend.

Usually it was possible to get a piper for the Ball from one of the Scottish Regiments engaged in the fight against the terrorists. On this occasion, however, there were no Scottish pipers available. We obtained the services of the pipe-major from the 7th Battalion of the Ghurkas who were stationed in the neighbouring state of Negri Sembilan. He had studied at the School of Piping at Edinburgh Castle and was reputed to be the best non-Caucasian piper in the world. At the Ball, it was my task to look after the piper. When he arrived, I asked him what he would like to drink. He replied that he drank whisky. We had all arranged to have bottles of spirits and wine to be placed on our tables. I poured him what I thought, was a generous measure and asked what he took with it. Most people took either water or soda water. He said that he drank it neat. My generous measure went down in one gulp, and off he went to pipe for a Scottish dance. He was indeed a brilliant piper. His timing was excellent and he had no need for a drummer to keep the correct tempo for the dancing. When he had returned to my table after the dance, my friend, Harry Mathieson, said that he would like to give the piper a drink and asked what he drank. I replied, 'Neat whisky.' Harry poured him an extremely generous measure. Again it was swallowed in one gulp. All through the evening people kept coming up to give the piper a drink. The measures got larger and larger until they were nearly full glasses. All were disposed of the same way. One gulp and they were gone. Every second dance was a reel, a strathspey or a schottische and the piper never missed a beat. The piping and drinking performance went on until three or four in the morning. The piping was brilliant. The drinking was phenomenal!

The Government of the State of Selangor had decided to build a completely new town called Petaling Jaya. The site was about seven miles from Kuala Lumpur, the capital of the Federation of Malaya. The Malay word for new is 'baharu' There had of course been previous settlements called 'new' such as Johore Baharu and Kuala Kubu

Baharu but this was the first time that a pre-planned town was being built to provide for residential, industrial and social needs. In some ways it was similar to places such as Harlow and Crawley in UK. They needed an engineer to take charge of the construction so I applied and was invited for an interview. On the day that Wyn and I went to visit Petaling Jaya so that I could be interviewed we left Douglas with friends, Jimmy and Isobel Miles. Jimmy was manager of a motor company. As a two and a half year old, Douglas was very bright. He spent the day looking at copies of 'Autocar' and other car magazines. One of the magazines happened to be a Motor Show edition and had sketches of all the cars in the Show. By the time that we returned he could recognise and name any car in the book. This recognition was very soon transferred to the vehicles on the road. One day we were coming out of a lunch party and he called out in great excitement 'Look, a Bristol!' The owner was astonished. It was the only car of that make in Malaya. He asked how Douglas knew the make. I replied, with a touch of pride, 'He reads the Autocar.' Douglas still has a great interest in cars. His latest acquisition is an Aston Martin. He also reads phenomenally fast and has a photographic memory.

I was successful in my application for the post of Town Engineer of Petaling Jaya. On the day after the St. Andrew's Ball, 1954 we bade farewell to Malacca. It had been a fascinating introduction to colonial life in a happy and relaxed environment.

Malaya's first modern New Town

On the 1st of December 1954 I took up my appointment in what for the next ten years I considered to be the best job in the whole of Malaya. Not many people get the chance to build a completely new town around themselves. It was the sort of appointment that in UK I would not have expected to get until I was nearly 40 years old. I was 28. The Petaling Jaya Development Corporation had sent a couple of lorries to bring our belongings from Malacca. I learned later that the drivers of the lorries had been told to make enquiries about me from the Malacca workers. Apparently, the verdict was that I was 'Very strict but very fair'. I often wondered if it was anything to do with my Solomonic disposal of the disputed Provident Fund.

The original general planning for the town of Petaling Jaya had been done by the Federal Government Town Planning Department. The word 'Petaling' is the name of a species of tree. 'Jaya' means successful or prosperous. I suppose that in the context of a tree it means fruitful. We were responsible for the detailed planning and everything else. I was in charge of all technical matters. I was at that time the only qualified engineer on the staff. I had quite a number of technical assistants and technicians of various grades, all Malayans of Malay, Chinese, Indian, and Eurasian extraction, and I was delighted to find that the majority were competent and very loyal. I also had about 400 road workers who were mostly Tamils. It was wonderful. There were very few systems in place. I had to set up systems for checking the labour, maintenance of vehicles and fuel consumption. When I started the system for checking fuel consumption some of the vehicles were showing 1 mile to one gallon of petrol. I had also to organise a planning and construction drawing office with a staff of over fifty.

Having been warned by Dr. McMahon in Malacca of the dangers of corruption, I believed that the way to reduce this as far as possible was to have good systems in place and to ensure that the systems were followed. This was what I set out to do. Hopefully I was reasonably successful. Certainly Petaling Jaya has been an enormous success. It has expanded so much that if I go there now I get lost.

Only once in all the time I was in Malaya, was I personally, offered a bribe by a contractor. He shot out of the door, jumped into his car, and sped off with a screeching of tyres and a smell of burning rubber when I furiously told him that he had thirty seconds to get out before I called the police. Naively I had thought that my squeaky clean reputation would protect me from any such approach. He must have been desperate. I was quite happy to attend dinners with the contractors that I worked with. It gave me the opportunity to explain my philosophy to them. That philosophy was that if I accepted a gift from them it could only be as a friend. I would then have to give them a gift at the appropriate time. Then as a friend they had to deal with me with scrupulous fairness. This was the basis on which I dealt with Tiw Wan, one of my contractors. We did a lot of work together and he never let me down once.

When I arrived in Petaling Jaya the roads consisted of red laterite, which was extremely slippery in the wet and sent up clouds of red dust when it was dry. The population was about 700 living in timber houses of various shapes and sizes. The important thing was that they owned the houses that they lived in. The Petaling Jaya Development Corporation had constructed three bungalows on top of a hill in the middle of the development area for its three senior officials of which I was one. The others were the Administrator, who initially was an expatriate member of the Malayan Civil Service, and the Development Officer, another expatriate who was in charge of selling land.

The Emergency was still on. About three miles away there was a New Village called Sungei Way, set up by the Government to resettle people who were squatting on State land nearby. The idea was to prevent them from coming into contact with the terrorists. Some of the people in the village were indeed Communist sympathisers. The Government wished to prevent them from supplying the terrorists with food and medicines. A friend in the police told me that one of the favourite medicinal drinks for the terrorists was Dom Benedictine. The police frequently came across it in food caches. The New

Village was surrounded by a high barbed wire fence. It also had a gate that was closed and locked at night.

Not long after we moved to Petaling Jaya we had a visit from the British Secretary of State for Defence. He arrived with a large retinue in a convoy of armoured personnel-carriers. When they stopped troops armed to the teeth jumped out and surrounded the Secretary of State's vehicle. Only when they were sure that there were no terrorists about was he allowed to get out. The party came to the Administrator's house next door to us for tea. Wyn was asked to lend our silver tea set for the tea. She asked the servants to polish the tea set before it was taken next-door. This they did but after polishing they did not wash it. The milk came out of the jug a horrible green colour. The visitors must have thought that it was one of the hazards of Malayan living to have to take green milk in your tea.

Wyn and I were there to answer questions about the Development. The visitors were keen to know how we were protected. They asked whether we had troops or police to protect us. We said that we had no such protection. They asked whether we had electric fences and floodlighting as they had at the management compounds on most rubber estates. We said that we did not. Quite horrified in view of the tight security around themselves the members of the party asked what we did about security. Wyn and I both gave the same answer, 'We are trying to grow a hedge round the garden.' Afterwards, when we compared notes, we decided that the visitors thought that we were either pulling their legs or that we were insane. In fact we were trying to grow a hedge of a variety called Onato. In the evenings we would go round the garden pinching the shoots at the top of the shrubs in order to thicken up the hedge. Strangely enough we never felt threatened.

Although there were terrorists in the area right up until 1960 they never came into Petaling Jaya. Apparently, because they owned their houses, the people of Petaling Jaya wanted nothing to do with Communism. Sometimes of an evening we would sit on our terrace and watch planes bombing terrorists' camps about four miles away. Where the bombs once fell is now a superb golf course. However other dangers were thought to lurk among the trees. One day whilst

I was inspecting one of the areas under development the drivers of the earth-moving equipment told me that a black panther had been seen in the area. They insisted that I carry a large heavy stick in case I was attacked. I had visions of behaving like a lion-tamer in a circus. The panther was never seen again. Perhaps the sight of me striding around with my big stick frightened it off. There is now a road called in the Malay language 'The Hill of the Black Panther'. There was plenty of other wild life around. Snakes were liable to find their way into the house. They usually came into the bathroom. One day however we found one coiled round a rocking horse. The amah screamed and called her husband. By the time he arrived the snake had disappeared. Eventually we found it lying between the mattress and the spring of one of the beds. Troops of monkeys often came out in the cool of the evening to play by the roadside. On one occasion a monkey got into one of the wardrobes in the children's bedroom and started eating the clothes. Close up even small monkeys are quite frightening when they are angry. We had quite a job to get the monkey out of the house.

The development system was that we cleared the land of the secondary jungle and old rubber trees. We then laid out the roads, put in the services, and sold sites for houses, shops and other purposes. The price of the land that we sold was very cheap. Initially however there was some reluctance to buy. Although it was only seven miles from Kuala Lumpur, people thought that it was too far. In one particular month we sold only six house lots. The fear was that if we did not sell we would have to stop. The initial capital put up by the State Government had been used to purchase the land. Fortunately demand started to increase and sales picked up well. Some time later, I persuaded the Development Corporation that we should build houses for sale. From the profits that we made we were able to improve the standard of development. The houses were sold at a very reasonable price and the demand was very high. The members of the Development Corporation, who lived locally, did the allocation and I think that they used the system to increase the number of their political supporters.

The atmosphere was very friendly. We were always being invited to house-warming parties and other local celebrations. There was none of the colonialist attitude of Malacca. All races mixed together to get the job done. On one occasion we were invited to the opening of a Buddhist nunnery. The food was prepared by the nuns themselves. It was served after the fashion of a normal Chinese dinner but all the courses were made from vegetables. We had imitation roast duck, imitation sharks fin and a variety of soups. Even today my mouth waters at the thought of it.

Badminton was an important sport in Malaya. Indeed the Malayans had held the Thomas Cup, which is the world team championship in the sport. Many houses had floodlit courts in the garden so that the game could be played in the cool of the evening. I became President of the Petaling Jaya Badminton Club. The standard was quite high—we even had a former Thomas Cup player as a member. Wyn's great claim to fame was that partnering him she reached the final of the club championship. We started a scheme to uncover local talent and found some very useful young players.

One of my priorities was to get the most used roads surfaced to eliminate the mud and the dust. Before I could do this however, one evening Wyn and I were sitting having a cup of tea. It had been raining heavily. I heard a car revving, obviously stuck in the mud at the bottom of the hill. I said to Wyn, 'I had better go and see if I can help.' When I arrived at the roundabout at the bottom of the hill there was indeed a car up to its axles in the mud. The driver, a tall Malay, was standing looking somewhat forlornly at his vehicle. His wife and son were with him. I asked if I could help. He introduced himself as 'The Raja Muda of Selangor'. Clearly he expected me to know what that meant. I'm afraid that at that time it meant nothing to me. I thought however that he looked as though he was some sort of VIP. The idea was helped by the fact that his car did not have a conventional number-plate. Instead it had a gold crown. To show that I was important also I announced somewhat pompously, 'I'm the Town Engineer of Petaling Jaya.'

The Raja Muda was very friendly. I said that if they would like to come up to our house I would arrange for a lorry to come and extricate his car. He and his wife and son came up to the house and we offered them a drink. In Malaya any visitor, whether in the home or the office, was as a matter of course offered a drink on arrival because of the heat. Wyn has never forgotten that our servants not knowing who our distinguished guests were, brought out the cheap glasses that we used every day. They were the kind of glasses that you used to get in petrol stations.

I rang up Charles Bolar the workshop foreman and he and Tan Huck Chuan the head storekeeper who lived next door to him, organised the release of the car from the mud and brought it to the house. When the Raja Muda was leaving, he asked 'Have you been to my Istana?' Neither Wyn nor I knew that an Istana was a palace. Malacca being one of the Straits Settlements did not have any palaces. My Malay lessons had not taken into consideration that I would be invited to palaces. We knew that whatever it was we had certainly never been to one. He then said, 'You must come to visit me. Can you come next Friday?' On the Friday we set off in good time to arrive at the appointed hour. Being new to Kuala Lumpur we got hopelessly lost. We were not too worried as often in Malaya people arrived at parties quite a long time after the supposed starting time. But we were horrified when we found that we were the only guests. We found out later that we had kept the heir to the Sultan of Selangor waiting for over an hour. Our embarrassment increased when we were served our drinks by the liveried servants in superb crystal glasses. Wyn and I looked at each other remembering the glasses that had been produced at our house.

We became firm friends. We often went on weekend trips to play golf or visit the seaside and it was in this way that Wyn and I improved our knowledge of the Malay language. In the company of the Raja Muda his wife the Raja Puan Muda and other Malayan friends both English and Malay were spoken interchangeably. If something was easier to say in English it was said in English. If it was easier in Malay it was said in Malay. On occasion, we would be sitting in a group and someone would make a reference to a 'Mat Salleh'. This is a slightly pejorative Malay way of referring to a European. If they realised that we were there, (and they did not always do so) they would be greatly embarrassed. Someone, usually the Raja Muda, would say, 'Don't worry, Frank and Wyn are not Mat Sallehs.'

Our proficiency in the language remains. When we visit Malaysia nowadays if we are on a Malaysian plane we start speaking it straight away. Not long ago we were visiting Kuala Lumpur when Michael our younger son was working there. While I was attending a meeting, Wyn had gone off to visit Rowena, our daughter-in-law. She had been chatting to the taxi-driver about where we had lived in Kuala Lumpur. The following day after I had been to another meeting, I picked up a taxi in the street and was chatting to the driver in Malay. Suddenly he said to me, 'Does your son live in Jalan Setia Kaseh Empat?' Surprised I said, 'Yes, how do you know?' The driver replied, 'Because I took your wife there yesterday.' I asked him how he knew it was my wife. He replied 'She speaks Malay too.' From all the taxi-drivers in Kuala Lumpur, a city of over a million people, I had picked him and he had linked me to Wyn because we both spoke Malay.

In the Malay language there is a particle 'Lah' which is often added to a word to give it emphasis. Even when they are speaking English many Malaysians, especially young people, add 'Lah' to an English word. I was doing an arbitration in Kuantan on the East Coast of Malaysia where less English is spoken than on the West Coast. Wyn was with me. She was chatting in Malay to the girl who was cleaning the hotel room. Suddenly the girl realised that they were speaking in Malay. She said to Wyn, 'Where did you learn to speak Malay like that?' As a joke Wyn said, 'I've been here three days already.' The girl paused then said, 'Cannot-lah! even if very clever.' Wyn then explained that she was only joking.

The barber at the Golf Club always told me that when he was talking to me, if he could not see me he would think that he was talking to a Malay. There are quite a large number of words in the Malay language that have been taken from English. There was a story told of the somewhat pompous British government servant who came across an old Malay boatman cleaning his out-board motor. The boatman had the carburettor in his hand. The government servant pointed to it and asked, 'What do you call that?' The old Malay smiled and said, 'I don't know what it is called in English, but in Malay we call it a carburettor.'

One of the wonderful things about Malaysia is the way that everyone celebrates everyone else's Festivals. We would visit our Muslim friends, including the Raja Muda, on the day after the Fasting Month Ramadan, ended. In Malaysia the day is called Hari Raya Aidil Fitri. At Chinese New Year we would call on our Chinese friends. When the boys were small they used to receive 'Ang Pows', the little red packets with small amounts of money in them. At Deepavalli, the Festival of Lights, we would call on our Hindu friends. Public holidays were all related to the religious festivals. As well as the main festivals everyone knew about The Prophet Mohammed's Birthday, Wesak Day (Buddha's Birthday), Guru Nanak's Birthday (Sikh) and Thaipusam (Hindu). These were days where the members of the particular faith could take what was called 'unrecorded leave'. For Christians such days were Good Friday and Boxing Day. It annoys me when I hear local politicians in Britain saying that we will upset our non-Christian friends by celebrating our Christian Feasts and that Christmas should be called 'Winterval'. I believe that in Britain we often allow the extremists to set the agenda.

At Christmas it was our turn to hold open house. Starting at about 6.30 in the morning we received a constant stream of visitors. Douglas once remarked that, for a long time he thought that Kumarasamy our driver was Santa Claus, because he was always in the house so early on Christmas morning. 'Samy' always turned up first bringing with him those of his growing family who were old enough to walk the half-mile or so from the labour lines where they were housed. Road-workers, lorry-drivers, mechanics, foremen, draughtsmen and engineers came to drink orange juice or beer and eat Christmas cake. All day long until about 6 o'clock in the evening they were kept refreshed by our cook. The food and drink then stopped so that preparations could be made for the dinner to which the Raja Muda, (and later when he became Sultan,) was coming. This was the pattern for as long as I was Town Engineer of Petaling Jaya.

Sadly not all Britons abroad know how to behave. On one occasion a group of British soldiers stationed near Petaling Jaya had arranged to give a Christmas party for some local deprived children. They asked the nuns at the convent to allow them to use their premises and gave the children a great party. Afterwards I invited them to our house for a drink. There were about eight of them. Samy was given the task of dispensing the drinks. He had apparently at one time had a part-time job as a barman near where the soldiers were based. When he heard me asking the lads if they would like a beer he warned me that I should not give them beer. He said that, in his experience when British soldiers drank beer they always ended up fighting. I pointed out that these were very nice lads. They had given up their time and had spent their own money to give the children a party. He was not impressed but he served them beers. When I offered them a second beer Samy became quite 'Bolshie'. However I persuaded him to let them have another. He made it quite clear to everyone, that there would be no more. He was not going to have a fight breaking out in his 'tuan's' (master's) house. Fortunately the soldiers had to get back to their camp, so there was no further confrontation. I thought that it was sad that the reputation of the decent British soldiers was so badly tarnished among the people of Malaya by the yobbish behaviour of a minority.

Heavy drinking and fighting was not of course confined to British soldiers. Sometimes on a pay-night after they had been drinking 'toddy' a potent brew extracted from the coconut palm, some of my workers would get involved in fights. These were on occasions quite serious. Pretty large cuts were sustained, from the long parangs (slashing knives) that they used as weapons. Instead of going straight to the hospital to get stitched up they would often appear at my gate in the middle of the night calling out for me, wanting to show me the damage that had been done to them. On the way from the Labour lines to my house they had passed the hospital. Now I had to get dressed and drive them to the hospital. In Malaya, it was the custom for most public bodies to provide housing for their labour-force. This was because the large majority of them were expected to return to India when they retired. After Independence when they became Malayan citizens, this was no longer the case. I persuaded the Petaling Jaya Development Corporation to allow our workers to purchase the houses. They had 'a right to buy' long before the Thatcher era. I also introduced a change in the way that the houses that they bought were identified. Previously, they were designated as unit numbers in blocks identified by letters of the alphabet. It was thus clear to anyone that the house that the person occupied was a 'Labour Line'. I changed this to house numbers in streets so that they were like everyone else.

By the time we had left Malacca Wyn was pregnant. When the time drew near for the baby to be born there were a number of false alarms. To try to speed things up I took to driving her over the roughest roads. The car springs never really recovered. Eventually I threatened Wyn that I would arrange for her to be driven across the undeveloped area in a tractor. That did the trick. On 25th July 1955 our second son Michael was born. Douglas had been the perfect baby. He was quite content to lie in his cot quietly and amuse himself. I think that even at a very tender age he was thinking about the ways to put the world to right. We of course attributed his good behaviour to our skill as parents. We smugly compared our success with the failure of other parents whose children behaved badly.

Little did we know. I think that Michael had had a previous existence. He was up to any trick to get attention. He walked when he was 8 months old. What a handful! We have cine-film of him playing football at a year-old. Before he went to kindergarten, at the age of three he was climbing trees up on to the roof of our house. He spent his first year at kindergarten helping a plumber to install new toilets at the school. He apparently did not go into the classroom very much. He was always taking his toys apart to see how they worked. If they broke he could fix them. There was never much doubt that he was going to be an engineer.

At an early age the boys learned to swim. Most weekends were spent at the swimming pool where they met their friends and had a curry lunch. It amused me that the cost for lunch for children was half that for adults. The children could eat twice as much. Later when the boys were at boarding school the staff at the swimming pool would ask when the boys were due on holiday. We reckoned that they wanted to know when they would need to order extra food for our 'eating machines'.

Monthly swimming and diving competitions were organised for the children. Both the boys used to take part and did well. Even at the age of three Michael would go up on the 5-metre board. He would stand on the high-board and smile at everyone before he dived off. Douglas reckoned that Michael's cheeky grin was worth at least one mark extra from the judges. When they came to boarding school in England their swimming was well ahead of their contemporaries.

Holidays were usually taken in Fraser's Hill, a holiday resort carved out of the mountain range that runs down the middle of the Malay Peninsula. The elevation is approximately 5000 feet. During the day the temperature is very pleasant. In the evenings it is cool enough to have a log fire. The last five miles of the journey was along a single-way road that was open for an hour in each direction. It was on this road that Sir Henry Gurney was ambushed and killed. He was replaced by General Templar who is credited with taking the country by the scruff of the neck and bringing the Emergency to an end. In their post-colonial phase most countries blame any deficiencies on the former colonial power. There was some of that in Malaya. In 1982 however I attended a function in London where the Malaysian government was celebrating twenty-five years of Independence. I was pleased to see that the guests-of-honour were Sir Gerald and Lady Templar.

During the Emergency on the road to Fraser's Hill cars were inspected to ensure that no food was being carried. The main attraction of Fraser's Hill was the somewhat tricky 9-hole golf course. Because of the weather conditions the course always seemed to be wet. You could lose a ball on the fairway because it would plug into the soft ground. Jungle walks were also popular and it was easy to imagine getting lost in the dense growth. It was in similar jungle at another resort Cameron Highlands that Jim Thompson, the famous exporter of Thai silk, was lost. There were beautiful butterflies with the most vibrant colours. There were also huge flying beetles that only existed at altitude. Unfortunately the numbers of butterflies have been reduced considerably as a result of people catching them. I hate to see these beautiful creatures mounted in glass cases and sold to tourists. How much nicer to see them flying freely in their natural habitat.

We also had holidays at Port Dickson, which was a popular seaside resort. It had a beautiful sandy beach which was later spoiled by the building of not one, but two, oil refineries.

Life in Petaling Jaya continued to be exciting. In 1955 as a prelude to Independence, elections were held. The Alliance, an amalgamation of a Malay party, the United Malay National Organisation (UMNO), a Chinese party, the Malayan Chinese Association (MCA), and an Indian party, the Malayan Indian Congress (MIC), swept the board. Tengku Abdul Rahman, a member of the royal family of the State of Kedah was leader of UMNO and he was elected Chief Minister. They say 'Cometh the hour, cometh the man'. Tengku Abdul Rahman was certainly the right man to lead Malaya to independence.

Malaya, with its mix of different ethnic groups, is probably unique. The proportions at that time were said to be approximately 45% Malays, 35% Chinese, 10% Indian and 10% others. There were delicate questions as to privileges for the ethnic Malays, which they enjoyed under the British regime. The citizenship rights for the other races, was another thorny issue. Before handing over power the British were anxious to see these matters settled. In Tengku Abdul Rahman they had someone to deal with who was trusted by everyone. He had no pretensions to being an intellectual. When I told him when I met him at a party in London in 1978 that I was studying for my Bar Exams, he told me that it had taken him twenty-five years to pass his Bar Exams. Tengku said that he thought that when he sat the exams in 1955, the examiners had found out his number and given him a pass because he had by then become the Chief Minister of Malaya.

At the same party, he asked me if I was still winning golf cups. This was a reference to the fact that twenty years before he had presented to me a cup called 'The Merdeka Cup'. The competition had first been held in 1957 to celebrate Independence. I was ashamed to tell him that I had won nothing since then. He was a lovely man and became known as ' Bapak Malaya'. (Father of Malaya). His birthday was the 8th February, which is the same date as mine.

The negotiations regarding independence took two years. On The 31st August 1957, the Malayan flag replaced the Union Jack. Tengku became Malaya's first Prime Minister. He, his Deputy Dato Razak, who was also the Minister for Education, and Dato Ismail, the Minister for Industry had all built houses in Petaling Jaya fairly close to our house. Both Dato Razak and Dato Ismail later received Malaya's highest honour and became 'Tuns'. We named the area where they lived 'Bukit Menteri' (the Hill of the Ministers). Tun Razak would pull my leg about the possibility of independence for Scotland. When he eventually succeeded Tengku Abdul Rahman as Prime Minister he said that when Scotland achieved independence he would want to attend the celebrations. The Parliamentary system that was set up in Malaya was modelled on the British system. The Speaker of the Parliament was Tun Razak's father-in-law Dato Haji Noah. He told me that his job appeared to be like that of a teacher in charge of a particularly unruly class of school children. I think that in this it also follows the British system very closely indeed.

In Malacca we had acquired a white and tan coloured spaniel that followed Douglas everywhere. She was called 'Snowball'. We had brought Snowball with us from Malacca to Petaling Jaya. One Sunday afternoon I was taking her for a walk. We were passing Tengku Abdul Rahman's house. There he was in the garden with a fire burning brightly. On the fire there was a whole lamb being roasted. He was having a party for his Cabinet colleagues that evening. Whilst we were having a chat I was terrified that Snowball would find the smell of the lamb roasting too tempting. It was typical of Tengku that he was himself making the preparations to entertain his guests. In the course of time I became friends with Tengku, Tun Razak and Tun Ismail.

Tun Razak's son Najib, Tun Ismail's children, Tawfik and Zailah, and our son Douglas all went to the same Kindergarten in Kuala Lumpur. Since Tun Ismail was travelling into Kuala Lumpur to his office he took Douglas with his own children. One day Douglas came home and announced that he was learning to speak the Malay language. We asked what he had learned. He raised his right arm and said loudly 'Merdeka'. (Freedom). This was the rallying call of the political parties involved in the discussions leading to Independence. Apparently Tun Ismail's driver had thought it fun to teach Douglas this. Najib has been Minister of Education and Minister for Defence in the Malaysian Government.

The transfer of power from the British to the Malayans was friendly. Tengku Abdul Rahman said that unlike Burma and Indonesia there would be no mass exodus of expatriates at Independence. A system was worked out for Malayans, as they became qualified, to take over from the expatriates who would be compensated for loss of office and would hand over. The system worked well. It is probably one of the reasons that Malaya progressed so well economically after Independence. Other Commonwealth countries were not so fortunate. The form of monarchy in Malaysia, devised in 1957 at the time of Independence, is unique. There are nine Sultans who are rulers of their states. They become the Yang DiPertuan Agong, (King) in rotation subject to a vote of approval by their fellow Rulers. The Agong, like our Queen, is a constitutional monarch acting on the advice of the government. He reigns for five years. The approval of the Agong and the Deputy Agong takes place at a meeting of the Rulers' Conference. Meetings of the Conference are held at fairly regular intervals to discuss constitutional and other relevant matters. The Rulers take it in turns to chair the Meetings. When HRH the Sultan of Selangor was Chairman on one occasion, he invited the other Rulers and their wives to a party at his palace in Kuala Lumpur. He invited Wyn and me to come to the palace for the dance after the formal dinner was over. It was an unusual situation to be in. Every man in the room, apart from me, was the Ruler of a state and every lady was a Ruler's wife. What with occasions such as this and golf matches, we came to know most of the nine Rulers. As guests of the Malaysian Government Wyn and I had the pleasure of attending the Installation of our friend of some forty-four years, HRH the Sultan of Selangor when he became King. When I thanked the Prime Minister Dr. Mahathir for inviting us he replied that as we were the King's oldest friends they had felt it was essential to invite us. We are the proud possessors of a unique sequence of medals from our friend: His Coronation medal as Sultan of Selangor, his Silver Jubilee Medal, and now, his Installation Medal as Yang DiPertuan Agong. Sadly my oldest friend in Malaysia, the Yang DiPertuan Agong, died suddenly in November 2001. Wyn and I were very glad that we had gone to Malaysia to the official celebration of his 75th birthday in June of the same year. When we were there, at the various ceremonies we were placed with the members of the Agong's family. For us that was a great honour.

The system of the succession of rulers in the nine States varies. In Selangor and a number of other States the succession is by primogeniture—the eldest son succeeds. In Perak the succession is through three families who provide the Ruler in turn. In the State of Negri Sembilan the system is akin to the old Celtic system of 'tanistry' that was used in Scotland until 1144. Under this system, the heir is elected by his peers. In Negri Sembilan, the heir is elected by the heads of four families who are territorial chiefs. Also in Negri Sembilan property is inherited through the female line. Interestingly the Negri Sembilan royal family has been generally recognised as the most enterprising and modern of the Malaysian royal families.

After Independence the demand for the housing land in Petaling Jaya had taken off. We could hardly keep up with it. I now had a fleet of earth-moving equipment and we had gradually replaced the old petrol-guzzling vehicles with diesel-engined lorries. Because diesel fuel was much cheaper than petrol there was less incentive to steal it. Besides we kept proper records of such things as the fuel that each vehicle used and how long tyres lasted on different vehicles. The workshop foreman, Charles Bolar was a Eurasian. He was extremely good at his job and completely honest in everything that he did. In the mornings when it was cool I would drive round the various sites where we were working. On one occasion when I was standing watching lorries being filled with earth, I noticed that the number painted on the tyre of one of the lorries did not correspond with the number of the lorry. When I visited the workshop later I asked

Charles about it. He was mortified. It appeared that the vehicle had had a puncture as it was leaving the workshop and they had put on it the first tyre that was available. It is on such little incidents that a reputation can be built. The word got round that I knew everything that went on.

Vickers who made the bulldozers and scrapers, which were my pride and joy, ceased making them after I had built up a considerable fleet. It was a great pity as in my opinion they had developed a first class machine at great expense. Just when they appeared to be about to reap the rewards of their labour they gave it all up. I believe that it had something to do with an American company defaulting on payments for Viscount aircraft. As we were trying to keep up with the demand for land my earth-moving equipment was utilised to its maximum capacity. I had two drivers for each machine. They worked twelve hours a day, two hours on the machine and two hours off. On their two hours off they carried out other tasks. They usually worked seven days a week. The drivers were a great team. They were of Indian, Malay and Chinese extraction and the leader was Thambirajah, a South Indian Tamil. He had previously worked for the Public Works Department and when I took him on I was warned by one of the Public Works Department engineers that he had had a reputation as a troublemaker. I tackled Thambirajah about it. He agreed that he had been a bit of a tearaway but said that he was now married and had settled down. He turned out to be a great help and we got on well together. Thambirajah was a good driver but not the best. The best was Arunasalam, another Indian. I think that he was a Malayalam. When Vickers sent out a representative from UK he brought with him a demonstration driver. Vickers reckoned that their man could handle their equipment better than anyone else. We put Arunasalam up against him. It was fun! We set up a race between two powerful tractors each towing a scraper with a capacity of sixteen cubic yards of earth. They had to fill the scraper, tow it about two hundred yards and go back for more. They did this half-a-dozen times. In the end, there was nothing in it. Arunasalam was up with the best.

The land that we were developing contained a considerable proportion of sand. Some of it had been mined for tin. Alluvial tin is found in that type of land. The sand took its toll on our earth-moving equipment. We were going through a bad spell when a number of the machines were under repair. The drivers knew that I hated to see the machines standing idle; so one Sunday morning they held a ceremony. It was a kind of exorcism. They sprinkled the blood from three chickens over the machines. They then made an excellent chicken curry to which Wyn and I were invited. I have to admit that our troubles seemed to decrease after this. In our workers' housing areas we tried to ensure that there would be no problems caused by religious differences. We did not want offence to be caused by say, a group of Chinese workers roasting a pig close to their Muslim neighbours. One day one of the Muslim drivers came to see me because he wanted to move house. As he was housed in the area next to other Muslims, I asked him why he wanted to move. He told me that his wife was having trouble with the neighbours. I pointed out that that sort of thing happened and would not normally justify a move. He explained that as a tractor-driver, working lots of overtime he was earning much more than the neighbours. The other wives were jealous of his wife and were making life very difficult for her. He wanted to live among the other drivers. We arranged for him to move as soon as we could.

When Thambirajah's first son was one month old he invited Wyn and me to a dinner to celebrate the naming of the child. We had another dinner to attend on the same evening but we promised to go along later. We arrived at the celebration after everyone had eaten. Despite our protests we were seated and with everyone else looking on we were served with huge plates of very hot curry. I tucked in to my second dinner of the evening, but poor Wyn, apart from having already eaten; she had an ulcer in her mouth. Every spoonful of curry was agony. I had recruited from UK a deputy, Bert Lodge, who had a local government background and a Malayan engineer of Sikh origin, Amer Singh Bhatt. We were all kept pretty busy trying to keep up with the demand for our land. On the industrial side we had applications from British firms such as Metal Box, Glaxo, Dunlops and numerous other companies that I was told were to be found in other newly independent countries around the world.

The system for long leave at the time was that you were entitled to four days of leave for every month that you worked. In addition you were entitled to two weeks local leave every year. In 1957 I had over six months leave due. The workers gave a party for me before I left. I was expected to make a speech. As we had Malays, Chinese, Indians and Eurasians and some of them spoke only a little English, I thought it best to speak in the Malay language. I said, as I have always believed that no matter what job you do in any organisation it is important to do it well. Perhaps I should have left it at that. Carried away by my own eloquence however I went on to explain that everyone could not be the Town Engineer but that it was important that everyone did his own job to the best of his ability. Later I was told that the general consensus among the workers was that no one wanted my job. It was much too difficult. I think that I failed to get my message across.

Fluency in the Malay language did however prove useful to me on one occasion. I was in a shop called 'Peiping Lace'. They sold craft goods made locally and from China. We usually bought some of these to take home as presents when we came back to UK. All our relatives are the possessors of Malay watercolour paintings, Chinese embroidered hand towels and various Royal Selangor pewter mugs and vases. On this occasion I was browsing. I noticed a man come into the shop and recognised from the way that he spoke that he was Indonesian. The Indonesian language is very similar to the Malay language and people in both countries can understand each other. The Indonesians however have a much stronger accent. The man produced two krisses (the long daggers with a wavy blade) that he wished to sell. After some bargaining a price of 100 Malayan Dollars was agreed and paid over. When the seller had left the shop I approached the man behind the counter. I asked him how much he wanted for the two krisses. Without hesitation he said, '300 Malayan Dollars each.' I let him know that I was aware of what he had paid for them and that I was quite happy that he should make a profit from carrying out the negotiation. Eventually we agreed on a figure of 150 Malayan Dollars for the two. Quite a bargain. On our trips to UK we were allowed to choose to sail or fly. On our first home leave we arranged to fly home. The plane that we flew in was an Argonaut. It had a very limited range. We seemed to stop at every bus stop on the way. In Colombo we were taken in a taxi round the town. The driver told us that he knew a jeweller who sold very good sapphires at very cheap prices. We bought a necklace, bracelet and earrings and they looked quite good to us. The jeweller was happy to take a UK cheque. This was in the days before cheque cards. Years later in London we were having Wyn's jewellery valued for insurance purposes. The jeweller told us that the sapphires were worth very little. We came back to Scotland and rented a house in Portobello for six months. We bought a new car, a Ford Zodiac. It was two-tone, white on top and black below. In Scotland it looked a bit flashy but light coloured cars were normal in Malaya as they reflected the rays of the sun instead of absorbing them. Later when air-conditioning came in the colour did not matter so much. One of the perks of the job was that you got an interest-free loan every three years to buy a new car. As you became more senior the size of the loan allowed increased so that you could buy a bigger car. We toured Scotland and generally enjoyed ourselves.

One of the dangers that faces expatriates who have long leave is that you bore people to tears telling them about the wonderful life you have with large houses, servants to look after you, constant sunshine and a good salary. Hopefully, we avoided that trap and our relatives always seemed glad to see us. Some of our friends came back from leave with horrendous stories of storming out of parent's houses after rows about their children's behaviour. We showed the films that we had taken in Malaya. There were films of children's birthday parties with children of all nationalities enjoying them-selves. There was also a film taken at the airport as we were leaving. Among those who had come to see us off, were Tun Ismail and his wife Toh Puan Neno. When my father saw them he said, 'I see that you mix with the natives.' We explained that the people in our films were as well educated as we were and were successfully running the country. Six months doing nothing was too long for me. I visited

New Towns in Scotland and England. I even took Wyn to visit a sewage works. By the time that we returned to Malaya the Independence ceremonies were over. The Duke and Duchess of Gloucester had represented the Queen at the ceremonies. When I was Sheriff of London, in 1988 Princess Alice Duchess of Gloucester was a guest at luncheon at the Old Bailey. She had obviously been well briefed. She asked me how it was that she did not meet me when she was attending the Independence ceremonies in Malaya. I made the excuse that we were home on leave at the time. The chances were however that even although I knew all the personalities involved I would not have ranked high enough to be invited to the official ceremonies.

When Michael went to kindergarten Wyn was asked to help the Catholic nuns who had opened a convent in Petaling Jaya. They were of the Order of the Franciscan Missionaries of Mary, evicted from China. They had started in a small house lent to them by a wealthy Chinese Catholic Tang Sze Wing. Sze Wing was very cultured, polite and punctilious. He seemed out-of-place in the rough world of construction, but he was a very shrewd businessman. We were good friends. Sze Wing's uncle had been a bishop in China and languished in jail for many years because he refused to convert to the Communist-dominated National Catholic Church. The uncle's story was somewhat similar to that of Thomas More and his relationship with Henry the Eighth.

Subsequently, the nuns had built themselves a convent and a maternity hospital. They were now anxious to open a school. So Wyn became a teacher. She enjoyed it very much and was a very good teacher. Coping with a class of fifty children many of whom did not speak English was a big enough task. However there were added complications. Some of the Chinese children would have a name that they had been given at birth. This was the name that was on their birth certificate. Sometimes, especially if the child had been sickly, she would be given a different name. This was to fool the evil spirits that were causing the sickness. But at home the child would be known by a pet name, which was different from either of the other names. Trying to sort out the class at the beginning of term was a nightmare but they always managed.

Another problem would be when one of the nuns would say, 'That's funny, these two children have the same address, the father's name is the same, but their dates of birth are only three months apart.' Wyn would look at the register and say, 'That is Mr Chew Loy. He has four wives.' Or it might be, 'That is Mr Tiw Wan he has three wives.' Chew Loy and his four wives lived in a large house that he had built in Petaling Jaya. He had organised a system whereby his card was inserted in a frame against the name of the wife that he was spending the night with. When we visited the house he proudly showed us how it worked. Everyone seemed quite happy with the arrangement.

For many Chinese businessmen having a number of wives became a status symbol. Tiw Wan was a case in point. He was a building contractor who eventually did quite a lot of work for me on oil-palm factories. I liked him and found him to be very trustworthy. One time, we were doing a site visit near Penang. I had told him that I was taking my wife with me and that I was going to spend the weekend in Penang. He said that he was doing the same. I invited him to have dinner with Wyn and me, at the Chinese restaurant in our hotel. He duly arrived at the hotel, not with one wife, but with three. Each wife had one child with her. The youngest wife was about eighteen. At first Wyn thought that her small baby was Tiw Wan's grandchild. During the dinner the conversation was in the Malay language, and the two older wives refused to talk to the young one. It was quite a fun evening. Sadly some time afterwards Tiw Wan died of cancer. It turned out that he was also keeping a mistress.

Another of our Chinese friends lived quite near us. He had what he called an 'upstairs wife' and a 'downstairs wife'. They both had children. When you visited the house you would have thought that the two ladies were sisters or very close friends. Apparently the man had been going to marry one of them when he lived in China. Before he could do so he had had an opportunity to escape to Hong Kong and then to Malaya. The girl was not allowed out of China and he did not dare go back. Eventually he had married in Malaya. Later when China opened up a bit he went back and visited his home village. He found that the girl was still unmarried. He brought her to Malaya and with the approval of his wife took her as his second wife. It sounded very romantic and everyone seemed to be very happy.

A well-known Chinese millionaire was reputed to have twelve wives. It was said that when he wanted a new wife he went off to China and brought one back. They all lived in a huge house in Kuala Lumpur. The house was later purchased by the Malayan Government as a palace for the Yang DiPertuan Agong. I played golf with some of his sons. I think that they must have all taken their looks from their mothers, as there was no family resemblance.

Once they had the primary school up and running the nuns decided to open a kindergarten. They asked Wyn to run it for them. This was a huge success and it was not long before they were running out of space. The nuns had started another project to build a teaching hospital. I tried to counsel them to exercise caution in the size of the project. With their implicit faith in God's bounty they proceeded to build a large hospital with no real knowledge of how they were going to finance the running of it. The burden on the nuns was tremendous as they tried to keep the cost of running the hospital within the limits of their finances. At the same time they were trying to pay off the debt incurred in building it. I could see that it was taking its toll on the health of some of them. One day I told the Reverend Mother that I would not work my earth-moving machines the way she worked her nuns. She took the hint and thereafter ensured that they could get a break from time to time in the coolness of the hill-resort at Cameron Highlands.

The nuns were in fact great fun. They always travelled in pairs and often got a lift into Kuala Lumpur from Wyn or myself. They always said a prayer at the beginning of a journey. One day after they had finished their prayer I said, 'That was rather a long prayer.' Quick as a flash the answer came back, 'It all depends on who the driver is.'

That particular nun was a tall Australian called 'Sister Augustine'. I told her that when we were children in Edinburgh there was a member of the City Council who held public meetings near where we lived. His party was called The Protestant Action Party. He was a sort of Ian Paisley without the charm. We would sneak along to hear his stories about Catholics. We thought that they were very funny. One of his stories was that whenever you saw two nuns together one would be tall and the other short. The tall one was a man in disguise. Sister Augustine laughed uproariously. 'I must be the man for the whole convent as I'm taller than anyone else.'

The nuns had been given a Land Rover for transport by one of the rubber estate management companies. They had nowhere to keep it. For a while it was kept in our garage. One day when Wyn and I were out of the house Tangachee, who had come with us from Malacca, decided that she would try to drive it. She managed to get it out of the garage but getting it back proved to be beyond her capabilities. She crashed it into the wall of the garage. Fortunately the damage to the vehicle was minor and the garage wall was not too difficult to repair. We suddenly realised that she was growing up. Not long afterwards her parents came to the same conclusion and she went back to Malacca. They arranged for her to be married to a young man who had worked for me in the Water Department. When we saw her a few years later she was very happy and had two children of her own. As far as we could see many of these arranged marriages seemed to work out quite well.

We were becoming quite involved with the nuns. We admired their dedication and the very useful work that they were doing. At one time our house seemed to be an annexe to the convent. Our garage was full of crates of powdered milk that had been donated to the maternity unit by a German charitable organisation. The French nun who was a doctor was on night duty. She was not getting any sleep because of building work on the school and she was sent to us so that she could get some sleep during the day. The Reverend Mother was a tiny Irish nun called Sister Columcille. When she had to go away for any length of time she would ask Wyn to keep an eye on the convent. The boys used to refer to Wyn as 'Our Reverend Mother', or 'Our Mother Superior'.

Wyn took Sister Columcille shopping in Robinsons, a large department store in Kuala Lumpur, one day. Apparently the store always gave the nuns a discount on their purchases. When Wyn bought something the nun said, 'You should give her a discount too as she is one of us.' Wyn was about seven months pregnant and it was very evident. She said to the Reverend Mother, 'You have just ruined the reputation of your convent.'

An ex-colonial in an independent country

The Sultan of Brunei built a palace in Kuala Lumpur. Taylor Woodrow the contractors, had to get it finished in something like nine weeks to coincide with the celebration of Malayan Independence. Somehow they succeeded. At the opening reception I found myself sitting at a table with Tengku Abdul Rahman and some other Malayan dignitaries. Tengku told us that the Sultan of Brunei never served alcohol. He said that when we were asked what we wanted to drink we should order soda water. We followed his instructions and after the soda water had been served he produced from inside his sarong a large flask of whisky that he proceeded to dispense generously. At least one table had an alcoholic jollity about it.

In Malaya there was ambivalence about the drinking of alcohol. Some people believed that it was forbidden by the Koran. Others took the view that it was the abuse of alcohol, like other excesses, that is condemned. Whichever it is, most of my Muslim friends who went on the Haj, the pilgrimage to Mecca, returned after an uplifting experience and never afterwards partook of alcohol. All Muslims are enjoined to make the pilgrimage at least once in the course of their life. In order to help them do so the Government in Malaya set up the Tabong Haji, which is the Pilgrimage Fund. It is run rather on the lines of a building society except that no interest is paid on savings. Under Islamic teaching receiving interest is usury and is forbidden. Capital gain from the fund's investments is however permitted. Most of the commercial banks in Malaysia have Islamic Banking units which work on the same principle. As part of the agreement on Independence, subject to certain conditions as to date of arrival in Malaya, non-citizens could apply for citizenship. For example if Michael had been born in Malacca he would have been entitled to apply for Malayan citizenship when he reached the age of eighteen. This would have been on the basis that he was born of parents who were British citizens in one of the Straits Settlements before Independence. Because he was actually born in Kuala Lumpur he was not so entitled. Our Malayan friends encouraged

Wyn and me to apply for citizenship but we remained stubbornly British. We did however become permanent residents. For non-Malays who wished to become citizens there was a language test. At one stage I was assisting with the language tests. We asked the applicants simple things, such as the word for nose or hand. The idea was to make it easy for non-Malays to become citizens. It is my belief that immigrants who wish to acquire British citizenship should have to learn to speak English and should also learn something of British customs.

I have never forgotten a stupid remark that I made early in 1957. I was sitting in the Royal Selangor Golf Club having a drink with a friend, Murray Allen. I said, 'I don't suppose that there will be many golf courses laid out in this country after Independence.' At that time there were only three non-European members of the Royal Selangor Golf Club. Like most Europeans I thought that golf was too much of an expatriate's game to require more courses. Since Independence there have been dozens of superb courses laid out. Among the earliest new courses was one in Malacca. It had been carved out of the jungle and was at some places close to the Malacca Zoo. It was quite disconcerting to be standing on a tee about to play when from among the trees came the roar of a caged tiger. Malaysians have taken to golf like ducks to water and are very good at it. The Royal Selangor is still the premier club and happily I am now an Honorary Life Member.

1958 was my 'Annus Mirabilis' as far as golf was concerned. I was playing about four times a week and my handicap went from 24 to 13 in less than three months. I played a lot with my friend Dr. Low Nan Hang who was a medical practitioner in Petaling Jaya. We entered a Foursomes Knock-out Competition together and reached the Final. In the final we had to play against two very good low-handicap golfers Patrick Lim and Leong Thoe Soon. On the last hole I conceded a short putt to them and they won the Competition. Dr. Low said that I should have made them putt out. He was probably right. In 1988 I was involved in an arbitration in Kuala Lumpur. As the hearing was scheduled for two weeks I had taken my golf clubs with me and had a round at the Royal Selangor Golf Club.

While I was changing afterwards someone mentioned that my friend Dr. Low was in the Card-room. I went in to meet him. Our erstwhile opponents Pat Lim and Leong Thoe Soon were also there. As soon as he saw me Dr. Low said, 'We were talking about you only yesterday. Do you remember the putt that you conceded to these two?' Thirty years had passed and they were still talking about it. By this time the putt was of course many yards long.

The Raja Muda became the Regent of Selangor in 1960 when his father the Sultan was elected Yang DiPertuan Agong. However shortly after assuming office the Agong was taken ill and within a very short time he died. I considered whether or not I should attend the funeral. He was the father of a close friend and also a very devout and gentle man. But as he was the Agong I decided that it would probably be a State occasion attended by VIPs only and I did not think that I came into that category. The Regent was proclaimed Sultan. A few days later when I met him, he asked why I had not attended his father's funeral. I had made a mistake. Even Sultan's find it comforting to have their friends present in their hour of grief.

On occasions I was invited to partner the Sultan for a game of golf against the King, who by this time was the Raja of Perlis, and one of his friends. The normal stakes in golf games were one ball on the first nine holes one ball on the second nine and two on the match. That is what the King's partner and I played for. However, the King and the Sultan regarded 'one, one, two' as one hundred, one hundred, two hundred. Occasionally they would decide to have an 'expensive hole'. This meant that there was a bet of four hundred balls on that hole. Whilst the King's partner and I were not involved in that bet nevertheless it was quite some pressure when you were standing over a six-foot put across a sloping green, knowing that your partner had the cost of four hundred balls riding on it.

HRH the Sultan from time to time would organise a team from among his friends to play against teams brought together by the King or another of the Sultans. HRH's team usually comprised members of other royal families living in Kuala Lumpur, the Prime Minister and senior government officials. I was often invited to play in these matches. The matches were sometimes played on the nine-hole golf course that had been laid out round the Sultan's main palace. This palace was located in Klang, which is the main port on the West coast of Malaysia. When we had a match we would be allocated rooms in the palace to change for the lunch after the match. When you were changing there would be a discreet knock on the door of the room by one of the palace servants to enquire whether you would like to have a cool drink. Visiting players had been heard to remark that it was the best clubhouse in Malaya.

On one occasion we went over to the northeast coast of Malaya to play against HRH the Sultan of Trennganu's team. We had a very enjoyable weekend. We discovered that it was considered disrespectful to wear shorts when playing with the Sultan in Trennganu, so long trousers it had to be. Some time afterwards HRH the Sultan of Trengannu was chosen by his brother Rulers to become the Yang Di Pertuan Agong. He had of course come to live in the Palace in Kuala Lumpur. One afternoon he had been playing golf at the Royal Selangor Golf Club, and afterwards he was sitting having a drink in the lounge. I had been playing with my friend Murray Allen and we were also having a drink. As Murray and I were leaving, the Agong called to me. He said that he had been in Kuala Lumpur over three months and that I had not called on him. To be honest the thought of calling on the King had never entered my head. I made some excuse about believing that he would be too busy to receive visitors like me. He said that I should make arrangements for Wyn and me to call on him. Later I got in touch with his secretary who said that His Majesty had told him that I would be phoning, and a couple of weeks later Wyn and I drove up to the palace. We were received as though we were members of the Diplomatic Corps presenting our credentials. Tea and cakes were brought and we spent a pleasant half-hour or so chatting with Their Majesties. The King and I were talking mainly about the prospects for the development of the State of Trennganu. Wyn during her conversation with the Queen was asked whether she played cards. Away from her home State, and finding time on her hands, the Queen had taken up playing Poker with some of her friends. She had become quite good at it. Fortunately Wyn is not very keen on card playing.

Some British expatriates because of their colonial attitude found it difficult to adjust to the new situation after Independence. They found it difficult to meet Malayans as social equals. The result was that when they were in the company of even very senior Malayans they unconsciously adopted a somewhat condescending mode of speech. Malayans had antennae a mile long and could detect this from a great distance. After one of our dinner parties a Malay friend said of the British chairman of a large company 'Mr X doesn't like Malays does he?' This was quite serious as the company did quite a lot of business with the particular organisation that the Malay was running. I pointed out that he did not get much opportunity to meet high-ranking Malays on a social basis and could appear awkward when he did. I believe that after independence Malays holding senior positions in Government had been warned about the dangers of accepting hospitality from commercial organisations. Some of them developed the habit of accepting invitations and not turning up. This was fine if the event was a large party but could cause a lot of trouble if it was a sit-down dinner. Because Wyn and I had Malayan friends at all levels who were comfortable in our company many of our European friends said that the only place that they could meet Malayan 'Movers and Shakers' was in our house.

Malayans of all racial origins have a great sense of humour. They also love parties. At Malayan parties segregation of the sexes was the norm but gradually this changed. We used to get involved with the Sultan's other friends in organising parties at the palace. The two most memorable parties were the 'Shipwreck Party' and the opening of the cinema. The 'Shipwreck Party' was a farewell for the Sultan and his wife the Tengku Ampuan who were going on a round-the-world tour. Everyone was told that unless they wore fancy dress they could not attend. We took over the palace in Kuala Lumpur for the night. Friends of ours who lived on a tin mine near Kuala Lumpur were in the habit of holding a party at their house at New Year and they decorated their house to a different theme each year. They were very good at thinking up themes and implementing them. They did a terrific job on the palace. I never found out where they got the fishing-nets, giant seashells and huge pieces of driftwood. The invitations were crudely written on scraps of paper, and I delivered the invitation to the Sultan and the Tengku Ampuan in a bottle. At the time Confrontation with Indonesia was at its height. The guards at the palace thought that the invitation was a bomb.

The highlight of the party was the cabaret that we put on. We had four ladies doing a very fancy Charleston. Two rather elderly gentlemen doing a balloon dance which in spite of its simplicity was extremely funny. The show-stealer was however the all-male 'Can--Can'. This had two Malays, a Chinese, and a very burly Sikh. I, the master of ceremonies, was having serious doubts as to whether we were ever going to get it going. From the area where the dancers were being dressed by their wives there were constant roars of laughter. Eventually the hilarious Can-Can came on stage. We were having dinner not long ago in London with the Agong's daughter. She was about eight years old at the time of the party. Thirty years on she was saying what fun it had been.

The opening of the Sultan's private cinema was another uproarious occasion. I wrote a Malay version of Romeo and Juliet, called 'Ahmat and Aminah' to be performed before the first film was shown. Basically the story was of the couple being found together in compromising circumstances. Unlike the Shakespearean version, the girl's parents insisted on a marriage taking place. There was great discussion about Ahmat's job and prospects. Arrangements were made for the wedding, but as it was about to take place the door opened and an irate wife with about a dozen children all calling 'Bapak' (daddy) came running in. We all finished up singing a Malay song entitled 'Ahmat and Aminah' which was popular at the time.

Petaling Jaya was used as a showcase for the burgeoning industrialisation of Malaya. Visiting dignitaries were brought to see what we were doing. Because of this we met King Bhumibol of Thailand and his very beautiful Queen Sirikit and many others. I was also invited to Singapore to make suggestions regarding their first major proposed development at Jurong.

Singapore, Sabah (British North Borneo), and Sarawak, joined with Malaya in 1963, to form Malaysia. Due to political differences Singapore left Malaysia in 1965.

Childless again—the boys at boarding school

Provision for primary schooling in Malaysia was good but it was usual for most older British children to be sent back to Britain to boarding school. In September 1960 it was time for Douglas to go to England to start at boarding school when he was eight years old. We had chosen Beaumont College, a school near Windsor run by Jesuits. It had the great advantage that it was close to Heathrow airport so the boys would be able to get a taxi there when they were coming to Malaya on holiday. Douglas's great ambition was to get to play at Lord's in the cricket match between Beaumont and the Oratory that took place annually. Unfortunately before he could reach that level the school was closed.

We had all been very sad when the date for Douglas's change of school came but tried to play it up as a great adventure. Wyn accompanied the boys to UK and arranged for clothes and other necessities. She settled Douglas into school and rented a house about half an hour away from the school, and I arrived about two months later. On the Saturday after I arrived Douglas was allowed out so that we could take him to the Motor Show at Earl's Court. We all enjoyed it, Douglas especially. When we arrived back at school in the evening, we were slightly early and not being very experienced we stayed around with him instead of saying 'Goodbye' straight away. He did not want to leave us and eventually we had to leave with him being held by one of the masters. He was calling out that he did not want to stay. As we drove home none of us could speak. Even the usually ebullient Michael was sobbing quietly.

As soon as we reached home we immediately phoned the school and spoke to one of the masters. He assured us that Douglas was fine. He had seen him in the Common Room showing the other boys the catalogues that he had picked up at the Motor Show. That was the only time that we had a problem taking the boys to school. Douglas always said that the worst thing about going to boarding school was the time between leaving home and getting into school. He said that once you were in school you were in a boys' world. The headmaster said that boys who were happy at home generally settled well at school. When the time came for Michael to go to boarding school Douglas was in the top class. Because they had always been good friends Michael had no problem settling in.

Wyn and I missed the boys terribly when they were away but knowing that they enjoyed school most of the time made the separation easier. Later when we spoke of returning to the United Kingdom to live they were horrified. Being quite independent they reckoned that they had the best of all worlds, coming out to Malaysia for two holidays every year. They thought that missing a few half terms or weekends out of school was worth it. Wondering what you can do for a seventeen-year-old when you are based on the other side of the world is no joke. Fortunately for us, both the boys are exceedingly clever so there was no doubt that both of them could go on to University. Douglas had two degrees from Oxford before he was twenty one years old and Michael took a First in Civil Engineering from Edinburgh. Both of them are very good at their professions.

Douglas reckons that one of the reasons that we all get on well as a family together is that, while the boys were growing up and going through the difficult teenage years, we saw each other for relatively short periods and we all tried to be nice to each other. From time to time we still all go skiing together. We enjoy each other's company.

While Wyn was in UK with the boys I had gone with the recently proclaimed Sultan of Selangor to see the new palace that was being built on a hill in Kuala Lumpur. Because I had traded in my car for the new Jaguar that Wyn was picking up in UK I was using Wyn's car which at that time was a 'Sit-up and beg' Ford Anglia. I drove to the Sultan's house in the Ford. As I passed through the gates the sentry on duty recognised me and gave a snappy salute. I parked the car. A few minutes later I was with the Sultan and his wife the Tengku Ampuan in their Rolls Royce and we swept out through the gates to another snappy salute. I thought that the contrast between my entrance and the exit was highly amusing.

The new palace had many louvered shutters of the style that we had had in the house in Malacca and I warned the Sultan that he would have trouble with the rain. The evening before I was due to fly home the Sultan and the Tengku Ampuan had invited me to the palace as they had just moved in. The Tengku Ampuan had had a gold brooch made with the Selangor crest and she wanted me to take it to Wyn as a present. I arrived and found the brand new sitting area in a state of chaos. All the furniture was soaking wet. There had been a rainstorm and as I had predicted the rain had come through the louvers. The Sultan said that it had been just like a waterfall. He asked how it was that I knew what would happen when the Public Works Department architect who had designed the building did not. All I could say was that he had probably never lived in a house that had the same problem. It taught me that when designing buildings you have to consider lessons learned in the past. When we were designing our various houses later we were very careful about such matters as orientation and providing shade from the sun. Whilst we were in England I received a letter from one of my staff in Malaya. He was very upset. My deputy Bert Lodge had been heard to say that I was not coming back and that he was taking over from me. It was the first that I had heard of it. I wrote and told the writer of the letter that as far as I knew I would be back in Malaya in a short while. Just in case there were any problems Wyn and I decided that it was time that we owned a house of our own. We wanted a house that needed little looking after and it had to be easily rentable when we were away. The next day we went out and bought one. Just like that!

The house was under construction on the outskirts of Wokingham. I rang the Letting Officer at Arborfield army camp, which was nearby and asked him if the army would be interested in renting the house if we bought it. He said that he had seen the houses and was sure that they would want it. So before we bought the house we knew that we would have no difficulty renting it out. As we were arranging the purchase we came to the conclusion that in any project there are 'up' days and 'down' days. On the up days completion dates, mortgages etc., seemed to be falling into place. On the down days snags seemed to arise one after the other. The main thing was to keep the project moving forward.

We decided to furnish the house from auctions. It was great fun. The first auction that we went to Wyn and I found ourselves bidding against each other. Another time I was bidding for a gas cooker and Wyn was shaking her head because there was a thick layer of grease all over the cooker. We were buying so many things and the auctioneer knew that we were together. He said, 'I wish you two would make up your minds.' We bought the cooker but I had to clean it up. Michael came to the auctions with us. He had learned that you had to watch when you bought furniture, that it did not have woodworm. When the carrier delivered a nice oak bookcase that we had bought into the house that we were renting, Michael said, 'Look! There's wood-worm.' The carrier said, 'Don't blame me. It was your father who bought it.' I believed that the worms were not active but just to be sure I treated it with a liberal dose of Copper Sulphate and it caused no trouble. We even bought an old upright piano which Wyn painted white and gold. Before we left for Malaysia we had a tenant for the house but the main thing was that we now owned a house.

The Chief Minister of the State of Selangor was Dato Abu Bakar. He was also Chairman of the Petaling Jaya Development Corporation, my employers. He had been an Inspector in the Police before he retired and went into politics. I do not think that he found it easy to adjust to the politics and the power that it gave him. I had some sympathy for him and we became quite friendly.

When I returned to Malaysia I was met by my Deputy (he who had been saying that he was going to replace me). He told me that both he and the Development Officer had been sacked. I was surprised. I knew that they had both been trying very hard to cultivate the friendship of some of the members of the Development Corporation. He said that the Corporation had become antagonistic towards the British employees so when I went to the next meeting I expected the worst. I found that the Chairman and the members could not have been more helpful. It was clear that my star was in the ascendancy. They knew that I did not like long leaves. They asked if I would prefer to have six weeks leave every year. This was just what I had been hoping for. By this time holiday cheaper charter flights were available. This meant that Wyn and I could fly to UK for one of the holidays and Douglas could come out to Malaya for the other two. In those days Wyn and I used to fly on separate planes in case the plane crashed.

It appeared that the members of the Corporation had become tired of the demands that my Deputy and the Development Officer were making. They felt it best to get rid of them. However I managed to persuade the Corporation that it would be fair to give them six month's salary so that they could have time to resettle themselves in UK. Amer Singh Bhatt became my Deputy and we brought in an assistant, another Malayan who was of Tamil extraction, V. Mahalingham. I was in loco parentis at both of their weddings and we are still all good friends.

A couple of days after we had returned to Malaya from UK the Sultan rang up to invite Wyn and me to have dinner with him and the Tengku Ampuan at the Lake Club. Just the four of us. I explained that as we had just returned from UK our servants had not yet come back and we had no one to act as baby-sitter to Michael. He suggested that we take Michael to the palace where he could sleep until we got back from the dinner. We took Michael and left him asleep in a luxurious bedroom in the palace with one of the staff on guard over him. When we returned from the dinner he was in such a sound sleep that we decided to leave him and fetch him the next morning. When we arrived next morning Michael had enjoyed the experience of sleeping in the palace so much that he announced 'When I grow up I am going to become a king.'

At one time I reckoned that I worked for the benefit of three organisations. The Malaysian Government got the first bite out of my salary as income tax. Next came the boys' school that got their fees. Every year a letter arrived saying 'Our accountants advise us...' It then went on to say by how much the fees had to increase. I said to Wyn that I wished that they would change their accountants. Third came the airlines that got the fares. There was not much left for Wyn and me.

Life continued to be hectic and I could see that in Petaling Jaya we would soon run out of land. I put together a proposal that meant that a new Corporation should be formed to take over the development of State land in the whole of the State of Selangor. Before it was agreed I think that it was becoming a bit embarrassing to the Corporation that seven years after Independence they still had an expatriate engineer in charge. All the other public engineering posts in the country were held by Malaysians. Besides, I think that my Deputy and my assistant were beginning to feel that their Malaysian contemporaries were leaving them behind. So in early 1964 I received compensation for loss of office and left to set up my own consulting engineering practice in Kuala Lumpur. The Government of the State of Selangor awarded me their Meritorious Service Medal for my work in Petaling Jaya.

Almost as soon as I had started up my consulting practice I was invited to join the committee that had been set up by Tengku Abdul Rahman to manage the construction of a new golf course at Subang just to the West of Kuala Lumpur. The Government had bought the land and would pay for the construction of the course. The money would be recouped from the sale of surplus land for development. By and large that is what happened. The result was an excellent golf course with truly magnificent greens. Tom Verity, a Yorkshireman who had been the professional at the Royal Selangor Golf Club since 1932, supervised the actual construction of the course. Tom, now in his nineties, is still alive and active in Malaysia.

Apparently at one of the meetings it was decided that they should have an engineer on the Committee. Tengku said that I had just started working for myself, and he thought that I would be happy to help out. Importantly he thought that I would be available free of charge. How could I refuse? I think that apart from the Cabinet it must have been the most powerful committee in the country. There were four Ministers including Tengku the Prime Minister as chairman and Tun Ismail as the deputy chairman. There were also four or five Permanent Secretaries to Government Departments. Among the others were Peter Cooper, the senior partner in a firm of accountants who was secretary of the executive sub-committee, the Director of Town Planning, Frank Watkinson, and me. I was appointed as a member of the executive sub-committee.

One morning I received a phone call from Peter Cooper. He asked if I could be at the Prime Minister's Residence at noon. I arrived at the residence at about fifteen minutes before noon, before anyone else. Tengku was the first to arrive. As we sat having a cup of coffee he explained that he was going off to Japan that afternoon to have a cataract operation and wanted to have a meeting about the golf course before he left. He added that he had just come from a Cabinet meeting. He said that Siew Sin (Tan Siew Sin the Minister of Finance) had been going on a bit and he had had to ask him to hurry up, as he wanted to get to the golf course meeting. From anyone else it would have sounded a bit far-fetched. From Tengku Abdul Rahman it sounded the most natural thing in the world to hurry up a meeting of the Cabinet so that he could get to a golf course meeting.

We both go into business

The convent kindergarten was overflowing, and they had no room to expand. It was agreed that Wyn should start a kindergarten of her own. She named it St Anne's, her own confirmation name. The first pupils would be the overflow from the convent kindergarten.

As we were going to need a house of our own we decided to buy two plots of land from a private developer adjacent to Petaling Jaya. One was for a house and the other for a kindergarten. In order to get the kindergarten started we erected a temporary open-sided building in our garden to use for the first term. Then Wyn made a joint bid with the owner of a commercial college for a share of the lease of the old Petaling Jaya Corporation office. The college was called the Goon Institute, the owner being Mr Goon. The boys thought that this was hugely funny. They called the kindergarten 'The Goon Show'. By this time we were designing our house and the new kindergarten. It was fun.

I had formed a partnership as a consulting engineer with a brilliant structural engineer from Singapore. This was very useful as the Kuala Lumpur office started off with work in hand. However the partnership did not last too long as our views on how we should develop differed considerably. He wanted to build a large organisation. In my role as Town Engineer I had seen the problems caused in consulting firms by too rapid expansion. Due to the cyclical nature of the construction industry rapid expansion was often followed by considerable retrenchment. I wanted to have a reasonable sized organisation that had sufficient work to keep it going through any low points in the cycle. We agreed to differ and went our separate ways.

We were sad to leave the house provided by the Petaling Jaya Development Corporation, which we had occupied for nearly ten years. Over that period our hedge had matured and trees and shrubs that we had planted had grown. As the house that we were building was not yet ready, a close friend, the late Ronald Fletcher, who at that time was chairman of Sime Darby one of the great trading and rubber companies invited us to stay in the guest-wing of his house.

When the building of our house was finished we started work on the school building. Wyn had definite ideas on what the best kindergarten in Malaysia should contain. Before it was finished it was already too small. After each term, we had to add another classroom until there were six. Fortunately we had obtained approval for the whole building at the start. We just did not think that it would have to be expanded so quickly.

By this time, our house amah was Ah Que. She was a tall well-built Chinese girl. She was very hard working and when the kindergarten building was ready for occupation she asked Wyn if she could move over to work in the school. Wyn had purchased a second-hand 22-seater bus from a local bus company to bring children to the school. It became a well-known sight in Petaling Jaya as it was painted in the kindergarten colours of yellow and white. One of Ah Que's duties was to act as 'bus conductor'. Since the kindergarten started at 9 am and finished at 12 noon Ah Que quickly spotted that there were possibilities to use the bus more economically. Other schools started earlier and finished later so the bus could be used to take children to these schools. She took driving lessons to obtain a Public Service Vehicle licence, bought Wyn's bus from her and started her business of transporting children to and from school. Ah Que was very successful. She was always smiling and the parents trusted her and it was not long before she needed a second bus. Needing another driver she decided that it was also time that she had a husband. She saw no reason why the same person should not fill the two vacancies, so she advertised in Hong Kong and found a husband who could drive.

The school had a terrific reputation. Deservedly so. Wyn had set up a system, which combined the best modern practice with recognition that the basic Three Rs were essential. She had children from fourteen different nationalities who started from the age of three upwards. Many of them spoke no English. In the top class the children had to learn the Malay language. At the age of six, many children who had been through the school could speak three languages, could read well and could add and subtract. One of the secrets of the success was that every class had a library of books suitable for the age group of the class. When they had finished the task which they had been set the children would fetch a book and read until the others were finished. That way they were never bored. There was plenty of learning by playing. The teachers in the convent primary school reckoned that they could always tell which children came from Wyn's kindergarten. They spoke very good English like Wyn.

Eventually Wyn owned three very successful schools and she took over our house as part of St. Anne's. Wyn with two ladies in the Malaysian Education Department was asked to draw up a syllabus for kindergarten supervisors throughout the whole of Malaysia. With encouragement from Wyn four of her teachers opened their own schools. The St Anne's system was spreading rapidly.

When Wyn took over the house for the Kindergarten we had to find somewhere else to live. For a time we rented a house belonging to the Sultan of Selangor near his own Palace. It had a badminton court and HRH and our other friends used to come in the evenings to play. HRH had an electric golf cart. Sometimes in the evening he would drive round with Tengku Ampuan for a cup of tea. One evening he came round. He had been at a lunch that day given by the King in honour of the President of the United States Lyndon Johnston. It had been quite clear that the President had been badly briefed. He thought that all the Sultans were the King's children. He had also committed the solecism in Islamic countries of crossing one of his legs over the other and pointing the sole of his foot at his host. The feeling was that he was 'kurang ajar' (badly brought up) and a bit of a rough cowboy. I think that a lot of Americans thought the same.

I was doing quite a lot of travelling around Malaysia and I had a driver called 'Ali'. He was an excellent driver. An Australian client after travelling in the car observed that Ali's relationship with the car seemed to be like that of a jockey with a horse. Drivers take their status from the cars that they drive and Ali was quite happy when he was driving the Jaguar that I now owned. He was even happier when we bought a Mercedes. At first, he was not too happy when I brought back from UK a Bentley S2. Then when he saw that the British High Commissioner's Rolls Royce Silver Cloud was the same apart from the radiator he was very happy.

I sold the Mercedes to a Finance Company. I was telling Tiw Wan that they were paying me cash and had asked me to meet them at a bank. He was horrified. He said that these people had links with gangsters for the purpose of enforcing payments and were quite likely to have someone waiting outside to rob me. He insisted that we should go in his car. After the money had been handed to me I walked to the car. He stayed two or three paces behind me. When we got into his car he showed me the automatic pistol that he had in his pocket. He was serious.

On the subject of guns, a friend who was a judge was sitting next to me at a Rotary Club Lunch one day. He had been saying that I should join the Shooting Club, as it would give me an excuse to get a licence to keep a gun in the house. I pointed out that I did not want a gun in the house, as I might be tempted to use it if someone broke in. The judge was called upon to speak. As he got up from his seat he said, 'Hang on to this for me.' In my hand he put a large automatic pistol. I sat through his speech holding the gun very gingerly. Wyn's driver was called Mohammed. He was a very happy character but he had a disconcerting habit of turning round to answer you, if you spoke to him whilst he was driving. The two drivers lived in Klang. Our new house was about 25 miles away in Kuala Lumpur. The drivers decided between themselves that only Ali should come with us to Kuala Lumpur. With Mohammed gone, Wyn was then able to indulge her taste for exotic sports cars, as she took to driving herself. She had a Triumph Spitfire, an Alfa Romeo GTV, a Ford Capri and a BMW Coupe at various times. The BMW was a very smart looking car. One day Wyn had gone shopping at the local Super-market. When she returned to the car there was a note on the windscreen saying that if she ever thought of selling the car, would she ring the telephone number given on the note. The boys were also catered for transport-wise. After motorbikes they had a Singer Coupe and then took over the Ford Capri. When we bought Douglas a motor scooter he had his first lessons from our Tamil gardener. Shortly afterwards the gardener seemed to disappear. We did not know where he lived. Much later we discovered that he had caught chicken pox and that he had died.

With a large number of expatriates still in Malaysia, there were lots of young people coming out from UK on school holidays. They were well catered for. There were rugby matches, cricket matches and parties. There was also the cross-country running club called 'The Hash House Harriers'. There are branches of 'The Hash' all over the world. I was talking to an American friend from Malaysia, Keith Kenaga recently. He still runs with 'The Hash' in Central Park in New York.

Both boys played for the Selangor Club at rugby at a fairly young age. They found it quite frustrating however, to come home from a party to find mum and dad waiting up for them. Douglas was moved to say, 'We spend most of the year half the world away and you have no idea what we get up to. Here you know exactly where we are and whom we are with. Yet you sit up late at night waiting for us to come home. Parents!'

On one occasion Douglas had arrived from university earlier than Michael who was still at school. Douglas had all the arrangements made by the time that Michael arrived. On Monday it was the Hash. On Tuesday it was rugby training at the Selangor Club. Wednesday was a soccer match. Thursday it was more rugby training. On the Friday Michael said that he did not know what was the matter but he felt tired. No wonder, without taking time to get over jet lag or to get acclimatised he was indulging in some very strenuous exercise.

We were arranging to build another house for which we had bought a site from a developer in Kuala Lumpur. Our second effort at house design was built in a U-shape enclosing a swimming pool. All the rooms opened on to the terrace round the pool. The water was pumped through the filter and ran down a waterfall back into the pool. It also had a pond in the entrance hall with a fountain in the middle of it. The fountain threw the water up into a conical shape and had a dark green marble plinth in the middle of it. We needed a statue between 18 inches and 24 inches tall to put on the plinth, and driving to London Airport to catch a plane after a visit to UK, we stopped off in Camden Passage. In one of the stalls we saw exactly what we wanted. It was a spelter statue of a boy carrying a water jar. I asked if they could send it to us in Malaysia. The dealer said, 'What! For a fiver?' I had omitted to ask the price. I carried it triumphantly on to the plane as hand baggage. On the plane I was sitting next to a Malaysian judge whom I knew and I showed him the statue. He said that he was building a new house and had been looking for a small statue. Without knowing what I had paid for the statue he said that he would give me twice what I had paid for it. It was not for sale.

From a 'feng shui' point of view the house design was very bad. The good luck which came in the front door flowed straight out and down the waterfall. In spite of this we continued to prosper. When we eventually came to sell it there was a young Chinese couple wished to buy it. The couple brought the man's father to see it. He was a Hakka from the town of Ipoh, a wealthy tin miner. I know none of the Hakka language but as he stood in the entrance hall talking in an animated fashion I knew exactly what the father was saying. I said, 'Feng shui m' ho.' This is Cantonese for 'The wind and the water are not good'. Or 'It is bad luck'. He laughed but they did not buy the house. This was a relief to Wyn and me.

The couple had a year-old child. We did not think that the house was suitable for a child of that age. A short time before friends of ours had moved into a house with a swimming pool. As they had young children they had arranged to have a fence put round the pool before they would move in. During a house-warming party in the middle of the day the gate in the fence was left open. Their two-year-old slipped through the opening fell into the pool and drowned. We were away at the time and did not hear about it until later. We were always extra careful when friends with small children came to visit.

My knowledge of the Cantonese dialect was picked up mainly at Chinese dinners. I can therefore ask for sharksfin soup, crabs, or duck. I can also ask a young lady sitting next to me in Cantonese 'Why is it that you are so beautiful?' Wyn found out the meaning of this latter phrase. I had to learn another. This is 'Mo hup cho'.

Literally it means 'Do not eat vinegar'. Colloquially it means 'Don't be jealous'. I did in fact decide to learn to speak Mandarin. This is the National Language of China. I enjoyed it but as I started my law course shortly afterwards, the language lessons lapsed. The Mandarin teacher said that I spoke Mandarin like a Cantonese. I do not think that he was being complimentary. However I made my name as a linguist with one of my Dutch clients when he heard me discussing with two Chinese ladies whether it was nicer to say 'I love you' in Cantonese or in Mandarin. Actually when we eventually visited China, because of my few words, the tour guide told Wyn and me quite a bit about life in China. I do not believe we would have heard about it otherwise.

When we had moved into the first house that we built, we employed a Hainanese cook, Ah Zoon, who was one of the best cooks in Kuala Lumpur. Ah Zoon and I had agreed that one day we would walk along the Great Wall of China together. Unfortunately he died a few years after we left Malaysia, so we never made our walk together. When Wyn took over the house for the school and we eventually moved to the new house, we acquired a new house amah, Ah Kum. Her duties were to look after the bedrooms and do the washing and ironing. Ah Zoon looked after the entrance hall, the lounge and the dining -room. When Ah Kum arrived we were not sure how we would get on with her. She was older than the amahs we had had before and she did not seem to smile very much. She turned out to be a real treasure and remained with us until we returned to UK, saying that if she had been younger she would have come with us. One of her most endearing habits was that if the boys were out late she could be seen with her joss sticks praying for their safe return.

Feng Shui comes up many times in relation to laying out house lots and designing houses. There is a house lot in Petaling Jaya, which was impossible to sell. It was triangular-shaped. It therefore had three corners with acute angles for the good luck to flow out. In one of the best residential areas of Kuala Lumpur a couple we knew had built a house but after they moved in they deemed that they were experiencing bad luck. They called in the geomancer to find out the cause of the problem. He said that the cause was a house that had been built on the other side of the valley. The house had a veranda with a sharp point that was facing directly towards our friends' house. It resembled the mouth of a dragon. The bad luck was being directed towards them. It was necessary to erect a mirror to reflect it back. A mirror was duly erected. Problem solved. Alas our friends had relations who lived further along the valley on the same side as the house with the veranda. They started having troubles. Their dog died. Their servant got sick. Time to get the geomancer again. The mirror was the problem. Instead of reflecting the bad luck straight back to the source it was diverting it to the relative's house. Another mirror was required to divert the bad luck to someone else. Presumably the bad luck is still bouncing around the valley. All the people involved were UK-educated engineers and lawyers.

Because I was submitting plans for factories for approval by the Petaling Jaya Development Corporation I was a frequent visitor to my old office that was now in a handsome modern building. I was always welcomed and given a cup of coffee. One morning while I was having a coffee with my successor Amer Singh Bhatt the Administrator Dato' Tahir came in. He told us that the Federal Government wished to replace Dato' Abu Bakar as Chief Minister of Selangor after the elections which were due shortly. They had approached the State Legal Adviser Dato' Harun to resign his post and stand for election in a safe seat so that he could become Chief Minister. It was all supposed to be a great secret.

That same afternoon I was sitting in my office that I had set up in Kuala Lumpur. The phone rang and to my surprise it was Dato' Abu Bakar. He asked me to go to see him as soon as I was free. It was not far from my office to the Chief Minister's office so I was there about fifteen minutes later. Dato' Abu Bakar said that he would like my advice as a friend. He said that he was trying to make up his mind whether or not he should stand again for election and he would like to know what I thought. I was a bit taken aback that he should ask me. However knowing that I had already been told that morning that he would be replaced I proceeded to outline to him all the disadvantages of taking on a further five-year term in a strenuous office. When I had finished he said that he was very glad that he had spoken to me and that he would follow my advice. That same evening I had occasion to call on the Sultan at his palace. I cannot remember why I had to meet him. After we had been talking for a while His Royal Highness asked me who I thought would be the next Chief Minister of Selangor. I did not know whether he knew of the politicians' plans so I made some remark such as 'It could be anyone'. He then said, 'Will it be a businessman or a government servant?' I deduced that he knew what was planned. I said, 'Tuanku (Your Royal Highness), you know and I know that it is going to be Dato' Harun.' He looked absolutely astonished and said, 'That is supposed to be a State secret. How do you know?' I told him that there were no secrets, State or otherwise in Kuala Lumpur. Certainly the identity of the next Chief Minister of Selangor was not a secret. I got it three times in one day.

On one of our visits to Scotland we were driving south. Wyn was reading 'The Scotsman' and came across an advertisement that said that there were plots of land for sale overlooking Muirfield golf course. We stopped the car at a telephone box and rang up. We bought one. It was a beautiful site overlooking the first fairway. When we got back to Malaysia I set about sketching what we wanted for the site. We had been given the name of an architect in North Berwick and sent the sketches to him to complete and to get the house built. Everything started off quite well. The plans were approved and a contract was signed with a local contractor. We were all very excited about the house that was supposed to be ready in nine months. It seemed that the architect lost interest and because we were overseas the contractor treated it as a 'hospital' job, working on it when he had nothing else to do. Each time that we were coming to UK we told the architect, and he would always try to persuade us to delay our trip. We had been the first to submit our plans to the Local Authority but ours was the last house in the row to be completed. At one stage the local rumour was that we had gone bankrupt and could not afford to finish the building. In all it took nearly six years to finish.

When it appeared that the house was going to be finished, we started to try to order furniture from manufacturers in UK. They were quoting delivery times of fifty three weeks, so we decided to design the furniture ourselves and have it made in Malaysia. This took us about three months. Wyn came home to Scotland a month before me. By the time that I arrived she had had several local tradesmen in to carry out extra bits of work. She had purchased the domestic appliances that she required, and had carpets laid throughout the house. The curtains had been made in Malaysia and were arriving in a container, which was due to arrive a couple of days after I arrived. While Wyn was in one of the department stores using her credit card so fast that it was in danger of overheating, one of the assistants asked if she would go up to the office. Apparently, they had grown worried that Wyn's card, which had not been used for months, was now being used at a furious rate. They were quite happy when she explained what she was doing. Ever since Wyn has had a higher credit limit on her card than I have.

I was extremely impressed by the driver of the container vehicle who delivered our furniture. The entrance gate opening was 8'-3" wide. His container was 8'-0" wide and he backed it in without hesitation. A real professional! When we received the furniture we soon settled in. We had a housewarming party before we returned to Malaysia. Before we set off for Malaysia we went round the local contractors in Gullane that Wyn had employed. We told them that we would not be back for twelve months and asked for their bills. They all said that was all right we could pay when we came back. Eventually after some persuasion we managed to get them to bill us so that we could pay them.

One of the areas of business that I was involved in was the design of oil palm factories. Many of the rubber estates were changing over to oil palm and they required a factory to extract the oil from the fruit. It was excellent business and my consulting firm was expanding. Malaysia was also attracting investment from the electronics industry and we were involved in designing factories for the manufacture of microchips. When the boys came to Malaysia on holiday they used to come with me to visit the buildings under construction.

They were both fascinated by the burgeoning electronics industry but from two different aspects. Douglas's interest was in the economics of the industry. When he came to write his thesis for his M.Phil. Degree he chose to write about the Malaysian electronics industry. The predictions that he made about its future at the time seemed to me to be in the realms of fantasy. They turned out to be astonishingly accurate. Michael loved to go on the sites where building was taking place. He was a very useful site supervisor.

One of my clients was a company called Ansul. They manufactured herbicides. They wished to erect a factory in Malaysia and we were commissioned to carry out the task. As I was going to UK on holiday it was suggested that I visit their factory in the United States to see how they operated. I decided that I would take Wyn and the boys with me. We flew to New York. After we had a meal we decided to go out and have a walk round Times Square. It was quite late in the evening but we did not worry. Next day we hired a car and headed west. When we eventually reached Chicago we turned north until we reached Marinette, which is in Wisconsin. We booked into a Motel for a week and proceeded to enjoy the enormous steaks for which Wisconsin is famous. The Motel had a sauna, which we all enjoyed. During one of our sojourns in the sauna we started talking to a group of businessmen who had come up from Milwaukee for a weekend of golf and fishing. They invited us to join them for dinner. I seem to remember that they spent most of the meal listening to Douglas telling them about American politics. He told them about the percentages of votes by which John F Kennedy had won the various states and what the reasons were in different cases. He also discussed with them the arguments for and against the Gun Laws. They were astonished that a schoolboy from England knew so much about what went on in America. Their surprise is understandable because Americans themselves are largely ignorant about what goes on outside America. You could have an event of worldwide importance consigned to a few lines on page seven of a newspaper. The banner headline on the front page would be something like 'Carpenters win 20 cents an hour pay-rise'.

After I had finished my business in Marinette we carried on driving North and crossed into Canada at Sault Ste. Marie. From there we phoned my cousin Isobel who lived with her husband Neil in Montreal and they invited us to stay with them in their lovely house near Lac Ste Louis on the outskirts of Montreal. While we were in Sault Ste. Marie we came across a shop that sold electric sauna units. We ordered a unit to be sent to Malaysia. We visited Niagara Falls. Douglas had been telling Michael that at night they turned off the white water in the Falls and sent down pink water. Michael was not fooled. We were having dinner in a hotel overlooking the falls. When it got dark the lights came on. They were pink and indeed the water took on a beautiful shade of pink.

Isobel and Neil made us most welcome. They had a Granny Flat in their house and Neil's father who was a widower was staying in it. They told us that he was from Uddingston, which is in Scotland halfway between Edinburgh and Glasgow. When we met him we all thought from his strong Scottish accent that he was in Canada on holiday. He had lived in Canada for fifty three years where he had been teaching Canadian children English. Presumably generations of Canadian children grew up speaking English as though they were from Uddingston.

When we returned to New York, I phoned another cousin who was a member of the New York Police. He came round to the Algonquin where we were staying and was horrified when he heard that we had been wandering round Times Square at near midnight. He thought that we were completely mad when we told him that we had walked to the docks to take a boat-trip round Manhattan Island and had walked back after dark. He said that if we had told him beforehand he would have told us to stay in the hotel until he came to fetch us. He told us that he always carried a gun even when he was off duty.

Living in a multi-racial country

It saddens me that the media in UK does not appear to realise the fine line that politicians in a country like Malaysia with its delicate racial balance, have to tread. Of course they do things differently from the way that we like to see them done in Britain but then circumstances are different. I do not believe that I see things Malaysian through rose-coloured spectacles. But I believe that the way that Malaysia has prospered since Independence has not been due just to good luck. They must have got more things right than wrong. From the early nineteen-sixties I had been predicting that there would be racial difficulties in 1969. I had said that we should leave Malaysia in 1968. However we were enjoying life and did not feel like leaving. As in UK Malaysian parliaments have a maximum life of five years. They generally run the full term. 1969 was due to be an election year. Although on the surface everything was going well tensions existed underneath. In spite of policies, which were supposed to improve the economic welfare of the indigenous Malays, only a small minority were seeing any real benefit. The vast majority had had expectations that they would benefit from independence. Their expectations had not been fulfilled. I believed that eventually there would be trouble and that the election in 1969 would set off the trouble. I thought that by 1969 it would become apparent that the indigenous Malays were not sufficiently integrated into commercial life while still having the overwhelming political power. This I considered to be an unstable situation. I propounded this theory to anyone including any Malaysian politician who was prepared to listen to me.

On 13th May 1969 the day after a general election it happened. It is a date most Malaysians remember. Racial riots broke out. A 24-hour curfew was immediately announced. Anyone seen outside was liable to be shot. Douglas was with us on a gap year before going to university and he was out playing cricket on the padang when the curfew was announced. Ah Kum got out her joss sticks. We all waited anxiously until at last we heard the sound of his motorcycle coming along the road.

After the first twenty four hours we were allowed out for an hour to shop for food. In the area where we lived there was a small super-market and we went there to get some supplies. There was quite a long queue and we wondered whether we would get served before the curfew was reimposed. A lady in front of us was buying toilet rolls. The shop assistant handed over those nearest at hand. They happened to be pink. She required green. She insisted and he went away, climbed a ladder to reach the top shelf, and fetched green ones. Everyone in the queue fumed. It was announced on the radio that volunteers were required to pack food in a depot near where we lived. The food was to be transported to areas that were still under 24-hour curfew. Wyn, Douglas and I volunteered. We were given Curfew Passes. Foolishly, we had not told Ah Zoon and Ah Kum what we were doing and by the time we returned after doing a stint at the depot, they were in a dreadful panic. They thought that we had all been shot. Later we heard that some of Douglas's old school friends had seen him on television working at the depot. The hours under curfew were reduced gradually but it was a long time before the curfew was finally removed. The total number of people stated to have been killed in the rioting was around 150.

One of the results of the riots was that politicians realised that using the 'race card' in elections was a very dangerous strategy. In subsequent elections generally they have dealt with racial issues sensitively. As time goes on and new generations come up the memory of the riots will dim. Race could again become a political issue.

I had known Dato' Harun before he became Chief Minister of Selangor. We kept in touch afterwards and sometimes had discus-sions about matters affecting the State. Sometimes he would ask me to drop a hint to HRH the Sultan on some delicate matter. One day he phoned me in my office. He asked me if I knew anyone at Harri-son and Crosfields. I said that Brian Joyce a close friend was a Director and that I played golf regularly with Philip Gunton who was the Chairman. Dato Harun then went on to tell me about an incident which had occurred on the Federal Highway between Port Klang and Kuala Lumpur. Apparently HRH the Sultan had been travelling on the Highway. As was normal in Malaysia, he had police outriders in front of his car. They came up behind a car and signalled to it to pull over to let the convoy pass. At first the driver refused to pull over. After some distance he was persuaded to do so and as the Sultan's car passed, the driver made what the police described as a rude gesture. The police had traced the ownership of the car. They had discovered that it belonged to an expatriate man who worked for Harrisons. Dato Harun said that the police were taking the matter very seriously but he hoped that if there was a suitable apology he could sort the matter out. I said that I would convey the message and I phoned Philip and told him the story. He was quite shocked. He said to leave it with him. Not long after I was playing golf with Philip and I asked him if the matter had been sorted out. He said that they had sent the man back to UK and added that a company like his could not risk employing people who did not respect the feelings of local people. It seemed a bit harsh to me but he was probably right from the company's point of view. An interesting sidelight on racial abuse occurred during an international football tournament in Kuala Lumpur. Dato' Harun was the President of the Malaysian Football Association and in the final Malaysia were playing a team from Australia. Before the match he told the team that whatever happened they must not get upset if the Australians swore at them. He said, 'If you lose your tempers you will lose the match.' He went on to explain that to Australians the word 'bastard' was often used as a term of friendship. As an example he quoted how on a visit to Australia he had met up with an Australian friend who was a judge. The judge said, 'How are you going on, you old bastard?' Dato Harun told the team that he had been a bit perturbed until he realised that the judge was not intending to be rude.

The match was a great success. At full-time the score was 2–2. After extra time Malaysia won 4–2. The teams absolutely shattered came off the field with their arms round each other. Later one of the Malaysian team, who was of Indian extraction, told the Chief

Minister 'Dato' it was a good job you warned us about the swearing. As soon as we got on to the field one of the opposition said to another, 'You look after the black bastard, I'll look after the brown one.' If you hadn't warned us there would have been a fight straight away.' Sometimes I wonder whether our methods of dealing with racial matters a bit too heavy-handed and cause more problems than they solve.

For many years the Malaysian government was reluctant to give permission to Malaysians of Chinese origin to visit China. Wyn and I visited China in the early Eighties and my view was that the Malaysian government should be quite happy to allow anyone to visit. There were very very few Chinese in Malaysia at that time who were not considerably better off than their counterparts in China.

For over thirty years Malaysia has been a model of interracial harmony. At Lincoln's Inn where I am a Bencher there are quite a large number of overseas students. You can always tell the Malaysians. You will have a group of young people of different colours and clearly different racial origins obviously comfortable in each other's company. Interestingly although the medium of education in the schools in Malaysia is Bahasa Kebangsaan (The National Language) the lingua franca is English. When I speak to them in Bahasa Kebangsaan they usually tell me that I can speak it better than they can. They are also fascinated to hear about the early days of Malaysian Independence. One student said to me, 'Dato' you are part of Malaysian history.' That comment did not make me feel any younger.

Racial issues do arise from time to time. When you are trying to change the economic structure of a society tensions are bound to arise. In the case of Malaysia the Government has been trying to bring the indigenous Malays more into the private business sector of the economy. To try to give the Malays a share of the economic cake while not taking away from the other races has required some delicate balancing. However it has been Malaysia's good fortune that almost since Day 1 of Independence the economy has been expanding at a steady rate. There have been minor hiccups but generally the trend has been upwards. The result has been that over the years the

Malays have been able to play their part in the expansion of the economy without causing disadvantage to the Malaysians of other racial origins.

There have of course been scandals and evidence of corrupt practice. After Independence there was an upsurge in industrial investment. The investors were committed to bringing in local capital, generally by floating companies on the local stock exchange. A certain proportion of the shares had to be reserved for Bumiputras (Ethnic Malays and other indigenous races). Most of the flotations were vastly over-subscribed with the result was that by the time trading in the shares started they were at a healthy premium. The Government set up a form of Unit Trust open only to Bumiputras to take up the reserved shares as and when there were sufficient funds available. As the shares were being taken up at the issue price you would have thought that they could not possibly lose. They nearly went bankrupt. What with high salaries and flashy offices they managed to get through an awful lot of money.

Dato' Harun was eventually convicted of corruption and sentenced to six years in jail. This was in connection with using shares in a bank of which he was the chairman to guarantee funds needed to finance the boxing match between Mohammed Ali and Joe Bugner. A syndicate of Malaysians had obtained the right to stage the fight. One day when I was at the Selangor Club watching Douglas and Michael playing rugby a lawyer whom I knew approached me. He wanted to know whether I wanted to be part of the syndicate. I asked what rights the syndicate had in connection with the fight. He said that they had everything except the television rights. I was surprised that some very smart people had allowed themselves to be put in the position where they had to bear all the expenses and the risk, while the promoters had retained the only part of the project that was certain to be profitable. I said that I would not touch it with a barge pole. Ultimately the Malaysians made a huge loss and Dato' Harun ended up in court.

For a while Malaysia seemed to attract con-men. Our first experience with one was in connection with Wyn's school. He was English and his wife was Chinese. They brought their two children along and ordered everything: uniforms; places on the school bus; and orange drinks at mid-morning break. With the tuition fees it came to a considerable sum for the term. Paying with a post-dated cheque the man explained that his account had not yet been transferred from Hong Kong. When the cheque was eventually presented it bounced. He managed to stretch things a bit by saying that there had been a minor difficulty but that it would be sorted out within a couple of weeks. After a couple of weeks the family disappeared. Wyn rang the bank to find out if it was worth presenting the cheque. Their answer was that if she found out where the couple were to let the bank know. The Bank was owed a considerable amount of money. It turned out that the couple had been moving around Kuala Lumpur running up debts then moving on. In Petaling Jaya they ordered beer and spirits for a farewell party the night before they left. The bill was never paid.

One Saturday afternoon I received a call from a man who claimed that he wished to talk to me about a major project at the port of Klang. He said that it was urgent that he saw me. I asked where he was staying and he told me the name of the hotel. I was immediately suspicious. It had a reputation as being one of the largest brothels in Kuala Lumpur. I said that I could not meet him there. If I had parked my Bentley there half of Kuala Lumpur would have been on the phone telling Wyn that my car had been seen there. I arranged to meet him at a cafe where we could have a beer. He was of Indian extraction and had a good command of English. From the story he told me the project was indeed large and would be very profitable for us. I thought that he must have been looking for a bribe so I said that we were not in the business of paying commissions or any other form of 'kick-back'. He replied that he knew of my reputation for straight dealing. I was beginning to feel that I had misjudged the man. Then he asked if I could lend him four hundred and fifty Malaysian ringgit. Not a large sum in con-man terms. I pointed out that I carried very little money, and what I had had paid for the beer. He did not appear to be very perturbed, and left saying that he would be in touch after his boss had arrived from Indonesia. I never saw him again. A few days later a story appeared in one of the newspapers about a contractor who had reported to the police that he had been conned. The story was the same as I had been told. He had believed it and had given the man four hundred and fifty Malaysian ringgit.

My next experience with a con was when a man came to my office. He was a Malay and claimed that he knew some people that I knew. He had with him a cablegram as confirmation that he could purchase a large quantity of crude oil at a price which was well below market price. He said that he had already got agreement that the Malaysian government would buy the oil at a price that would show a large profit. I did not understand what the Malaysian government was going to do with a large quantity of crude oil. I asked him why he had come to me. It was the usual story that comes in those letters that come from Nigeria. He had been given my name as someone he could trust and he wanted me to be involved. When I enquired how he wanted me to be involved he said that he needed three thousand five hundred Malaysian ringgit to set the deal in motion. I pleaded poverty and he left. I was telling the family about it and Douglas's comment was that I must have been becoming part of the Malaysian establishment with the con men seeking me out.

A Scotsman Abroad and a New Development

Curry tiffins (lunches) were one of the great social institutions in Malaysia. They were nearly always held on a Sunday. There was an area in Sussex where there were a large number of people who had retired from Malaysia, known as 'the Curry Tiffin Belt'. As the security situation in Malaysia improved people thought nothing of driving fifty or more miles to attend such a lunch on a rubber estate. The guests would start to arrive around noon. Serious drinking would take place from then until lunch was served around 4 o'clock. At that time there were no drink-driving laws. Most estates had a number of contractors who were employed to carry out a variety of jobs on the estate. It was customary for the contractors to give the manager of the estate cases of whisky and brandy at Christmas. Nothing but the best was good enough. The result was that most estate-managers would only drink single malt Whiskies or VSOP Brandy. At one such lunch that I attended I heard a planter telling the house servant, 'I would not wash my car windows with that stuff.' He had committed the ultimate solecism of producing a bottle of Johnnie Walker Red Label instead of Black Label.

Wyn and I were staying with friends on an estate in North Johore. We were invited with our host and hostess, to a lunch on another estate. The manager of the estate, had built a 17'-6" boat. He said that he wanted to sell it, as he was unlikely to get to anywhere that he could use it. From time to time, the boys had suggested that we should join the Yacht Club and buy a boat. Whether it was the brandy I know not but I, the worst sailor in the world, who gets sea-sick going through a car-wash, agreed to buy the boat if it could be delivered to the Yacht Club at Port Swettenham (now called Port Klang). Thus it was that we acquired a boat. We needed an engine. It was about this time that there appeared stories in the papers about a Catholic priest in Kerala in South India who was sending young girls to Italy to become nuns. He was receiving US $300 for each girl that he sent. The boys and I discussed whether we should sell Wyn to get the money for the engine. After all she had acted as a Reverend

Mother in charge of the convent on a number of occasions. She should thus be extremely valuable, but we decided against the idea. I arranged to buy a 75 HP engine and we finished off the boat by getting carpeting for the deck and cushions for the cabin seats. By the time the boys arrived on their next holiday we were ready to sail.

We decided to go for a picnic to one of the offshore islands. Someone in the club warned me to make sure that I had sufficient fuel. I thought that I had sufficient. When we reached the island we had only used about a third of the fuel that we had taken on board. Because I was at the helm I had no problem about being seasick. After a lovely picnic we started on the return journey. What I had not realised was that when the tide is running against you the fuel consumption just rockets up. We ran out of fuel. It was quite scary. After drifting for a bit we were given a tow to another island where we were able to get fuel to take us back to the Club. It was a salutary lesson and I bought a couple of spare tanks so that it could not happen again. The currents in the area were extremely strong. On one occasion we were cleaning the boat and were tied up to a buoy. Michael was doing some painting. He dropped the paint-pot into the water and it started to float away. Without a second thought he dived in to retrieve it. Although a very strong swimmer Michael had great difficulty in getting back on board. This was another lesson learned. Everyone must wear a decent lifejacket. I like designing houses and so does Wyn. One day I was talking to a Malay friend who said that there was a very nice house site for sale in an area of Kuala Lumpur, which had originally been developed as a diplomatic enclave. It had now been opened to others. I decided to have a look at the site and liked it. At first Wyn was not terribly keen. That same day she had had a lunch for her teachers. One of them had remarked as she floated in the pool, 'If I lived here I would not want to leave the house. I would stay in all day.'

I had sketched out what I had in mind and Wyn agreed that we should go ahead. When we told Ah Zoon and Ah Kum that we were thinking of moving house Ah Kum said that Ah Zoon had said only the previous week that he thought that we would be moving soon as we never stayed too long in one house. He had already seen us through three moves.

The new house had four air-conditioned bedrooms each with its own bathroom. It had a large lounge downstairs and a smaller air-conditioned sitting area upstairs. The lounge and dining room had large glazed sliding doors that opened on to a deep terrace shaded by the upstairs veranda. The dining room could also be air-conditioned. The swimming pool was quite large and we had changing rooms and a sauna beside it. We also had a floodlit badminton court. There was no need to leave the house to keep fit. Our curry lunches took on a new dimension. Wyn was looking at the house plans one day. There was a space behind the garage. She enquired what was going to be there. I said that it was just a space. She said, 'Why don't we have a Japanese garden?' A Japanese garden it was, with access from the house through a door that looked like a Japanese screen. On one of our trips in the boat Wyn came across a large piece of driftwood. She decided that it was just what she needed for her Japanese Garden. It was waterlogged and floated just below the surface. It was very, very, heavy. The boys and I could not lift it up on to the deck of the boat so we towed it back to the club. A friend who had a van transported it to our house. We still have that piece of driftwood, now considerably dryer, at our house in Scotland.

Wyn had taken up a variety of art subjects. She did screen-printing, copper tooling and enamelling on copper. She now had a studio to work in. She appeared on television demonstrating her skills. It got to the stage where they would ring her up to find out whether she was doing anything new. She also started to grow roses around the badminton court. The plants were bought from a leper hospital outside Kuala Lumpur. The patients lived around the hospital and their main occupation was growing plants for sale. The disease is largely eradicated but those who have had it find that because of prejudice it is better to live at the hospital.

A Scottish rubber planter, the late Duncan Kidd, who was manager of an estate nearby, gave a lot of his spare time to assisting the patients in growing their plants. I was very happy when as a result of my recommendation he was awarded an MBE by the Queen.

Wyn used to water the roses in the morning with ice cubes and sprayed them with some highly toxic substance which seemed to be banned everywhere except Malaysia. The roses flourished but unfortunately after we left our tenants did not look after them and they all died. She also grew a number of varieties of orchid in the garden. Beautiful white Dianas and many brightly coloured types grew in great profusion. It was a lovely house to live in. With its correct orientation and wide veranda it was remarkably cool. Apart from the bedrooms we hardly used the air-conditioning. We had imported all sorts of things such as wallpaper, special wall tiles, marble floor tiles, and toilet fittings. Using coloured perspex Wyn created a 'stained-glass' window in our bathroom. She also tooled designs on sheets of copper, which were the fixed to the entrance door.

We had a house-warming party not long after we moved in. Among the guests was to be HRH the Sultan of Selangor. As they always did when going to a place that they had not been to before, the police outriders who were to accompany HRH came to our house one evening before the party. Apparently they had stopped outside the gate. A Malay watchman at the house opposite asked what they were doing. When they told him, the watchman asked why the Sultan was coming to visit us. Later the watchman told Ah Zoon our cook that the policemen had said that the Sultan and I were very good friends. In fact we were like brothers. I suppose that to people at the palace it could have seemed like that.

We had given our dog Snowball to a friend when we went on one of our long leaves and she had settled so well that we did not have the heart to take her back so we had subsequently acquired a chocolate-coloured standard sized poodle. She was quite large. We named her Fifi. Like most dogs Fifi had remarkable hearing. In the afternoons she would lie stretched out enjoying the cool marble floor. As soon as she heard my car coming up the hill about a hundred yards away she would get up to greet me. When she rose Ah Zoon knew that it was time to boil the kettle for our afternoon tea. His aim was to get the tea to the table on the terrace overlooking the pool before I came in the door. We thought that it might be a good idea to breed from Fifi and we were told of a Chinese family who had a male standard poodle. We contacted them and they agreed that they would bring their dog when Fifi was in heat. When the time arrived we rang them and they brought the dog over. The poor dog was very scrawny. Fifi took an instant dislike to him. It was agreed that the dog would be left with us overnight. Fifi was genuinely in heat but she would have none of him. We spent the whole evening trying to get them to mate. When we lifted the dog on top of Fifi he would slide off. It was a complete pantomime. Eventually we decided to leave them together in a veranda, which had a folding sliding gate. Next morning the male had gone. We found him asleep in the garage. He had managed to squeeze through the narrow openings in the gate. Obviously impregnating Fifi was not one of his priorities.

In Kuala Lumpur in addition to the St. Andrew's Society we had what we had nicknamed 'The Tribal Societies'. These were the St. George's, St. David's and St. Patrick's Societies. There was also a Malaysian/Australian/New Zealand Society. Each Society would have social events and a golf match against the 'Rest of the World'. The other Societies had a President, but the St Andrew's Society had a Chieftain. In 1971 I was elected Chieftain.

As in Malacca the Society's main social event was the St Andrew's Night ball. It was always a very grand affair. Also as in Malacca the Scottish dancing was taken very seriously. Practices were started some months in advance. Members were expected to invite to the practices the guests that they intended to invite to the Ball. The trick was to invite as your guests members of the other societies so that you would be invited to their functions. Interestingly the St. Patrick's Society had members from both the North and the South. BOAC (as British Airways was then called) flew out a supply of haggis. I was also fortunate in that British Caledonian Airways flew their pipe band to Kuala Lumpur for our ball. I had to sign a bond that the musical instruments that they brought into the country would be taken out again. They also brought Christine, a Scottish Champion dancer and a lovely girl. The band played at the Scotland versus the Rest of the World rugby match. They also held what might be called master classes for Malaysian pipers. Members of the Society hosted and entertained the members of the band. One of the bandsmen was heard to say, 'If anyone asks me what I saw of Kuala Lumpur, I will have to reply that everything I saw was through the bottom of a whisky glass.'

The Chieftain's speech was expected to be of a high standard. It was closely studied by the members for length and content. It was truly a major opus. I started preparing mine several months in advance. I put it on tape. It sounded awful. The content was banal, the humour was pedestrian and the delivery was full of ums and ahs. To say that it was rubbish would be flattery. I worked at it and eventually I had what came to be regarded as a very creditable speech. It, so I was told, took twenty minutes and twenty-one seconds to deliver. This was acceptable, as I had had to wait for the laughter to subside on a number of occasions.

The guest of honour was of course my friend, HRH the Sultan of Selangor. There is an apocryphal story in Kuala Lumpur that on one occasion the St George's Society had invited the Sultan's father to their celebration of St George's Day. They were holding it in the Lake Club. At that time there were no Asian members of the club. The Society, it is said, was told that they could not invite him, as Asians were not permitted to attend functions in the Club. I never met anyone who could confirm the story.

Normally St. Andrew's night was held in the Selangor Club. The previous year we had decorated the club as a baronial hall. One of the members of the Society Andy Anderson had brought a stag's head from Scotland. We christened it Hector. The Sikh community were celebrating the Guru Nanak's birthday two days after our celebration. They asked us to leave our decorations up, as there were buildings of the same style in northern India. We were happy to do so.

Because of the numbers coming to our celebration in the year that I was Chieftain we had to hold our function in the large Chinese dining room of one of the hotels. There were large columns in the room with writhing golden dragons winding round them. To cover up the dragons and give a Scottish atmosphere we wrapped the columns in any cloth that we could buy which looked like tartan. As the cloth was made in Japan we decided that it must be the MacMitsubishi tartan. The British High Commissioner Sir Jack Johnson was the guest speaker so we exchanged speeches in advance. That way the 'spontaneous' jokes could be arranged.

It is quite amazing what unexpected problems can arise on such occasions. After the pipe-band had performed and Christine had danced, one of the Committee members came to me and told me that Christine was very upset. I immediately left the top table and went to find her. She was in a corner sobbing her heart out. It turned out that she had been told that the coach that was taking the band and her to Singapore next morning was leaving very early. The poor girl was worried that she would have to leave without saying 'Thank you' to the couple who were looking after her. She said that they had been so kind to her and she could not bear the thought of leaving without seeing them. She was staying with the New Zealand High Commissioner and his wife who because of another engagement were not attending our Celebration. I promised her that I would deal with it. Later I dropped her off at the High Commissioner's house. I woke their cook and told him to wake up his employers with a cup of tea early enough for them to see the young lady off. In the event it all turned out beautifully but for a while it had me worried.

One evening purely by chance I was talking to a man at a cocktail party. We had never met before. We were talking about land development. He said that his company wished to sell ten acres of land practically in the heart of Kuala Lumpur. I asked him how much they wanted for it. The price was very reasonable but much more than we could afford. I asked him if he could give me a couple of days to put in an offer for it. He agreed. I worked out an arrangement whereby payments were made on the occurrence of specified events after we paid the initial 10% nonreturnable deposit. However I needed the support of the bank in case any difficulty arose. I took it along to the Hong Kong and Shanghai Bank. The manager Dickie Smorthwaite and his deputy Ian Sim were old friends. They were a bit doubtful about the scheme but they said, 'If you think it will work we will agree.' Michael had a gap year between leaving school and going to study Civil Engineering at Edinburgh University. He came to Malaysia on his way to Australia. Michael's comment was 'It looks a great scheme, who loses?' The answer was that like any transaction where both the buyer and the seller are satisfied there were no losers.

Michael had the job of delivering the proposal to the Company. He had bought an old Norton motorcycle, which he intended to take to Australia with him. However when he went into it he found that taking it to Australia was going to be difficult and expensive. When it came time for him to leave he took the bike back to the shop from which he had purchased it. They offered him a very low price. He protested that he had only had it for a few weeks. The answer that he got was that it was an awful bike and he should not have paid so much for it. 'Caveat Emptor' with a vengeance.

Our land deal worked extremely well. In fact the company asked me to take on an office development scheme with them. I felt that we had committed ourselves to an extent that would stretch our resources and declined. Later they told me that they had worked with someone else but that they wished that they had waited until I felt free to go ahead with them. Wyn and I had great fun. We designed houses of various types. We worked out colour schemes and interior designs. As in the case of our own house we imported the wall tiles and toilet fittings from UK. More than twenty-five years later the houses that we built are still regarded as among the best of their type in Kuala Lumpur.

In March 1973 HRH the Sultan of Selangor decided to honour me by making me a member of the Order of Royal Dato's. It is as a result of that that I am called 'Dato' in Malaysia. In foreign office terms it is regarded as equivalent to a knighthood in UK. Each of the Royal Dato's has a title denoting the function that he would carry out for the Sultan. As an example 'Dato' Laxamana' is the Admiral. He would be in charge of the Sultan's boats. My title is 'Dato' Seri Selera'. In days gone by I would have been the Sultan's Food-taster.

I imagine that at some periods this could have been a dangerous occupation.

The ceremony for becoming a Royal Dato' is in two parts. The first part which takes place at the palace on the Sultan's Birthday 8th March is where the Sultan presents the new Dato' with a weapon to go off and fight the Sultan's enemies. In the case of Malay Dato's they receive a Malay kris. Non-Malays receive a ceremonial sword. On receiving the weapon the Dato' carrying the weapon at eye-level walks out of the throne-room without looking back. He leaves the State of Selangor for one week. Looking back is supposed to incur all sorts of bad luck. Malays when wearing full ceremonial dress carry a kris tucked into their sarong. When they approach the Sultan they have to remove the kris that they are carrying and lay it on the ground. I wore my kilt for the first ceremony. Before approaching the Sultan I removed my Skean Dhu from my stocking and laid it on the ground. The Malays in the audience thought that it was a nice touch.

The second ceremony, which takes place a week after, the first is again at the palace. Here the new Dato' arrives dressed in his uniform carrying a gift sewn into yellow silk. This signifies him arriving back after defeating the Sultan's enemies and bringing with him booty and trophies won from them. Wyn and I spent the week between the two ceremonies in Singapore and purchased a piece of silver as a present. Wyn found sewing it into silk a trifle difficult. I have in fact two uniforms. One is to wear in the daytime and the other is for eveningwear. The daytime uniform is made from white drill cloth. It consists of a tunic, which is closed at the collar and buttons down the front with brass buttons. The buttons have the crest of the State of Selangor on them. The headdress is a white Malay songkok decorated with braid in the State colours of red and orange and a gold badge of the State crest. The sword is worn with this uniform. The evening uniform is a military style white 'monkey' jacket with black trousers that have a gold stripe down the legs and are worn with a red cummerbund. When we went to Malaysia for the Installation of the Yang DiPertuan Agong I had to take my uniforms with me. I was delighted to find that even after nearly twenty seven years they still fitted.

In Malaysia yellow is the royal colour. Invitations to Royal events warn guests that they should not wear yellow. On such occasions the Sultan is invariably dressed in yellow. When he processes into the throne room liveried retainers carrying yellow umbrellas precede him. Malay dress is very colourful. For formal occasions both men and women wear clothes made from 'Kain Songket'. This is brightly coloured silk cloth into which gold or silver thread has been woven. For men a short sarong and tanjat (head-dress) of kain songket and a tunic and trousers of the same material but without the gold or silver thread completes the outfit. Ladies wear sarongs and tops with intricately woven designs.

It was about this time that I first got involved in arbitration. I was asked to do one or two small disputes. These went well and I enjoyed the experience. Then I was asked to arbitrate in a large dispute in Brunei. It was very complicated and I found the work intellectually stimulating. There were QCs, junior barristers, and solicitors from UK and expert witnesses of all sorts. I loved it. One of the QCs was Roger Parker who became Lord Justice Parker but is now retired. At the time we started the arbitration Roger was Chairman of the Bar Council. He found it difficult to be out of England. We agreed that when it was economical to do so we would have some of the Hearings in England. The other QC was Desmond Wright. He was Head of Chambers at 23 Old Buildings in Lincoln's Inn. They specialised in construction cases. It was in Desmond's Chambers that I eventually became a pupil after I was called to the Bar. Roger and Desmond were my sponsors when I was elected a bencher of Lincoln's Inn.

When I was in London for one of the hearings I had arranged for my Bentley to have its paintwork touched up. The idea was that when my car came back Wyn would put her car in to have it done. One evening I decided to phone Wyn. For some reason I forgot that Malaysian time was ahead of UK and I phoned at 7 o'clock in the evening. I thought that Wyn would be at St. Anne's Kindergarten. There was no reply so I rang our house number. A very sleepy voice answered. I said, 'I rang the school but there was no reply.' Wyn said,

'I'm not surprised. It's three o'clock in the morning.' By this time she had woken up and she decided that there was no time like the present to get in her bad news. She told me that my car had come back from the paint-shop that day. I said, 'Good'. She said, 'Not so good.' It turned out that after my car had been returned Wyn had decided to go out. She got the Bentley up the driveway then she lost control of it and hit a wall. She rang the paint-shop and asked them to return her car. The paint-shop people said that they had not even started to work on her car. She said that she knew that but they had to take the Bentley away again as she had damaged it. It all sounded so funny that I laughed. Wyn had thought that I would be very annoyed but as usual her timing in breaking the news was impeccable. The Brunei arbitration must have been my most successful arbitration ever. I heard later that *both* sides were satisfied. Often one side thinks you are good but the other thinks that you are useless. After I had given my award (judgement), I decided that if I was going to do this in a serious way I should take a course in English Law and I started on a correspondence course. leading to the first part of the English Bar Examinations. At that point I had no great ambitions to sit any exams. I put the material on tapes and I used to listen to them in the car as I drove along. It was fine whilst I was driving but it seemed that whenever I stopped at the traffic lights, the speakers would blare out something like 'Buggery is an offence' under some Act or another. I got the feeling that people were looking at me in a strange way.

When I had completed the course work we were coming back to UK on holiday and I decided to join Lincoln's Inn and sit the first Bar exam to see if I had learned much. My sponsors to join Lincoln's Inn were two Malaysian High Court judges. One of them, Tun Hamid, later became head of the Malaysian Judiciary.

A Dining Term meant having dinner at the Inn three times during term time. During the exams, I did a 'double dining term'. This meant that I dined six times in one week. The food and wines at Lincoln's Inn are excellent but six dinners in one week is a bit much. I passed the exams. When I got the results back in Malaysia I said to Wyn, 'I could become a barrister if I wanted to.' Now I tell people

Above: The Family
l to r: Rowena, Michael, Lady
Winifred, Sir Francis, Ianthe and
Douglas. In front, Christopher

Right: Christopher
in the Golden Coach

Below: the family skiing
l to r: Michael, Ianthe, Sir Francis,
Rowena, Christopher,
Lady Winifred, Douglas

v

The Lord Mayor in the coach

Above:
The *'Annus Horribilis'* lunch

Right:
The Late Very Rev Eric Evans,
Dean of St Paul's gives the
Lord Mayor a blessing
on Lord Mayor's Day

Above: Inspecting damage after the Bishopsgate bomb

Left: The Master of the Worshipful Company of Loriners (HRH the Princess Royal), Sir Francis and Lady Winifred after the Lord Mayor's Show

With Prime Minister John Major at the lighting of a beacon at H.A.C. ground in the City of London, 1993

Right: Sir Francis in Dato's uniform with Lady Winifred at the installation of the Sultan of Selangor as Yang Dipertuan Agong, 1999

Centre: The Malaysian Float in the Lord Mayor's Show

Sir Francis and Lady Winifred with the Australian Mayors

that I was going through the male menopause at the time and that it was a case of changing either my wife or my career. I add that Wyn persuaded me that changing my career would be cheaper than changing my wife and that being Scottish I took the cheaper option. I think probably that it was that I needed a new challenge. My clients were all personal friends. I had good staff. Really my only worry was my golf handicap, which was going up, although I thought I was playing better. I never did manage to get it down.

We agreed that we would come back to England so that I could become a full-time student for two years.

Starting a new life back in the UK

When Douglas was reading PPE at Oxford we visited him in the house that he was sharing with some other students. Wyn was horrified with the state of it. We decided that when he started to read for his next degree we would buy a house in Oxford so that he would have a decent place to live. This we did and once again had fun at auctions. Douglas lived in the house while finishing his studies. When he took up his first post with the Confederation of British Industry in London he rented it to other students.

Wyn had come back to UK before me. Douglas told her that the house in Oxford was vacant and arranged to take her to Oxford to see it. It was in a dreadful mess. Wyn removed all the bedding and curtains to a nearby laundrette, commandeered all the machines and washed everything. She got a gardening contractor to cut the grass and tidy up the garden. By the time I arrived about a month later, the house was looking excellent. She already had it on the market for sale. The first person who came to see it agreed to pay the price we were asking for it. I met him some years later at a dinner in the City of London and he remembered me. He reckoned that he had got an excellent bargain. We used the house whilst we settled down and prepared to start our own studies.

Wyn had decided that after twenty three years in Malaysia she needed to learn to cook so she had enrolled in the 'Cordon Bleu' school of cookery in London. She did two courses and as the students took what they had prepared home with them we fed very well. When I started my studies at the Inns of Court School of Law we were both travelling to London every day. One evening we were invited to a party by HRH the Sultan of Selangor who was in London at the time. We decided to stay the night in London and when we returned to Oxford the following day we opened the door of the house. Standing in the hallway was the small television set that we had bought a short time before. I said to Wyn, 'Hang on a minute! Don't touch anything.' I went straight through to the kitchen and saw a broken windowpane. We called the police. By the time they arrived we had discovered that the main thing that had been stolen was jewellery that belonged to Wyn. She had been wearing some of her better pieces for the party but there was some good jewellery in the leather pouch that had been taken.

The thief had turned out the drawers in the dressing table and chest of drawers in the bedroom. There he had found the jewellery. There were also letters that he had apparently read. These had our Scottish address on them. We worried that he might realise that our Scottish home was unoccupied and make a trip there. The police rang not long after to say that an informer had told them that the jewellery was to be handed over to a fence in a car park in Oxford. They had set up an operation and had caught the thief and had recovered most of the jewellery. For some time afterwards whenever Wyn wanted to wear any of that jewellery she had to go to the police and borrow it as it was required as evidence.

Wyn received a letter purporting to come from the thief. It was written in a beautiful copperplate hand. In it the thief apologised for the theft saying that he had just come out of jail and had wanted to get something for Christmas for his wife and daughter. He now realised that said wife and daughter were his most valuable possessions. He added that he had not expected to find such valuable jewellery in the house. Wyn was full of sympathy for him. She was all for going out to try to find him employment. When she told the policeman who was handling the case about the letter he came to see her. He showed her a copy of the thief's handwriting. It was nothing like that in the letter. I reckon that the thief had persuaded a forger pal to write the letter. Eventually the thief was brought to trial. He pleaded guilty and asked for fifteen other offences to be taken into consideration. He had committed them whilst he was on bail.

Being a mature student can be a humbling experience. I had spent a considerable part of my life, telling people what to do and how to do it. When I turned up on my first day at the School of Law I was directed to a desk occupied by a young clerk. She looked as though she was just out of school and she proceeded to issue instructions as to what I should be doing and when I should be doing it. It is probably good for one's humility but it does seem strange at the time.

We had now started to look for somewhere to live in London. As usual we quickly found a property that we liked. It was a maisonette in a conversion of one of the Nash houses in Regents Park. We needed a solicitor to make the purchase. We asked the porter in the block who other people who were buying flats in the property were using. He gave us the name of Raymond Bellenger. Raymond turned out to be a very good solicitor and a very good friend. I think that he saw us as innocent colonials who needed to be protected from developers. He decided that we were offering too much for the property. The developer would not reduce the price and in the end we did not buy it.

Next we found a flat in Berkeley Square. There were minor dilapidations to be seen to under the lease and Raymond would not let us buy. Then, Wyn found a flat in St. John's Wood that she liked. We were 'gazzumped' on it. It was then that Douglas suggested that we try the Barbican. He suggested that we rent a flat there until I had passed my exams. Then we would know what we intended to do. Later Wyn came to the conclusion that our guardian angels were pushing us towards the City.

Our house in Kuala Lumpur had been rented to the Turkish ambassador. The Turkish government kept the house for ten years. At that time the Turkish economy was in a dreadful state and they were always late with the rent. Douglas reckoned that they had to go to the International Monetary Fund for a loan whenever the rent was due. After the ambassador left we sold the house. Because of our status as permanent residents after I had passed my exams Wyn and I would still have had the option of returning to Malaysia. I could go back either as an engineer or as a lawyer. So long as she worked for herself Wyn could also work. I would also have the options of working in UK as an engineer or as a barrister. In the event I took another option. I decided to stay in UK and practice as an Arbitrator. Our Malaysian friends could not understand why we did not return to Malaysia. When Sylvia the lovely daughter of Amer Singh Bhatt came to visit us in London she said to Wyn, 'Auntie when are you coming home?' Even today, His Majesty the late Yang

DiPertuan Agong's and our other Malaysian friends' children and grandchildren, call us 'auntie and uncle'.

With Douglas we went to the Barbican Estate Office. At the time Douglas was living in a shared house with several other young people. We were shown a number of flats. They seemed quite nice. The girl then said, 'There is a penthouse in Shakespeare Tower which has just been completed. Would you like to see it?' The penthouse was on the 39th, 40th and 41st floors. It had five bedrooms. Whilst we were viewing it Douglas said, 'If you took this I could come and live at home.' That clinched it for Wyn. Having lost her children to boarding school when they were young here was a chance to get them back home. We negotiated a five-year lease with the City of London Corporation. Raymond scrutinised it and was satisfied. We then set to the task of purchasing furniture and carpets for this huge penthouse. It was like having a house in the sky. During the furnishing of the penthouse Wyn and I had to make a trip to Malaysia. In spite of the lack of carpets and furniture Douglas and Michael decided to have a party. I do not know how many they invited but over the years I seem to have met large numbers of people who have commented what a great venue it was for a party, and what a fabulous party it was.

One thing that concerned Douglas was that having been used to a busy social life in Malaysia we would feel very lonely in London as we did not know anyone so he used to get his friends to invite us to their parties. Douglas always seems to be concerned about the welfare of the rest of us.

Almost as soon as we moved in there was a form put through the letterbox. It suggested that we join the Residents' Association. I completed the form, which included a question about your occupation. I think that they must have been attracted by the fact that I was a civil engineer who was a bar student because back came a letter from the Secretary Tom Fripp. He asked whether I would be prepared to stand for election to the Association committee. My very ancient Engineering Degree from the University of Edinburgh had given me exemption from two subjects in that year's exams: The History of the English Legal System and Company Law. Why this was so I did not know but because of it I felt that I would have time to help, so I agreed. I think that there were twelve names for twelve places and I was duly elected.

At the first meeting of the committee I was asked to be chairman of the sub-committee for matters of common concern. This sub-committee dealt with all the aspects from a residents' point of view of the services and maintenance of the whole complex of 2100 flats and houses that were owned by the Corporation of the City of London in the Barbican. It was quite a sizeable brief. I decided that I needed a secretary to help me so I offered the job to Wyn. I did not however, wish to pressurise her into taking it on. I therefore said that if she did not wish to take it on I would see if the girl next-door would do it. Living next-door was Paul Raymond, the owner of the Raymond Revue Bar and a number of other strip-joints in London. His live-in girl friend was a stripper called Fiona Richmond, who roared around London in a spectacular yellow E-type Jaguar. Its number plate was FU 2. When we had visitors we used to take them down to the underground car park to see it. I think that Wyn felt that it would be inappropriate for me to have a stripper as my secretary so she agreed to take on the task.

I had no idea how the City of London was governed. Taking on this sub-committee was the start of a learning curve, which eventually took me to the Mansion House. Years later when I was Sheriff of London I managed to trace Tom Fripp. By then he had long since moved from the Barbican. I invited him to lunch at the Old Bailey and told him that it was in no small measure due to him that I had become involved in the City civic.

The City Corporation had a committee, the Barbican Residential Committee, which was responsible for the running of the Barbican estate. The relationship between the Corporation and the residents had at times been quite stormy. Not long before we arrived in the Barbican there had been talk of a rent strike. However by the time that we arrived things had calmed down a bit. The chairman of the Barbican Residential Committee was a lovely man, the late Gordon Wixley. He was a semi-retired accountant and very sharp, we always got on well together. Gordon and I were eventually joint chairmen of a liaison committee, which contained members of the Common Council and residents of the Barbican. We took turns at chairing the committee. I learned a lot from him about getting people to agree with you.

Later when I became a member of the Common Council I used to watch Gordon in action. If he was not satisfied that a proposal before a committee had been fully justified he would start off by saying something like 'I am sure everyone else understands what this proposal is about but I wonder if someone could explain to me why....' He would then put a question that went to the heart of the proposal. The official who had been hoping to flannel his way through would now know that unless the proposal could be fully justified it was a dead duck. In most cases if Gordon could not understand it none of the other members could.

Our first year in the Barbican was very pleasant and passed very quickly. Because of my exemptions I was not overburdened with work. When Wyn finished her cookery classes she went to classes at the City Lit. Among the subjects that she studied were 'Country Houses and Their Contents' and 'City Livery Halls'. Wyn and I dined regularly at Lincoln's Inn. As a student I had the advantage of partaking of the Inn's excellent meals and wines at a very reasonable price. The tables are divided into 'messes' of four people. Each mess was provided with a carafe of white wine, a carafe of red wine and a carafe of port. If the other students in the mess that we were in just happened to be Muslims who did not drink Wyn and I shared the wine between us. We often dined in the same mess as Malay students who are of course Muslims. As we had walked from the Barbican there were no drink-drive problems.

I found that very quickly my young classmates accepted me as one of them even though I was dressed in a suit and tie and they mainly wore tee shirts and jeans. When they asked where I lived I told them that I had a Council flat in the East End of London. This had them puzzled as they wondered how I had qualified for Council accommodation. The Malaysian students were especially intrigued by this old Dato' who spoke fluent Malay. More than one of them came to me and said, 'My father thinks that he knows you.' Some of them did.

One day one of my fellow students was complaining about how unfair life was. He was criticising some of our fellow students for their designer clothes and flamboyant life-styles. I am afraid that I rather tore into him. I pointed out to him that he had just finished a University degree and was now embarked on his Bar vocational course. These were great opportunities that many many people would never have. I persuaded him that he should be grateful for what he had. He was a bright lad and he got the message. When he wrote a couple of books a few years later he sent me signed copies of them. At Christmas I invited a few of my fellow students to our flat for a drink. I think that Wyn and the boys were somewhat uncomfortable with the manner in which these students treated me. It was as though I was the same age as them. Later when Wyn did a business course at Paddington College she found that it was not long before the other students who were teenagers were treating her as though she was a teenager also. It is quite rejuvenating.

When we had moved in to the Barbican I had discussed with the Manager of the estate David Amies the problems arising from having so many people moving into an area at about the same time. Because nobody knew anyone else, it was sometimes called 'New Town Syndrome'. I had suggested that the various blocks should have parties so that people could meet their neighbours. One day David told me that Shakespeare Tower was now full. He more or less said, 'What are you going to do about it?' Wyn and I decided to take up the challenge. We put up a notice on the board in the foyer of the block saying that it was proposed to have a party in the block and would anyone who was willing to help put their name on the list attached. We then went off to Scotland for two weeks on holiday. When we returned we found that only two couples had put their names on the list. We decided that there was little interest in the idea of the party so we took the notice down. We thought that we would invite the two couples up for a drink.

No sooner had we taken the notice down than the porter rang to say that people were asking what had happened to the notice so we put it up again. Within a couple of days there were a dozen names on the list. We invited them all to a meeting in our flat to form a committee. Among them were Roy and Joyce Nash. Roy was a journalist and author. We have copies of two lovely books that he wrote. Unfortunately Roy died not long ago. Joyce had been a headmistress in Yorkshire. She is a highly respected member of the Common Council, and has been Chairman of a number of important Committees.

Recently she was to our great delight, honoured by Her Majesty the Queen with an OBE. Stanley and Frances Johnson are also happily still very active in various causes although they have moved away from the Barbican. Recently, we attended their Silver Wedding celebration. Frances teaches French at Emanuel School. When I was invited to the school as Lord Mayor the main topic among the girls before the visit was whether Mrs Johnson would get a kiss from her friend the Lord Mayor. She did. When we attended Stanley's 80th Birthday party we were seated next to two of our other old Barbican friends Bob and Jill Gibbens, looking just as they did over twenty five years ago.

In most committees you get the talkers and the doers. It turned out that we had a committee of enthusiastic doers. In no time at all we had volunteers for arranging for food, drinks, looking after money and entertainment. The party itself was a huge success. More importantly people started to talk to each other in the lifts. In all we had three parties in Shakespeare Tower, and some of the other blocks followed our example. When I was Lord Mayor we invited to a private dinner party as many of the original Shakespeare Tower committee as we could contact. It was fun. So much had happened in the fifteen years that had passed.

I knew that my second year with the Bar Finals at the end of it was going to be tough so I told the other members of the Residents' committee that I would not have time to carry on as chairman of the sub-committee. However they asked me to stand for election to the main committee again. At the first meeting of the main committee the members unanimously invited me to be chairman of the main body. I was flattered but reluctant. They persuaded me that it was for the good of the residents because I had established such a good working relationship with the members of the Corporation on the Barbican Residential Committee. I eventually agreed but insisted that sub-committee chairmen/chairwomen would take responsibility for the work of their sub-committees. This caused one interesting incident. The wife of one of the chairmen approached me about the amount of time that her husband was spending working for the Association. She accused me of using people. I agreed with her that that was what I did and I explained that delegation is all about finding out what skills people have and what they like to do. Then you allow them to use those skills. I added that very often people are good at what they like doing, or that they like doing what they are good at. I think that I left her slightly bemused by the whole concept.

I managed to juggle my time between my studies and being chairman of the Residents' Association. As more families with children were coming to live in the Barbican I asked for the construction of play facilities. We also obtained the use of the tennis and badminton facilities at the City of London Girls School and the swimming pool on the Golden Lane estate, which is owned by the City Corporation. I started an initiative to get the Corporation to allow residents to buy their flats. I hoped that as a result of having a nucleus of owners we could build up a stable community. It was some time before this eventually came to fruition. Although not bound to do so as the flats were not covered by the Housing Act, the Corporation gave the same discounts as set out in Mrs Thatcher's 'Right To Buy' legislation. This was a major triumph.

I also decided that we should have a 'Village Fete' in the Barbican. We had a ready-made Charity on our doorstep, St. Bartholomew's Hospital. We chose the Children's Oncology Unit at the hospital to receive the proceeds. Again there was no shortage of volunteers. Led by a lovely lady called Miriam Griffith we had all the fun of the fair and raised £1,500 in one afternoon. Miriam was a tower of strength and did so much to help everyone. Nothing was too much trouble for her. When I was Lord Mayor I recommended her for an honour but she died shortly afterwards. I was honoured to be invited to speak at her memorial service.

Called to the Bar

I studied quite hard for my exams deciding that with so much ground to cover I could not hope to go into every subject in depth, I took the view that I should go for breadth rather than depth. Michael had arrived from Edinburgh to do his final studying and the drill was that we would have breakfast then repair to our respective rooms to study. One day Michael came down in the middle of the morning to get a cup of coffee and he found his father watching a Test Match on television. He said quite forcefully, 'I don't know how you can expect to pass your exams. If I studied the way that you study I would get nowhere.' A chastened father beat a hasty retreat to his studies. There had never been any doubt that Michael was going to get a First in his exams. His course work had given him very high marks so he would have to have done very badly in his Finals to have achieved anything lower.

The Bar final exams were like a medieval 'Trial by Ordeal'. You sat ten papers, two papers on each of five consecutive days. As people take different subjects you only meet your friends occasionally during the week. When I went to sit my final paper, which was in Labour law, I met two of the young people, a boy and a girl, who had been in my tutorial group. They were recent graduates and to me they seemed intelligent enough to have no trouble with the exams. They had been sitting the same papers together all week and had obviously had been feeding on each other's fears. They were in a terrible state of nerves. The boy told me that he had been so convinced that he had already failed that he had decided not to make an appearance that morning. His landlady had poured him a very large whisky, ordered a taxi, and almost literally pushed him into it. They both passed.

I was not very confident that I would pass all my papers. In the first exam I had spent too much time on one question and had not left enough time to complete all the other questions. Learning the subjects is one thing. Learning to sit exams is another. I felt that over the week I had got better at the sitting aspect. The results of the exams are posted at the Council for Legal Education premises at Gray's Inn on a Wednesday evening. They come out too late to get into Thursday's papers. The result is that many students go to Gray's Inn to get their results as soon as they are posted up. On the evening when my results were coming out I was chairing a meeting in the Guildhall. Michael fresh from achieving a first-class engineering degree at the University of Edinburgh was delegated to go to see my results. I was convinced that I would get either a conditional pass which meant that I would have to sit one paper again, or if I was lucky a third-class pass. A very large majority, some 70% to 80%, of those who pass the Bar exams get thirds.

Michael described the scene when he arrived at Gray's Inn. There were dozens and dozens of people milling around. They appeared to be knee-deep in cigarette-ends and fingernails. First he looked at the conditionals. Dad's name wasn't there. Then he looked at the Threes. This went from A to Z four times. Dad's name wasn't there either. Worried that he might have to announce that I had failed he looked at the Twos. There among them was Francis McWilliams—Class2 Grade2. There were no Class1s, and not too many Class2 Grade1. I reckoned that I was in the top 20% to 25% of those who passed. This was away beyond my expectations. Michael came round to the Guildhall and handed in a congratulations card that he had bought in anticipation. I opened the envelope very nervously. He had written in it 'Class2 Grade2'. I could not believe it. I was sure that he had got it wrong. However I finally convinced myself that he was fully conversant with the system. When the meeting was finished Gordon Wixley and the rest of the committee insisted that we retire to a pub and have a celebratory drink. By the time I reached home the champagne was on ice and Wyn had a superb dinner ready. Michael's comment was, 'Dad I am not going through that ordeal again. If you decide to sit any more exams can you go and get the results yourself?'

I have never found a group of students so uptight about exam results as Bar students. I was sitting next to a young girl at a dinner one evening in the City. She had just passed her Bar exams and she told me that she was so afraid to go to get her results that she had waited until after dark. She had to climb a large gate and while she was standing reading the lists by the light of the torch that she had brought, she heard a noise behind her. It was male student who had climbed over after her. Unfortunately he had failed. She said that he was very distressed.

The Ceremony of Call to the Bar at Lincoln's Inn is followed by a Garden Party. At the Garden Party on the day that I was called a young Malay man came up to Wyn and said, 'Datin you won't remember me but I attended St. Anne's Kindergarten.' Wyn said that made her feel really old. The day after my results came out we were off to Edinburgh to attend Michael's graduation ceremony. Rowena, Michael's girlfriend was graduating in History of Art from Edinburgh at the same time and we met her parents there. Her father was celebrating his fiftieth birthday. One of my nephews, Gordon Hunter, was graduating too. Each evening there was a cele-bratory dinner. Michael commented that it was like a Malay wedding. They often last for a week.

Michael had worn mainly tee shirts and jeans for most of the time that he was at university. They went with his thick shoulder-length hair and what I think was a long, German Air Force officer's coat bought from a charity shop. He decided that as he was going to be looking for a job he needed some new clothes. Wyn and I were delighted. We were even more delighted when he announced that he would have to get his hair cut. He applied for three jobs and was offered all three and decided that he would accept the one based in London. So he came to live in the Barbican. Later Rowena came to live with us too. We had a full house.

I had decided that in case I wished to appear in court I would spend twelve months doing a pupillage, and became a pupil to one of the senior juniors in Desmond Wright's chambers, Humphrey Lloyd (now His Honour Judge Lloyd). During my pupillage Humphrey took silk. As QCs do not have pupils I had to find another pupil-master. I asked to go with Colin Reece, a very fine young barrister who also had a great sense of humour. The pupil usually gets the job of going for the coffee. Colin was a bit embarrassed about it but I had no hesitation about doing the same as other pupils.

It was fortunate that I undertook a pupillage because some time later I was asked by Param Singh Gill, a Malaysian lawyer whom I knew, to act as his junior in an appeal to the Privy Council. At that time the Privy Council was the final court of appeal for Malaysian cases. It was a Hindu Family Law case. I swotted up the subject and prepared the petition to the Privy Council. Later I prepared the Case for submission. After a few alterations this was sent off. A couple of weeks before we were due to appear my leader arrived in England. We spent a considerable time in Lincoln's Inn library preparing what he was going to say. When the great day arrived, considerably excited, I donned my genuine horsehair wig and gown. I had purchased them second-hand and the wig had required extensive repair and cleaning. It now looked very presentable but not too new looking. My leader and I turned up at Number 12 Downing Street where the Privy Council sits. That day the bench consisted of the Lord Chancellor the late Lord Hailsham and four other well-known Law Lords.

We were first on. Before my leader could start, Lord Hailsham said, 'Mr Gill, we have read the petition and the Case, unless your learned opponent can show… (he then set out the things that our opponents required to show to rebut our case) …you have no problems.' My leader was not about to be deprived of his opportunity to address the Privy Council. He started off but after three or four minutes the Lord Chancellor looked over his glasses and said, 'Mr Gill there is one rule which applies in any tribunal and that is, when you have the tribunal on your side, you stop.' My leader got the message. He thanked their Lordships and sat down. But they are very polite and helpful at the Privy Council and in accordance with their custom the Lord Chancellor asked, 'Does your learned junior have anything to add?' I had been hoping to give them ten minutes on 'estoppel', which I thought was a very important part of our case. In view of my learned leader having been told, albeit very politely, to sit down I decided that silence was the correct course. I stood up, bowed and said, 'I have nothing to add your Lordships,' and sat down again. That was the extent of my career as an advocate. We won the case. As a result I can claim to be the most successful barrister in England. I practised only in the Privy Council and I never lost a case.

One day during my pupillage in Lincoln's Inn I ran into a young lad whom Wyn and I had met several times whilst we were dining. We had had drinks with him and his sister in the students' bar on a number of occasions. He told me that he was now chairman of the Lincoln's Inn Students' Association. Then he said, 'I'm glad I met you. You must come tomorrow night.' I asked, 'Why?' He replied, 'We are having a disco.' It was clear that all he saw in front of him was a fellow student because he added, 'There are some smashing birds in first year.' When I returned home that evening I said to Wyn, 'You'll never guess what I've been invited to tomorrow.' When I told her it was a disco she said, 'What! With your back' and we had a good laugh but I did not go to see the 'smashing birds'.

When I had completed my year as chairman of the Residents' Association I had expected to stand down. Until then no one had served as chairman for more than a year. However the committee asked me to continue. I agreed on the understanding that it was only for one more year.

One of the great problems at the time was the noise and dust resulting from the construction of the Barbican Centre. We secured a rate reduction for those flats affected. From our penthouse we looked down on the site and had a birds-eye view of what must have been the worst organised construction job that I had ever seen. I was horrified. If one person was working there would be three or four standing watching. There were four large tower cranes that cost £1,000/day. It was a busy day if one of them did a couple of lifts. It looked from where we were that the work would never be completed. It had been going on for eight or nine years. It had started out as a 'target price' contract and had developed into a 'cost-plus' contract. Alterations were being made all the time and extra work ordered. I later calculated that once a price had been set by the quantity surveyor for an extra piece of work the 'plus' was 28%. There was no incentive for anyone to finish the job.

We decided to celebrate the tenth anniversary of the arrival of the first residents in the Barbican with a party was to be held in the City of London Girls' School hall. I wrote to the Corporation and suggested that the Lord Mayor might like to attend. I received a somewhat snooty reply that said more or less that it was not considered an appropriate use of the Lord Mayor's time. I replied that at that time the City needed all the friends it could get and that getting its residents on its side would be good start. I believe that some members of the Court of Aldermen were not too happy to be told this in such blunt terms. Sir Kenneth Cork, who was Lord Mayor, saw the sense of it and agreed to come. Wyn baked a huge cake for the party and constructed a copy of the Barbican logo out of very hard icing. I was told to warn Kenneth not to try to cut this when he was cutting the cake. I forgot. Of course, he tried to plunge the knife straight into the logo. The knife skidded across the cake. Fortunately no one was impaled.

Before I finished my pupillage I had decided that I would practise as an arbitrator. I took steps to register on the various panels. Because of my engineering and legal qualifications I started to be appointed to conduct arbitrations both in UK and overseas. I enjoyed the work and there appeared to be plenty of it. On one occasion in Sri Lanka a President's Counsel, the equivalent of a Queen's Counsel in UK, appeared with no less than five juniors. They all sat in a row. Questions and answers were passed back and forwards along the row. It was highly entertaining but it must have been very expensive. The case was in connection with an irrigation scheme. Sri Lanka from very early in its history had used irrigation schemes in order to grow rice. A number of small reservoirs, which were known as 'Tanks' had been built. Over the years many of these tanks had silted up and had been buried. A scheme had been designed to build a large dam and a series of canals to distribute the water to the padi fields. When they were digging the foundations for the dam they came across the foundations of a dam, which had been built on exactly the same spot 2500 years before. The modern engineers with their computer technology and simulations had come to the same location. I thought that this was an impressive example of the skills which had existed so long ago but which had subsequently fallen into disuse. When we went on a site-inspection we saw a huge crocodile swimming in one of the canals. It was trapped and nobody knew how to get it out.

The day before I left Colombo, I saw an advertisement in a newspaper for a local Charity called 'Friends in Need'. The purpose of the Charity was to give basic artificial limbs to those who could not afford them for themselves. The advert said that it cost 1000 Rupees to provide an artificial foot that would enable someone to walk. I happened to have a 1000 Rupee note (at that time worth £25) that I knew I would not be spending. I put it in an envelope and arranged for it to be sent to the Charity. Later I received a very nice letter, which told me that the money had been used to make a foot for a 17 year-old girl who had lost her foot in a railway accident. I reckoned that it was the most worthwhile £25 that I had spent that year. My fellow arbitrators in that dispute were an American engineer and a Sri Lankan engineer. Later when I was Lord Mayor I had a letter from the Sri Lankan enclosing a copy of a photograph of Wyn and me, which had appeared in a newspaper in Sri Lanka.

Sri Lanka is a beautiful place. Indeed they say that it is where the Garden of Eden was located. It is sad that a state of civil war exists there. It is not difficult to see why it happened. The majority of the population is Singhalese. During the period when the British were in charge Tamils manned the civil service. After Independence the Singhalese with their majority formed the government. They felt that they should not have to rely on the Tamils to implement their decisions. The Tamils felt that they were being pushed into an inferior position and eventually started to agitate for a separate Tamil State in the North of the island where the Tamils are in a majority. It is difficult to see how it will all end. Strangely enough the last King of Sri Lanka was a Tamil.

I conducted arbitrations in the Middle East and in Malaysia and enjoyed travelling to new places. At the time of one of my visits to Malaysia in connection with an arbitration there was considerable disquiet among the members of the Malaysian Bar. It was believed that the Prime Minister was interfering with the independence of the judiciary and the incumbent head of the judiciary had been removed from his post on what appeared to be some manufactured charges. In a case not long before he had found against the ruling party and it was believed that the Prime Minister was getting his revenge. My friend Tun Hamid had been appointed in his place. The Bar got up a petition against the appointment and the young lawyers in my arbitration wanted me to sign the petition. I pointed out to them that Tun Hamid had been one of my sponsors when I joined Lincoln's Inn. They wanted me to apply to the Inn to have him disbarred. I told them that while they had my sympathy, if I did what they suggested they would probably find that I would not be allowed into the country to finish the arbitration.

Around this time the Foreign and Commonwealth Office were seeking my advice with regard to Malaysian matters. The Malaysian Prime Minister, Datuk Seri Dr. Mahathir Mohamad, had taken umbrage regarding adverse comment in the British media in relation to the take-over of a major British company by a Malaysian group. He had introduced a 'Look East Policy'. This meant that British firms were being barred from tendering for Malaysian Government contracts. After the policy had been going for some time Dr. Mahathir was paying a private visit to UK because his son was at boarding school in Britain. Mrs Thatcher had arranged a private dinner party for him at 10 Downing Street. Wyn and I were invited.

Before the day of the dinner both the Malaysian High Commissioner and the Foreign Office were worried as to how the two Prime Ministers would get on together. They asked me what I thought. My view was that either there would be an explosion within the first two minutes or they would get on extremely well. I suggested that as Dr. Mahathir would have been at a Non-aligned States Conference in New Delhi on his way to UK Mrs Thatcher could start off by asking what had gone on at the Conference. They got on very well together. At the dinner Mrs Thatcher announced that she had persuaded the Treasury to make £40,000,000 available to alleviate the problems caused by the decision to charge overseas students the full cost of their education at British Universities. The Malaysian Government had been very upset when the British Government had introduced the policy at short notice. With over 15,000 Malaysian students in UK many of them on Government scholarships the increased costs to the Malaysian Government were a considerable embarrassment. Also some families with two or three children studying in UK had had to make some hard decisions as to which of the children should be allowed to complete their studies because the increase in fees made it impossible for them all to go on.

It is fun to get into a taxi and say to the driver, 'Ten Downing Street'. The dinner was a great success and Dr. Mahathir became a great admirer of Mrs Thatcher's achievements. After Dr. Mahathir had left Mrs Thatcher was saying how amazed she was that he was the same age as she was but that he did not have a grey hair in his head. Wyn said that they have a saying in Malaysia, 'The engine is still good we might as well give the body a re-spray'. Wyn and I were very impressed that Mrs Thatcher was so natural. She was very different from her public persona. 'The Iron Lady' was human after all. However like most people who have been in office for a long time she began to think that she knew all the answers. Anyone who knew a little history and had experience in Local Government knew that a poll tax was a bad idea. It had been tried in the year 1379 and 'The Peasants' Revolt' had caused it to be abandoned. Whatever the deficiencies of the rating system, it had two great virtues. One was that it was based on property and property does not move. People move around. The other virtue was that it was cheap to collect. I was sad that she got herself into such a mess over the poll tax.

Aldersgate Ward

It was suggested to me that it would be a good idea if I stood for election to the Common Council. The theory was that I would then be able to put forward the residents' point of view directly. This as I later discovered was indeed important. There were members of the Council who seemed to have a deep dislike of the residents. They regarded them as a nuisance and out of place in what they regarded as purely a commercial area. The inclusion of residential accommodation in the Barbican Development had been forced on the Common Council by the Secretary of State. Some of the members still resented it.

The Common Council is like the parliament for the square mile of the City of London. Indeed when Simon de Montfort called the first parliament at Westminster in the year 1265, he modelled it on the Common Council. If Westminster is the 'Mother of Parliaments' the Common Council is the 'Grandmother'. The City is a federation of twenty five Wards. The boundaries of the Wards have remained more or less the same for centuries. Each Ward has an Alderman and a number of Common Councilmen. In the past the Alderman was the Ruler of his Ward. The Aldermen eventually came together and elected one of their number to be the Mayor.

The term 'Common Councilman' is used irrespective of gender. The numbers of Common Councilmen representing the different Wards varies. The largest number for any ward is twelve and the smallest is four. The numbers of electors in the Wards varies from 23 to nearly 4000. There have been proposals before Parliament to make some far-reaching changes to the electoral system of the City. It is hoped that these will be passed in the not too distant future. At present as well as residents members of business partnerships have a vote. It is proposed that companies should also have a vote.

The Barbican estate is divided between the Wards of Cripplegate and Aldersgate. Cripplegate has twelve Common Councilmen and Aldersgate has six. Shakespeare Tower is in Aldersgate Ward. I decided to stand for election in that Ward. The elections are held every year in December. In other local authorities elections are held every four years in May. There had not been a contested election in the Ward of Aldersgate for some time. Many of the Wards had not had contested elections for many years. In some cases it had been so long since they had had a contested election that the Ward Clerk whose job it was to conduct the election had forgotten the procedure. The Ward Club was a sort of filtering system, which had to be negotiated by anyone aspiring to become a Common Councilman. The Ward Club members were usually voters in a Ward or people who worked in the Ward. In most Wards, if you did not have the Ward Club members on your side there was no point in standing for election. In Aldersgate, however, most of the voters were not members of the Ward Club. Although the Club had some influence the main influence was with the residents.

There was a gentleman's agreement that you could put out a leaflet telling the electors about yourself but you did not attack anyone else. One candidate that I knew put as part of the information about himself 'When I came down from Oxford'. The inference was that he had studied at Oxford University. He had lived in Oxford, and had come to London to work. Nobody challenged him. As chairman of the Residents' Association I was of course well known in Aldersgate Ward. With Wyn as my election agent and Douglas, Michael and my friends in Shakespeare Tower helping, to the consternation of the sitting members, I came top of the poll.

Some of the older members of the Common Council were of the opinion that new members should wait until they had been on the Common Council for about three years before they got up to speak. For me, at my first meeting, even if I had agreed with them, which I did not, a debate on the spiralling costs of the Barbican Centre was too much of a temptation. Since the Centre was to be the London home of the Royal Shakespeare Company I thought it appropriate to start off by quoting from Shakespeare's Macbeth 'Tomorrow, and tomorrow, and tomorrow, creeps in this petty pace from day to day, to the last syllable of recorded time.' I then went on to explain why the costs were escalating to such an extent.

It was not long before I found myself on the Barbican Development Committee, which was responsible for the construction of the Centre. Later when the late Hugh Olson, a very shrewd and nice man, was asked to become Chairman of the Committee he said that he would do it if I would become Deputy-Chairman. By that time I was an Alderman and it was not usual for Aldermen to be elected Chairmen or Deputy-Chairmen but the committee members were, because of my qualifications, very happy to have me as Deputy-Chairman. From then on I found myself on any committee that was charged with constructing anything.

At my second meeting of the Common Council I again felt constrained to speak. I think that when I stood up some of the other members must have been thinking that the new member for Aldersgate was a bit of a 'Smart Alec'. However it was necessary for me to speak to save the Lord Mayor Sir Kenneth Cork and the Corporation from considerable embarrassment. The Lord Mayor was going to pay an official visit to Malaysia and in accordance with custom he was taking with him an address of greetings from the citizens of the City of London to the citizens of the Malaysian capital Kuala Lumpur. The address was read out by the Town Clerk in Common Council for approval. Normally this was a formality and this one was fine until the Town Clerk came to the point where he said, 'We were sad to hear of the recent death in office of His Majesty the Yang Di Pertuan Agong. We remember with pleasure his friendliness and dignity when he visited us at Guildhall.'

As I listened I realised that the Agong who had visited the Guildhall was the Sultan of Kedah. He had completed his five-year reign. The Agong who had recently died was his successor the Sultan of Kelantan. I had to 'rise in my place', as the phrase is and say that whilst I was in agreement with the sentiments expressed, I felt constrained to point out the error. The Town Clerk said that the information had come from the Foreign Office. It was eventually left that the wording of the address would be subject to the agreement of the member for Aldersgate, Mr Francis McWilliams. That afternoon the Town Clerk rang me and said that he had spoken to the Foreign Office. They had apparently said that the Agong had died in London and that I was probably right. I had to point out to the Town Clerk that it was not the Agong who had died in London but the Malaysian Prime Minister who by that time was Tun Razak. The Agong had died in Malaysia. We decided to leave out any reference to the death of the Agong. Afterwards Geoffrey Rowley, the Town Clerk used to say 'On the Common Council we can find experts on everything, even the Constitution of Malaysia.'

I enjoyed the Common Council. Apart from Gordon Wixley and Hugh Olson, there were many other people of high calibre, giving up their time to ensure that the City of London remained one of the great financial centres of the world. Many of them had worked in the City all their lives. Members of the Common Council unlike members of other local authorities do not receive any allowances. The meetings are all held during the day. They are timed to take place either before or after lunchtime. Members are given their lunch. Being in their own or their employer's time members did not like to waste time in meetings. Normally a member was only allowed to speak once on any topic. The Chairman's permission had to be sought if a member wished to speak a second time. Repetition of what another member had said was considered very bad form. You noticed the difference if you found yourself on joint committees with members of other local authorities. Repetition and filibustering were the name of the game. This was especially so if the meeting had gone on for some time and it needed only a short time more to take the time into the next period for an increased allowance.

One of the best-known members of the Common Council was Bernard (Bunny) Morgan CBE. He was chairman of a construction company but spent a great deal of his time either at the Guildhall or the City Livery Club. In order to fit everything in he rose very early in the morning. One of the duties that he loved to perform annually was Secretary of the Aldermanic Sheriff's Committee. When it was my turn to have such a committee if the telephone rang in the morning but it was after eight o' clock somebody would say, 'It can't be Mr Morgan. It is too late.' When I was first elected to the Common Council in 1978 Bunny was Chief Commoner. He went out of his way to make me feel welcome. Sadly he died a couple of weeks before the luncheon that the members of the Common Council had organised to celebrate his ninetieth birthday. Whilst the Common Councilmen are liable to have to seek re-election every year, Aldermen once elected by the Ward remained in office until they reached the age of seventy years. Formerly they had been elected for life. The electorate for Aldermen is the same as for Common Councilmen. Again in most Wards the Ward clubs play a part. Most people who seek to be elected as Alderman for a Ward also seek the support of the Ward's Common Councilmen. The choice of the electorate is however subject to approval by the Court of Aldermen. This in recent years has been the cause of considerable criticism. In most electoral systems there is some form of preliminary screening of candidates before they can stand. There may be a Committee of a Local Association of a political party, which chooses a candidate to represent the party in an election. Or there may be some qualification that candidates must fulfil. For Aldermen any Tom, Dick or Harry could put himself or herself forward for election. Other than the screening imposed by the Court of Aldermen itself, there was no screening. Once you are an Alderman you are on the ladder to become Lord Mayor so each new Alderman is a potential Lord Mayor. From the Court of Aldermen's viewpoint, to protect the future reputation of the City, it is therefore essential to ensure that Aldermen are suitable in every way to become the Lord Mayor of London. Previously there had been in place a system whereby the Senior Alderman interviewed potential candidates. He also took soundings from members of the Common Council who he thought would know the candidate. He then reported back to an informal meeting of the Court of Aldermen. They then decided to indicate to the potential candidate whether or not he, or she was likely to be approved if they were elected. They were given 'a red light' or 'a green light'. The system was private and worked reasonably well as generally people who were given 'a red light' did not stand for election. It did however give rise to the criticism that the Court of Aldermen was a self-perpetuating oligarchy. Later The Court of Aldermen was advised that, from a legal point of view, this system of pre-judging was indefensible. It was therefore discontinued. A system was introduced whereby a list of standard questions was put to the person elected. After these were answered the members of the Court of Aldermen would discuss the answers and vote on the candidate. I understand that even this has been considered unacceptable in this 'democratic' age.

The Court of Aldermen consists of 'Aldermen past the Chair' i.e. those who have already held the office of Lord Mayor and 'Aldermen below the Chair' those who have not yet held the office. Before he can have the support of his brother Aldermen to go forward for election by the Liverymen of the City as either Sheriff or Lord Mayor an Alderman must be interviewed by some of the Aldermen past the Chair. They then make a report to a Committee, which is composed of all the members of the Court of Aldermen. The Committee then votes as to whether or not the Court will support the candidature of that particular Alderman. Members of the Committee can be very critical of their brother Aldermen.

Sir Gilbert Inglefield, the Alderman for the Ward of Aldersgate was approaching his seventieth birthday. This meant that he would soon be submitting his resignation to the Court of Aldermen. I was approached by a Common Councilman, Edwina Coven. She told me that she intended to stand for election as Alderman when Sir Gilbert retired. Being somewhat new to the City I wondered why she was talking to me about her plans. Next I was approached by another Common Councilman Donald Silk who told me that he too intended to stand for election as the Alderman. Donald lived in the Barbican and was a member of Common Council for Cripplegate. He had always had a fairly high profile. As with Edwina I wondered why he was telling me. I must have been quite naive. It was some time before it dawned on me that they were trying to find out whether I was thinking of standing for the Aldermanic vacancy when it occurred. At that stage the thought had not entered my head at all. I was happily building up my practice as an international arbitrator.

As the time for Sir Gilbert's resignation approached things started to heat up. There was much discussion about both Edwina and Donald. It turned out that previously both had been advised not to stand for election to the Court of Aldermen. Edwina decided that she would not stand in the election. She was eventually to achieve the distinction of becoming the first lady to hold the office of Chief Commoner. She also became a Deputy-Lieutenant. Donald had different ideas. He had determined to stand for election and fight the Court of Aldermen. The Court of Aldermen knew it was going to be a tough battle and set about trying to find a suitable candidate who had a chance of beating Donald. Eventually, someone must have suggested that the only person who had any chance of doing so was the recently elected member for Aldersgate. He who had had the cheek to insist that the Lord Mayor attend the residents' tenth anniversary party. They probably decided to grit their teeth, hold their noses, and make the best of a bad job.

The suggestion that I stand in the Aldermanic election first came from a friend Bill Linton. Bill was Scottish and he lived in the Barbican. He ran his own printing business and had printed the leaflets that I had sent out when I stood for election to the Common Council. He was keen that I should be the first Scottish-born Lord Mayor since Sir James Miller. Uniquely, Sir James was Lord Provost of Edinburgh before he became Lord Mayor and Bill suggested that I do it the other way round by becoming Lord Mayor of London first and then going for Edinburgh. Whilst I was willing to consider the first I had no intention of doing the second. I do not think that I would be good at politics, local or otherwise, because I usually try to see the other person's point of view. Some of the other members of the Common Council suggested that it was in the interest of the City that I should stand for election as the Alderman for Aldersgate.

Donald had suggested to me that the reason that the Court of Aldermen was against him was that he was Jewish. I assured him that if that was the case, there was no way that I would stand against him. It turned out that his most implacable enemy on the Court of Aldermen was a past Lord Mayor, Sir Bernard Waley-Cohen, himself Jewish. He was also the Senior Alderman. When Sir Bernard heard that I was considering standing for election he asked me to go to see him in the Guildhall. During a chat, among the things that I asked him was the question of whether the Court of

Aldermen was opposed to Donald because he was Jewish. He assured me that this was not the case. Sir Bernard then asked if he could meet my wife so I rang Wyn and told her that I was bringing the Senior Alderman across to the Barbican for a cup of tea. She said, 'That's lucky, I've just finished baking a cake.'

We made our way to Shakespeare Tower and Sir Bernard enjoyed the cake. As he was leaving he said that he hoped that I would seriously consider standing for election as Alderman for Aldersgate. I'm sure that it was the cake that did it. On many occasions afterwards he said, 'Your wife bakes beautiful cakes.' Sir Bernard liked his food and he was grossly overweight. He had been a keen horseman when he was younger. He told me that he had once won a race putting up fifty six pounds overweight. It must have been some horse that he was riding.

Wyn and I discussed the possibility of my standing for election as Alderman with the boys. They were pleased to hear about it and promised to help in any way that they could. I decided to stand for election. In the Common Council elections where I had topped the pole it had been relatively easy. The elections were fairly relaxed affairs but Donald had been working towards becoming an Alderman for nearly ten years and he took it very seriously indeed. I think that we became a bit complacent. When I went round the Barbican canvassing some of the residents said, 'Why are you wasting your time canvassing? You will win by a street.' Some of my Jewish friends in the Barbican told me that they were upset to receive letters that more or less said, 'We Jews must stick together.' I was not very happy about that either. On the day of the election Donald got a slot on local radio. I suppose that I could have claimed equal time but of course it was too late. Donald won by eleven votes.

When we were canvassing we had always stopped at nine o' clock. One evening at about eight-thirty Wyn and I had arrived at a flat in one of the tower blocks. It was a Jewish family consisting of the parents and four adult children. They were all voters. We were invited in for a drink but we said that we had to get on to visit other flats in the block. The father said that having secured six votes in that flat we had done well for that evening and we could now afford to relax. We capitulated and finished our canvassing for the evening. On the day of the election the whole family arrived at the polling station with Donald. It was quite clear where their votes were going. We had fallen for one of the oldest tricks there is in electioneering. Keep the opposition candidate talking to you for as long as you can. When he is talking to you he is not winning any votes. The six votes in that flat were the difference between winning and losing. We counted up afterwards. There were three hundred and ninety five people who had said that they supported me but did not turn out to vote. We learned that it is crosses on ballot papers that count not assurances on the doorstep.

When Donald was presented to the Court of Aldermen for approval he was rejected. He decided to seek judicial review of the Court of Aldermen's decision. The court decided that the Court of Aldermen had a duty to consider candidates who had been elected. They had the right indeed the duty to reject anyone that they did not consider suitable. There were precedents. A candidate could try three times and if the Court of Aldermen rejected him three times they could then appoint someone of their own choice. After the court case there was another election. This time as well as Donald and myself there was a third candidate David Shalit. I think that David was related to Sir Bernard. Donald won but was again rejected. In the third election it was back to Donald and me. At each election the turnout was getting larger and larger. To the media the story was about Donald Silk and the Court of Aldermen. I was of little interest to them, but by this time we had learned a bit about electioneering. During the day there were people coming to vote that we had never seen in all our canvassing. Wyn and I had discussed the situation and were convinced that I had lost again.

After each election we had had a party in our penthouse for our helpers. My sister Helen had come from Cambridge. She said that she would find the count too nerve-wracking and had stayed back with our daily-help to prepare the food for the party. Apparently Helen had suddenly let out a yell. She shouted, 'We've won! I can hear Wyn's voice. She's just said we've won.' Helen was on the 39th floor of Shakespeare Tower, which is about a quarter-of-a-mile from where the count was taking place. I do not think that Wyn's voice could carry that far. Spooky! She threw on her coat and arrived at Ironmongers' Hall in time to hear the result being announced by the Lord Mayor Sir Peter Gadsden.

I had indeed won—by twelve votes. We were asked not to make the result known but to allow the Lord Mayor to make the announcement. When we returned to the hall after the count the look on Donald's face left everyone in no doubt that he had lost. In some ways I felt sorry for Donald. I felt that he had become too obsessed with the idea of becoming Lord Mayor and that this had clouded his judgement to some extent. I believe that he would have made an excellent parliamentary candidate.

I had to appear before the Court of Aldermen to seek their approval. I answered the questions that were put to me and was then invited to address them. I cannot remember much of what I said but I do know that I told them that my two childhood heroes had been Robert Bruce because of his tenacity and Thomas More because of his integrity. So it was that, within four years of my return to UK, I was on the ladder to become Lord Mayor of London. The Lord Mayor is the holder of, probably, the most prestigious civic office in the land. Life is full of strange twists and turns.

The Court of Aldermen

I had to get a full kit of clothes. Scarlet gown with sable fur trim, violet gown with bear fur trim (I wonder if anyone makes such things these days), velvet court suit with breeches and normal court suit with breeches and also trousers for less formal occasions. The court suits were worn with black tights. Some of the Aldermen said that when they had first become Aldermen they had worn stockings and suspenders. Someone, I think that it was one of my predecessors Sir Robin Gillett Bt. GBE who has a gift for words, once described the Court of Aldermen as 'A group of middle-aged men poncing around in medieval drag.' I have to confess that I never felt embarrassed about wearing my Aldermanic robes. I looked on them as my uniform that I wore when I was on duty.

In the past the Alderman was responsible for the keeping law and order in his ward. For that purpose he had a beadle, a uniformed official who carried a mace. The mace would have been used to bang on the head anyone who was behaving badly. Nowadays the beadle for each Ward carries a gilded mace and accompanies the Alderman on official occasions. Such occasions are ward elections, the election of Sheriffs and the election of Lord Mayor. He also walks beside the carriage bearing his Alderman in the Lord Mayor's Show. The Ward beadle for the ward of Aldersgate was Cecil Haynes who had become beadle when Sir Gilbert Inglefield had first become Alderman for Aldersgate. He was a very nice man and remained beadle until I retired from the Court of Aldermen. I was informed that he had died recently but nobody had thought to inform me so that I could pay my respects to a very fine man.

One of my predecessors as Alderman for Aldersgate was Sir Thomas Bludworth who was Lord Mayor at the time of the Great Fire in 1666. He was criticised for delaying the order to pull down houses to form a firebreak. When he did give the order it was too late. Samuel Pepys wrote that when he met him, 'He cried like a fainting woman, Lord! What can I do?' I hoped that I would perform better if I became Lord Mayor and had to face an emergency.

Life was rolling along very nicely. I was jetting around the world arbitrating and sometimes Wyn came with me. Douglas and Michael had married to two very nice girls, Ianthe and Rowena. There was just the two of us at home so when the lease on the penthouse expired we decided that we would take a smaller flat in the Barbican. At the same time we would look for a place outside London that we could go to at weekends. Eventually we found what we were looking for.

We had gone to an estate agent in Canterbury and explained what we wanted. He looked through his books and was about to say that he had nothing suitable. Then he said, 'We have this place. It has been on the books for nearly two years. Although a number of people have looked at it, we have never even had one offer.' Wyn and I looked at each other. Was it worth looking at? It did not sound too promising. We decided to take a look and the estate agent gave us the keys and directions on how to get there. Normally estate agents will not allow you to visit a property alone. They have to be careful about squatters. He seemed to be implying that this place was so awful that even squatters would not be tempted.

We duly arrived at an imposing brick building, a Queen Anne house with extensions by Lutyens. It was located in the village of Barham, which is south of Canterbury. The front door to the ground floor, which was for sale, was double-leafed and made of mahogany. It opened into an entrance hall of reasonable size. From there we went into a large drawing room. When we opened the shutters on the long windows we could see cobwebs hanging everywhere. It looked like the perfect set for a horror movie. The walls were wood-panelled, painted white many years before but time had taken its toll. They were now a dirty yellow. We expected to hear ghostly music at any moment but we moved on. Next we came to a large hall with a black and white marble-tiled floor. The walls were panelled in oak, which had clearly been neglected. The wood was very dry and dull. The hall too had large shutters hung with cobwebs. It also had a beautifully carved staircase leading nowhere.

The staircase had been partitioned off when the house had been split. There was also a large door leading out to the garden. To Wyn and me so far there was nothing that we could see wrong with the place that could not be remedied with care and attention. We thought that there must be some disaster area still to come but, apart from the neglect, there were no problems in the other three rooms, kitchen and bathroom. The garden was said to be two acres in extent. We could only get a short way into it because it was so over-grown.

It all seemed a suitable challenge for us so we went back to the estate agent. We said that we would take it. His reaction was, 'Are you sure?' We offered £500 less than the asking price. I think that if we had offered £5000 less it would have been accepted. We got in touch with our solicitor, Raymond Bellenger and told him that we wanted the place. We asked him not to make a fuss about the lease. We had seen it and it was not very clever.

What fun we had. Every weekend we would leave the Barbican and don our overalls. Gradually the flat came to life, responding to our cleaning and painting. We engaged a local plumber who was responsible for installing a central heating system and a new bath-room. Dave a local builder was a huge man who carried out partitioning and other such work. We had however to stop him help-ing with painting the windows because he was burning off the existing paint and breaking the Georgian panes. He said that the glass was not very good as it had imperfections in it! We told him that we would finish the painting ourselves. We bought a tower, which was made of galvanised steel poles fitted together, and had wheels for moving it around. Wyn would climb up on to it and perform her Michaelangelo act. She picked out the ceiling mould-ings in blues and golds and had a wonderful time exercising her artistic talents.

One weekend we were driving to Barham and Wyn remarked that it would be a relaxing time for the next couple of days as most of the work was complete. When we got through to the hall we could hear the sound of running water. It was coming from the newly installed bathroom. The door was stuck closed. When I forced it open I found hot water flowing out of one of the pipes. We had left the heating on to dry everything out and the pipe had been giving forth hot water for over a week. The floorboards were warped, the vanitory unit holding the washbasin had collapsed in a heap and the bath-panel had curled up into a most peculiar shape. What a mess! We called the plumber. He dashed round, turned the water off, and proceeded to sort it out.

The final part of the work was to restore the oak panelling in the hall, which we had decided to use as a dining room. Someone had advised us that a mixture of linseed oil and some other oil whose name I have forgotten would do the trick. We managed to find what was required. A few days before Christmas we went to Barham. Michael and Rowena were at that time living in Zambia and Douglas and Ianthe were off skiing. For the first time since we had returned to UK we were spending Christmas on our own. Douglas and Ianthe ever thoughtful had prepared a box, which contained all the requirements for a Christmas celebration. There were personalised paper hats, coloured candles and, of course, champagne and presents.

We started work on the panelling applying the oily mixture. At first because the panelling was so dry the oil was being absorbed as quickly as we applied it. We had to keep going back over and over again. By Christmas Eve we had finished. We decided to have our Christmas dinner on the evening of Christmas Day. There we were in front of a large log fire by candlelight sipping champagne, enjoying our achievement. The panelling seemed to be glowing. The atmosphere was wonderful.

We all liked Barham Court. It was hard work. The garden was completely overgrown and we hacked away for about two months. Eventually we reached where the vegetable garden had been and found a large Scout Hut and a greenhouse that we had not known about. We bought a large bag of some kind of weed-killer and had to sign for it. Apparently it was the type of chemical that the IRA used for making bombs.

Once I had been accepted by the Court of Aldermen it was suggested that I should become a Liveryman. There are now 102 Livery Companies in the City. These are derived mainly from the ancient City Guilds such as the Mercers, the Saddlers and the Butchers, to name but a few. However there are now modern companies such as the Engineers, the Actuaries and the Information Technologists. There are craft Guilds in other cities throughout UK and Europe, but the Livery is strongest in the City of London. Whether they are ancient (the Weavers' company's charter is dated 1155) or modern (the Information Technologists are number 100) the role of Livery companies today is threefold:

(1) to support the trade or profession.

(2) to support the City and the Lord Mayor.

(3) to support Educational and Charitable work.

To many outsiders the Livery companies are wining and dining clubs but most companies have a Charity Fund to which their members contribute. Such funds are used to carry out the duties of a Livery company. Nowadays the Court of Aldermen will not agree to the grant of Livery to a Company unless it has been in existence for a considerable length of time and has built up a sizeable Charity fund. Between them Livery companies donate well over ten million pounds every year to educational institutions alone, in the form of direct contributions, scholarships or prizes. Schools and universities benefit from such contributions. In all, in the year 2000, Livery companies gave over thirty-eight million pounds to charities. They are also responsible for the running of almshouses providing homes for the needy.

Many Livery companies are actively involved in the education of apprentices in their particular trade. The Plaisterers' Company maintains a list of qualified plasterers who are called associates. This list is made available to architects and others seeking persons with the required skills. The Plumbers' company organises a diploma in plumbing. The Waxchandlers' company organises a diploma in bee keeping. Many of the other companies have similar education schemes. For over 700 years the Goldsmiths' company has been responsible for the quality of precious metals used in London. The Assay Office is still at Goldsmiths' Hall.

A number of the members of the Aldersgate Ward Club were also Liverymen of the Worshipful Company of Loriners. In days gone by Loriners were the makers of the metal parts for horses' bridles such as the bits and also stirrups and spurs. It was one of the duties of the company to ensure that inferior metal was not used in the manufacture of such items. The Loriners' company was responsible for the course in Lorinery at Cordwainers' College in the East End of London. This has now been moved to Capel Manor another educational establishment. Every year the Master of the company presents a set of harness made by the prize student on the course to the winner of the Loriners' Trophy, a riding competition which is competed for annually by members of the armed forces. The presentation was made at the Royal Tournament at Earls Court. In this way the company promotes both the making of the harness and the standard of riding.

My experience of horses and riding consisted of two afternoons spent on the back of a particularly obstreperous large grey horse. I had been inveigled into this, to me, dangerous form of recreation by Wyn who spent weekends and summer evenings riding around the outskirts of Edinburgh on horses that appeared to me to be far more docile than the one that was allocated to me. The sole intention of my horse appeared to be to dump me backwards over his tail. This he contrived to do by rearing up. If I had not been so busy hanging on I might have been tempted to call out after the fashion of the Lone Ranger, 'Hi! Ho! Silver!' Notwithstanding my lack of experience I was invited to become a Liveryman of the Loriners' company. I accepted the invitation. Later when a Company of Arbitrators was formed, as I was the only member of the Court of Aldermen at that time eligible to join I became a Founder Liveryman of that company. The following year a Company of Engineers was formed and I was persuaded that I should become a Founder Liveryman of that company also. I have been Master of all three companies.

The Worshipful Company of Plaisterers has its beautiful hall in the Ward of Aldersgate. The hall contains examples of most different forms of plasterwork. It is one of the largest livery-halls in the

City. I am an Honorary Liveryman of that company. Wyn, always a keen gardener, is a Liveryman of the Worshipful Company of Gardeners.

At the same time that it was suggested that I become a Liveryman it was also suggested that I become a 'name' at Lloyd's. To be a name you have to have a certain amount of assets. Insurance policies are written and the names are carrying the risk. Names are subject to unlimited liability. This means that all the name's assets are at risk. Unfortunately in recent years a large number of people have found out just what 'unlimited liability' means. Quite a number have been driven into bankruptcy and there have also been several suicides. Before taking any action in the matter I decided to check out the system at Lloyd's. I visited Lloyd's and discussed with the people there, scientific methods of risk assessment. Some appeared to have a vague knowledge of the subject but to others I might as well have been talking in Serbo-Croat. When I returned home I discussed it with Wyn and the boys. The unanimous opinion was that I should have nothing to do with it. In view of the subsequent problems experienced by Lloyd's names I am glad that we came to that conclusion.

The late Sir Colin Cole who was Garter King of Arms was a member of the Common Council. Some time after I was elected as an Alderman he suggested that it would be a good idea to start thinking about a family Coat of Arms. It was usual for the Sheriffs to have a Coat of Arms to put on the various invitations that they sent out and hopefully I would eventually be elected Sheriff. We set about putting together a suitable design. We wanted to divide the shield with a Saltire (a St. Andrew's Cross). Apparently that is not permitted. Instead there are reversed blue and white chevrons. It looks a bit like a St. Andrew's Cross. This divides the shield into four sections. Two of these sections are blue and two white. In the blue sections we have yellow Hibiscus flowers. The Hibiscus is the National flower of Malaysia. In the white sections we put two towers. One tower represents Engineering and the other my birthplace Edinburgh which has its very distinctive castle. At the top is an oriental crown to represent my connection with HRH the Sultan of

Selangor as a Dato' DiRaja (Royal Dato'). Above the crown is an arm in the sleeve of a barrister's court dress. The hand is holding a sword to represent the City. On the sword is a mill-rind to represent Lincoln's Inn. Right at the top is an alder wreath to represent my Ward of Aldersgate. At the bottom are shown the star of the Order of Royal Dato's and the Pingat Jasa Kebaktian (Meritorious Service Medal) of the State of Selangor. Sir Colin suggested that most people have mottoes in English, Latin or French but it might be appropriate in my case to have the motto in the Malay language. I agreed with Sir Colin. I decided on 'Perundangan Asas Kebebasan'. This translates as, 'Law is the Foundation of Freedom'. It thus incorporates my two disciplines Law and Engineering (foundations). Later when I was awarded the GBE I was entitled to add Supporters to my Coat of Arms. For these I chose on one side a Scottish lion rampant on a representation of Arthur's Seat the hill in Edinburgh where I used to play as a child. On the hill are symbolic bunches of heather and thistles. On the other side there is a Malaysian tiger on a representation of Fraser's Hill in Malaysia. On it are hibiscus flowers and orchids.

When the Coat of Arms was ready Sir Colin suggested that we have a small handing-over ceremony at the College of Arms. It so happened that two very nice friends of ours Bob and Phyllis Gottschalk were in England on holiday from America. They were thrilled to come along to see the handing over and to have a drink with the Garter King of Arms. Bob and Phyllis were also invited to the Lord Mayor's Banquet.

Recently the *Sunday Times* produced amongst the myriad bits and pieces that go to make up the huge plastic-wrapped Sunday papers a list of the richest men of the last millennium. A surprising number of those named had been involved in the City of London many of them had been masters of Livery companies. Several of them had held the office of Lord Mayor. I suppose that that is why everyone thinks that, if you have been Lord Mayor you must be rich. In my case this is certainly a fallacy.

Among the more famous names in the list were those of Sir Francis Child and Sir Thomas Gresham. Sir Francis Child was the founder of Child's Bank and became Lord Mayor in 1698. According to the *Times* his year of office cost him £4,000, which would be around £800,000 in today's value. Sir Thomas Gresham was the founder of the Royal Exchange. He was a Mercer. In his will he left the Royal Exchange building to the Mercer's company and the City of London jointly. The rents received from the present building amounting to nearly £5,000,000 per annum are divided between them and used for charitable purposes. The most famous Lord Mayor of all is of course, Dick Whittington. He did not make the list but he was a wealthy man. So much of what is written about him is fiction that people have come to doubt that he existed but there was indeed a Sir Richard Whittington. He was the third son of a squire in Gloucestershire. When I was Sheriff of London in 1989 we went with the then Lord Mayor Sir Christopher Collett to visit Poultney, Dick Whittington's birthplace. The visit was part of the celebration of the 800th anniversary of the Mayoralty. Dick Whittington was elected Lord Mayor three times and he stepped into the breach in 1396 on the order of King Richard, when the Lord Mayor died in office. He was a Liveryman of the Mercer's company. He was well known for his good works.

One of the most famous of these works was paying for the construction of a large public lavatory over the Fleet River in the City. A copy of his will is in the library at Lambeth Palace. He had no children and when he died in 1423 he left the residue of his estate to the Mercer's company for charitable purposes. This sum amounted to £6,000, probably equivalent to about £2,000,000 in modern terms. Over the years this money has been carefully invested, to a large extent in property, by some pretty shrewd operators. According to Sir Alexander Graham, a past Lord Mayor and past Master Mercer, being Master of the Mercers' company today is like being the chairman of a large property company. All of the income of the company is used for educational and charitable purposes.

When I was Lord Mayor I received a cheque from the Mercer's company for my Lord Mayor's Charities. The cheque was drawn on the account of 'The Whittington Bequest'. Nearly 570 years had passed since Sir Richard Whittington's death and the bequest was still being administered as a separate account. This is the kind of massive continuity that strikes you again and again with regard to the City of London.

The Lord Mayor's role has changed over the years. Even in the time that I was a member of the Court of Aldermen I saw great changes. Initially the thinking appeared to be that the Mayoralty and the City Corporation should not get too close to the City financial. The reasoning behind this view was that there had been a number of scandals involving insider dealing and share-price rigging. These included the affairs regarding Barlow Clowes, Blue Arrow, Guinness and Polly Peck. Some of the Members felt that too close an involvement with the financial City could impair the image of the Lord Mayor and the Corporation. To me it appeared that the main reason for the continued existence of the Lord Mayor and the Corporation was to provide the infrastructure and the favourable conditions so that the financial City could flourish in an increasingly competitive world. That is the view that is generally held today.

Another role of the Lord Mayor is to be the leader of the City's Livery Companies. With this end in view he attends as many Livery functions as possible. These days it is becoming more and more difficult to do so because of overseas visits and other functions, which are of national importance. Livery functions tend to be lunches or dinners, which include a presentation of prizes or cheques to charities. It is also a way of reminding members of the various companies of the role that they are supposed to play in the City.

One of the privileges of Aldermen and Common Councilmen is that they are invited to a fascinating range of events such as Banquets and Honorary Freedom Ceremonies. The Banquets include the Lord Mayor's Banquet and Banquets for visiting Heads of State. These are white-tie and tails affairs and are very formal. The Honorary Freedoms are usually held at lunchtime. One such was given for Lee Kuan Yew the Prime Minister of Singapore.

Lee Kuan Yew had been a brilliant law student. He was a Queen's Scholar at Cambridge. He became leader of the Peoples Action Party (PAP) in Singapore. The PAP was regarded by many expatriates in Singapore as a crypto-Communist organisation. Certainly before the pre-independence elections it appeared to be a very radical party. Old Singapore hands were saying that if the PAP won the elections Singapore as a commercial centre was finished. The PAP duly won with a huge majority and Independence Day was set for the end of August 1958. Two weeks before the independence celebrations were due, Lee Kuan Yew declared Independence. Although nominally a Socialist party the PAP strategy was geared to attracting investment from overseas. Before independence there had been Communist-led strikes in the bus companies that had almost paralysed the economy. Lee gradually gained control. Communists who would not recant were jailed under emergency regulations and there may indeed be one or two who remain incarcerated to this day. He ran a very tight ship. Any opposition was dealt with ruthlessly. By providing a stable environment Singapore began to attract investment in the burgeoning electronics industries. The Singapore Housing Authority built thousands of flats that were gradually sold off to the tenants. Hotels were built and tourism flourished. Never was the prosperity of a country so dependent on the vision and personality of one man. By the time that the second elections came along, those who had been fearful of his being elected originally were saying that if Lee Kuan Yew was not re-elected Singapore was finished.

In Singapore it was believed that drug culture was related to long hair. Males were not allowed to have their hair below the level of their shirt collar. A nephew of mine who was passing through on his way to Australia had to have his hair cut by a friend at the Causeway in Johore which joins Malaysia and Singapore. On the plane on one occasion Wyn and I met a young man whose hair was in a ponytail. He said that he had just come from Singapore. We asked how he had managed to keep his hair so long. He rummaged in the haversack that he carried and produced a short wig. A team of hockey players came from Hong Kong to Malaysia on a tour. They were mostly Chinese and sported long hair and were due to go to Singapore. They were not keen to get their hair cut just for a hockey game so they borrowed turbans from the Sikh lads that they had played against in Kuala Lumpur.

For all his autocracy Lee Kuan Yew was a deserved recipient of the Honorary Freedom. The ceremony took place in the Guildhall. Lee knew his audience. Referring to the Falklands War he said, 'For eight weeks last year Britain found its Soul.' At the end of the speech he received a tremendous ovation.

I do not know whether or not Mr Lee knew that the City Corporation after the conclusion of the Falklands War had held a large lunch in Guildhall for the returning troops. The Great Hall, the Crypt and the Old Library were all full with members of the armed forces and guests. Of course the guest of honour was Mrs Thatcher. I was hosting a table in the Old Library and around me were soldiers, sailors and airmen. They said that they were surprised at the warmth of the reception given to them by the crowds as they marched through the City's streets. As one lad put it the crowd had lifted him so much his feet didn't touch the ground all the way. One of the soldiers told us how his aunt had a pub in I think Newcastle. The Saturday evening entertainment during the Falklands Campaign was to collect 10p pieces from the people in the bar. Someone had obtained a Buenos Aires telephone directory. They would phone up a number and when it was answered they would stand round the phone singing 'Land of Hope and Glory'. The members of the Forces all enjoyed the lunch and Mrs Thatcher made a cracking speech. The lads were very happy when we managed to get a case of beer for them to take back on the coach. Another visitor to speak in the Guildhall was Ronald Reagan. It was the first time that I had seen an auto-cue. It was brilliant. He spoke for about 45 minutes. Later when you saw it on television it looked as though he had no notes. Afterwards when you asked yourself what he had actually said you discovered that the speech itself was fairly inconsequential but the delivery was superb.

Brian and Anne Jenkins had invited Wyn and me to lunch at the City of London Club after Reagan's speech. They were very helpfully briefing us on what we should expect in my up-coming shrieval year. For the speech we Aldermen had been asked to turn up dressed in formal morning dress of tail coat, black waistcoat and striped trousers. For lunch I had changed out of the tail coat into a short black jacket and I was still wearing the striped trousers. We arrived at the club before Brian and Anne. When I told the doorman that I was lunching with Brian he said that I would need to get permission to go into the dining room, as I was not wearing a suit. I asked what he meant. He said that my trousers did not match my jacket. I found it highly amusing that what had been known for years as formal City dress was not regarded by the doorman as formal enough for lunch at the City of London Club.

The following year when I was Sheriff we had a visit from Mr Gorbachev. Because Reagan had spoken in the Guildhall Gorbachev had to do likewise. The speech had more substance than Reagan's but he did not say anything earth shattering. His bodyguard looked like parodies of the film version of Russian spies, all wearing leather coats with tied belts. Just after his car left Guildhall Mr Gorbachev decided to do a walk-about. He got out of his car and started to shake hands with the people who were lining the street. The bodyguard were still boarding their vehicles. When they saw Mr Gorbachev getting out of his car there was a mad dash to get to him. Seeing all these leather-coated tough-guys chasing along the street was like a scene from 'The Third Man'.

Part of the duties of an Alderman was to become a magistrate. After suitable training I was appointed to the City bench. Most of the cases related to traffic offences or fraud on the Underground and on the Railway. It is amazing the lengths that people will go to cheat on their fares. We have had people who had season tickets between the first two and the last two stations on a lengthy journey. I think that that fraud has been eliminated by the use of computers. Occasionally we could be in at the beginning of a huge drug smuggling operation. One such case was smuggling £150 million (a whole ship-load) of marijuana.

Because I lived in the Barbican I made myself available for Saturday duty. On Saturdays you sat on your own instead of in a Bench of three. The cases were usually drunks who had been picked up on the Friday evening. On one particular Saturday I had two cases. One was a gang of housebreakers; the other was a bank fraud where the sum involved was US$40 million. This was a considerable change from the usual £10 rail-fare fraud. Wyn and I were due to go to a wedding in the afternoon and there were long arguments about granting bail. Eventually I managed to get it all sorted out and I made the wedding. It was a most unusual Saturday morning's work.

As a magistrate the one thing that worried me most was when there was someone before the court who really should have been having care in a mental institution. He had probably been discharged from such an institution and should have been having medication. With no supervision the medication was not being taken. There did not seem to be any support. Often the person before the court was a persistent offender and the only remedy available to the magistrates was to send him to prison. 'Care in the Community' was a myth.

It is unfortunate that the magistracy can be and often is criticised as being white and middle-class. This is not the fault of the magistrates but the system of recruitment. On the City Bench we were fortunate to have people of different racial origins and the standards of intelligence and integrity were extremely high. In one case a lady magistrate was on a bench trying a case involving Lloyds of London. At the end of the first day she remembered that her husband was a Name at Lloyds. He did not of course have anything to do with the case in hand but she immediately disqualified herself from the case and, because she considered that she had fallen below the standard expected of a City magistrate, she immediately tendered her resignation from the bench. It is interesting to compare this course of action with that of a Law Lord who, having been guilty of a gross error of judgement in a high profile international case, remains in his post with the approval of the Lord Chancellor. I suppose however, that when the Lord Chancellor himself cannot see what is wrong about him soliciting contributions to his Party, from lawyers whose futures he holds in his gift, one could hardly expect it to be otherwise. I was a magistrate for eighteen years. I reckoned that my duties as an Alderman took up an average of about a day and a half a week.

Sometime after I became an Alderman I was invited by the World Federation of Burns' Clubs to attend their Conference Dinner. I was told that I was to receive on behalf of the City a flag from the city of London Ontario together with a book on the history of that city. Shortly after the invitation had arrived the organiser of the event telephoned to ask whether I would wear my dinner jacket, as the other guests at the top table would be so attired. He spoke with Wyn. She assured him that it would present no problem. She then asked whether I would be required to speak. The organiser said that I would only have to say, 'Thank-you' for the book and flag. Some time later he phoned again to confirm the timing of the event. I checked with him that I would not be expected to make a speech.

When the evening of the dinner came the top-table was duly assembled. With great ceremony we were marched into the hall behind a pair of pipers. When we sat down I became slightly uneasy. I was seated between the Federation President's wife, and the man from London Ontario. This appeared to me to indicate that I was somewhat more important than I had expected. There must have been six or seven hundred people in the hall from USA, Canada, Australia, New Zealand, as well as all parts of the United Kingdom. I asked the man from Ontario if he had prepared a speech. It appeared that he had done so. He had ten foolscap sheets of it. So much just to hand over a book and a flag! I checked on the menu card. My neighbour was not only handing over the book and the flag, he was proposing a toast to 'The City and the Metropolis of London'. I was down to reply to the toast on behalf of London.

I was in a bit of a panic and I said to the President's wife after the fashion of Victor Meldrew, 'I don't believe it! I have been told that I am not making a speech but I find that I am replying to a ten-page speech.' Her reply was that if she were in my place she would just stand up and say that she was not prepared to make a speech under the circumstances. As an Alderman of the City I did not feel that was an option at an international gathering. During the meal I persuaded the Canadian that ten pages was a bit too much for the occasion. He agreed and eventually cut it down to about four or five. I then had to start constructing a speech in reply.

I made a few notes on the back of the menu card about the occasion. Digging into my memory, I was able to regurgitate large chunks of the speech that I had made as chieftain of the St. Andrew's Society in Kuala Lumpur some twelve years before. The result was a crisp ten minutes about Scots especially Scots abroad. It was appropriate to the occasion and went down well. Indeed my sister Patricia in Edinburgh was later complimented by a friend who had been present on the excellent speech that her brother had made at the dinner. It was very fortunate that the speech for the St Andrew's Celebration in Kuala Lumpur had been so awful and had taken so much work to get it right.

It was just after Wyn and I had reached the age of sixty, that Douglas and Ianthe suggested that we should go skiing with them to St Anton in Austria. We had once tried to go skiing at Aviemore in Scotland. The weather had been so bad, that the chair lifts were closed. The result was that we only spent twenty minutes on the ski-slopes in the whole week. We decided to give it a go. We enjoyed the experience and have gone skiing nearly every year since. At the start I always found it difficult to stop. When we went to Meribel the French ski instructor told me that I frightened him by going very fast and then throwing myself on the ground. I told him that as a result of my rugby playing I was very good at falling and it was the only way that I could stop. Eventually I learned to stop without falling. Nowadays we tend to go to Colorado where the pistes are wider and there are fewer queues for the chair lifts. Also over-seventies used to get a free pass for the chair lifts. In France over-seventy fives get a free lift-pass.

We lived in our Barbican flat during the week and went to Barham at weekends. We usually left the Barbican late on Friday after the traffic had cleared and returned late on Sunday. Although we loved Barham Court it was just too far to commute on a regular basis and we decided that we would like to live in a rural area throughout the week. Wyn scoured the pages of *Country Life.*. One day she came across a picture of Praewood House a lovely dower house on the Verulam Estate near St Albans. It was not for sale but there was the possibility of negotiating a long lease. She arranged to go and see it.

I could not go with her as I had a meeting in the City to attend. When she returned Wyn said, 'You will love it.' She was right. Built in 1904, the house needing considerable refurbishment, had four and a half acres round it. The design was very logical. It had seven bedrooms and four bathrooms. It also had other cloakrooms and gardener's toilets. Having been brought up in a house with seven other people in it and only one toilet this was for me the height of luxury. It had a cottage in the grounds for a housekeeper and gardener. Unusually, the driveway, which was about 300 yards long, came off a public roundabout

We were interviewed by the Countess of Verulam to ensure that we were the right kind of people. It turned out that she had shared a room with our daughter-in-law Ianthe on a school trip abroad. We started to negotiate a ten-year lease. Raymond Bellenger again acted for us. We were not too worried about leasing as opposed to buying. At the time, house prices were high and rents had not yet caught up.

Wyn and I had a tremendous time refurbishing our leased house. Colour schemes had to be decided upon. Acres of carpets had to be ordered and yards and yards of curtain materials chosen. The cost of having curtains made eventually persuaded Wyn to start making her own. She bought a book on the subject and proceeded to make all sorts of fancy curtains, pelmets and swathes. She went to the 'Ideal Home Exhibition'. There she purchased a kitchen and a bath-room. We moved in as soon as it was possible to do so. The workmen were still around. From long experience we knew that the only way to get them to complete everything within a reasonable time was to move in and chase them. I suppose that we probably spent more than we should have on a house that had only a ten-year lease but we thought that it was worth it. It was a lovely house to live in and we enjoyed putting it all together. St Albans is transport-wise one of the best places in England to live. It is close to both the M1 and the M25. Also the train services are frequent and fast. Like Canterbury the City of St Albans has a nice atmosphere.

We advertised for a gardener and housekeeper in *The Lady* maga-zine and received sixteen applications. Eventually we settled on John and June Anderson. John had studied Art at the Slade and had become a Graphic Designer. Eventually he had decided to open a print shop. He was persuaded to lease all sorts of machinery. There was little call for most of the machinery that he leased but he was tied into five-year contracts. Inevitably he went bankrupt. John and June had to sell their home and at an age when most people would be looking forward to retirement they had to seek new employment. When they came to us, because there was an empty building in the grounds June who was a good seamstress, with the help of Wyn's book, was able to start up a business making curtains. By the time we left Praewood House the business was flourishing and they were back on their feet. It certainly was an example of what people who have courage and initiative can do. John is in fact a good painter and we arranged for him to do a painting of Wyn and me when I was Sheriff.

Whilst we were living in Praewood House a cousin of Wyn's arrived from Canada with her husband. We were having dinner with them at Wyn's sister Edith's house in Edinburgh and were showing photographs of our house. The husband said 'I know that house.' He had been a pilot in the Air Force during the war. His navigator had been injured and had been sent to Praewood House to recuperate. The house had also been a school for spies. They were trained there before being dropped into occupied Europe. One day we had a Frenchman and his daughter call in for a cup of tea. He was on a nostalgic trip to St Albans. He had spent some time at the house before being dropped into France. The author Nigel West rang one day to say that he had a group of former spies who might be calling in. Apparently they were pushed for time and just drove past.

Rugby has been one of the great loves of my life. In 1986 when my sixtieth birthday was looming Wyn asked Douglas what he thought that I would like as a birthday present. Douglas suggested that she and I should pay a return visit to Lansdowne Road, which we had visited on our honeymoon, to see the Scotland v Ireland rugby match. Wyn set about using all her contacts to make the arrangements and Douglas arranged the flights. A friend of his arranged the hotel. Having got this far, the remaining problem was to get tickets for the match. She spoke to John Hart who had been secretary of the Rugby Football Union and explained her problem. John told her to leave it with him. A couple of days later he rang to say that the tickets were on the way. We found that our seats were in a great position. We were behind the Irish team's substitutes bench. I told Wyn that if the Irish scrumhalf came off, she would have to go on. Scotland won and we had a terrific weekend with Irish friends who had been in Malaysia.

Once at a dinner when I was Sheriff I was seated next to a man from Wales. We were talking about rugby and I mentioned that I had watched international rugby at Murrayfield, Twickenham and Lansdowne Road but never at Cardiff Arms Park. A couple of months later I received a letter telling me that he had a ticket for the Wales v Scotland match if I wanted to come. He said later that he had never received such a quick reply to a letter. We had lunch in the Cardiff Club then went to the ground. The atmosphere was tremendous. The singing in the closely packed crowd was wonderful to hear. I wonder whether the atmosphere in the new National Stadium is the same.

The next time I visited Cardiff Arms Park was when Wyn and I were invited to the Barbarians v New Zealand match. After a superb game we attended the dinner in the evening. Wyn was sitting next to Sir Denis Thatcher. He is very knowledgeable about rugby and has a good sense of humour. Altogether we had a very enjoyable trip to Cardiff.

The Aldermanic Sheriff

In June 1988 I was elected as one of the Sheriffs of the City. No Alderman can be elected Lord Mayor unless he has served in the office of Sheriff. There are two Sheriffs who are elected on Midsummer's day and take up office in September. Usually one of the Sheriffs is an Alderman and the other is not. The non-alderman is usually referred to as the 'junior' or 'lay' Sheriff. The office of Sheriff is the oldest of the public offices still in use in the City, dating back for over a thousand years. Originally the Sheriff was the King's man. He was appointed to keep the peace and to collect taxes due to the King. The most famous Sheriff is the Sheriff of Nottingham. One of my predecessors took his children to see pantomime Robin Hood. The Sheriff was, of course, very, very, nasty. His daughter said, 'You are not like that are you, daddy?' 'No,' he replied.' That was in Nottingham.'

The Sheriffs are elected by the Liverymen of the City. More often than not there is no contest. Occasionally however two or more people are nominated for Lay Sheriff. In such cases in their election-addresses they say, 'Please give one of your votes to me and the other to the Aldermanic candidate.' Such contested elections although superficially very gentlemanly are very fiercely fought. When I was elected Sheriff I was very conscious of the historic nature of it. It is humbling to think of the many great men who have stood in the place that you are about to occupy. A thousand years is a lot of history.

Simon Block and I were elected without a contest. Apart from playing rugby together in Malaya, Simon and I had in common that we were both lawyers, he a solicitor and I a barrister. In addition Tishy, Simon's wife, was the daughter of a former General commanding the Malayan armed forces. So we had all lived in Malaysia.

It is customary for a Sheriff's Committee to obtain donations from the Sheriff's friends, towards the cost of the Sheriff's badge and chain. Each badge and chain is unique. It is specially designed and manufactured for that particular Sheriff. A few Sheriffs like Alderman Sir David Howard Bt. (Lord Mayor in 2000/01) whose father and grandfather both held the office of Lord Mayor inherit a badge and chain. That is unusual. The badges contain references to the Sheriff's life, career and interests. My badge was made by Toye, Kenning. It contains elements of a suspension bridge and is adorned with the shields of various bodies. These include the Institution of Civil Engineers, my Livery Companies and Lincoln's Inn. Interestingly when Toye, Kenning asked Lincoln's Inn for permission to put a shield with the Inn's Coat of Arms on my badge, no one could find any record of such a request being made, in the long history of the Inn. I do however know of one member of the Inn who was Sheriff not too long ago.

On the day that the Sheriffs are installed in their office the outgoing Sheriffs arrive at Guildhall by Rolls Royce. The in-coming Sheriffs arrange their own transport. After the installation ceremony, the new Sheriffs take over the Rolls Royces. The out-going Sheriffs have to make their own arrangements. A lunch is held in one of the Livery Halls. It is known as 'The Sheriffs' Breakfast'. Both pairs of Sheriffs are present. The in-coming Sheriffs are the hosts. When we were choosing the menu Simon and I decided that we would have Bread and Butter Pudding as the pudding. Wyn had a great recipe for it. The fruit was soaked in Vodka overnight and we instructed the caterers to follow Wyn's recipe.

The Sheriffs take it in turn to preside at the Old Bailey. The Sheriff who is not presiding accompanies the Lord Mayor on his duties. In the case of the Aldermanic Sheriff this is part of the training to become Lord Mayor. He sees at first-hand what duties the Lord Mayor carries out. All writs issued from the Old Bailey are served by the Under-sheriff in the name of the Sheriff who happens to be on duty on that particular day. On one of the days that I was on duty a writ was slapped on the side of an airliner at Heathrow in my name. The plane was full of passengers. The Sheriff on duty also hosts the luncheon for the judges at the Old Bailey. Guests are invited to these lunches. Usually about once a year, a member of the Royal Family comes as a guest. Invitations to lunch at the Old Bailey are readily accepted and are great fun. For the judges it is a welcome relief from the strain of the often very sordid trials that they have to conduct. For the guests it is a chance to see that the judges whom they have read about are not the stupid out-of-touch caricatures that they are portrayed.

There is usually an Alderman on duty at the lunch to represent the Lord Mayor. Once when I was duty Alderman I arrived at the Old Bailey to be told that the guest of honour was to be the late Princess of Wales. It was the first of a number of occasions that I met her. I thought that she was even more beautiful than her pictures and not nearly as dumb as she made out. When we met we chatted quite freely. On one occasion we were at Victoria Station to meet a foreign dignitary. The Princess and I were chatting and she was saying that she was feeling hungry. She said that she had a 'Mars' bar in her car. I offered to go and get it for her. She thought that I was somewhat overdressed to be looking for her car to retrieve her 'Mars' bar. We were also discussing the picture of her that had appeared in the press a day or two before. She was wearing a baseball cap. She said that a great deal of fuss had been made about her choice of head-gear but that no one had asked her why she was wearing it. The reason was that she had been exercising and her hair was a dreadful mess.

The second week of my Shrievalty we attended the dinner, which is given by the Lord Mayor's Livery Company to celebrate Her Majesty the Queen's approval of the Lord Mayor's election as Lord Mayor for the year ensuing. This approval is conveyed at the House of Lords by the Lord Chancellor. In the past it was the day on which the Gazette notification appeared of the award to the Lord Mayor of the honour of Knight Grand Cross of the Most Excellent Order of the British Empire. Traditionally oysters and salmon are served at the dinner. I do not like oysters so I had the salmon but Wyn had eaten some oysters. The following day when we drove home to St Albans Wyn was in agony. I eventually had to call out the doctor to her. She has not touched an oyster since. The following week we attended another dinner where a cheese soufflé was served. This turned out to be contaminated with Salmonella. The Lady Mayoress and at least 150 people in the City were very ill. Wyn and I were both affected and poor Wyn began to think that being ill every weekend was part of the job of the Sheriff's wife. Some of those affected by the Salmonella never fully recovered. Fortunately we did not suffer any further problems of that nature. The year as Sheriff is a very pleasant year. You go to places with the Lord Mayor that you would not normally visit. You also go on overseas trips where the Lord Mayor is acting as ambassador of the City as the financial capital of Europe. As the Sheriffs and their wives are thrown very much together it can make life very difficult if any of them is incompatible. Wyn and I were very fortunate that Simon and Tishy were two very nice people. We all got on famously. The Sheriffs take up office in September and Lord Mayors in November. Thus the Sheriffs' year straddles that of two Lord Mayors. We were also lucky with our two Lord Mayors and their Lady Mayoresses, Sir Greville and the late Lady Sheila Spratt and Sir Christopher and Lady Anne Collett.

The Sheriffs and the Lord Mayor share the responsibility for the Lord Mayor's Banquet. At the tasting for the Banquet nobody was entirely happy with the suggested puddings. It was decided that the caterers, the Lady Mayoress and the Sheriffs' wives would bring along a sample of a suggested pudding and we would all taste them. Wyn's suggestion was a 'Scotch Flummery'. That was the one that was chosen and she gave the caterers her recipe.

We travelled to the Netherlands with Sir Greville. Not long before our visit the British ambassador had been shot and security was very tight. We were instructed that, when we returned to the embassy after a visit outside, we should immediately get out of the car and get into the house quickly. The driver always radioed ahead and, as we approached the gates swung open, then closed immediately behind us. On one occasion we drove along a motorway with three armour-plated Jaguars in line and two Mercedes in the adjoining lane. As the cars were about two feet apart and doing well over eighty miles per hour, it was very exciting indeed. I was told that all the drivers were former police drivers.

During the year of my Shrievalty the City was celebrating the Eight Hundredth Anniversary of the Mayoralty. The first mention of Henry Fitzalwyn as Mayor is in the year 1189. It is possible that he was already Mayor before that date. He remained Mayor until he died. As part of the celebration Her Majesty the Queen and HRH the Duke of Edinburgh came to a lunch in the Guildhall. It was a great event, which is recorded in a painting, which hangs in the Guildhall. The names of all the Lord Mayors since 1189 are recorded in the windows of the Guildhall. It is fun to be able to point out one's name in a window. Mine is in a window near the west end of the Great Hall.

Another great event in the Guildhall while I was Sheriff, was the granting of the Honorary Freedom of the City to Mrs Thatcher. She appeared to be very moved by the occasion and Denis played his usual supporting role. She made two excellent speeches. The first was at the actual Ceremony and the other in the Mansion House at the Lunch afterwards.

It was interesting to compare the parts played by His Royal Highness the Duke of Edinburgh in relation to Her Majesty and Denis in relation to Mrs Thatcher. The Duke, of course carries out many public engagements on his own account and has a reputation for making gaffes when he speaks. I have met him on quite a few occasions and always found him to be very easy to talk to. We usually had a good laugh about something. When he is with Her Majesty he is like a supporting actor in a film and slots into his role effortlessly. Denis on the other hand does not do many separate engagements. Those that he did were usually connected with golf or rugby. Most of the time he seems to merge into the background providing support for Mrs Thatcher if needed. He too seemed perfectly comfortable in that role. He always appeared to be very solicitous about his wife's well being.

Our visit to the Bahamas with Sir Christopher Collett was less exciting than the Netherlands but fascinating. I had forgotten that the Duke of Windsor was Governor there during the war. We saw some of the memorabilia of that period. One of the problems of the Bahamas was drug smuggling. They showed us the wreckage of light planes that had been crashed by the smugglers. Apparently because the profits were so high it was worthwhile writing off the planes and making off with the cargo. When we were visiting one of the smaller islands I was asked by a boatman if I knew Sir Frederic Bennett. Sir Frederic keeps a boat in the Bahamas. We have been guests of his at his house in Wales on a number of occasions.

Simon and Tishy went with the Lord Mayor to Canada. Sir Christopher told us that, late one evening, in their room in the hotel the smoke alarm started to bleep. He called reception and they sent a man to look at it. He asked Sir Christopher to hold his ladder whilst he climbed up to check the alarm. Already in his pyjamas Sir Christopher obliged. (Contrary to rumour Lord Mayors do not wear their chains of office to bed). The tradesman said, 'Do you know that the Lord Mayor of London is staying in this hotel?' Sir Christopher replied, 'Yes and he is holding your ladder at this very moment.' The man nearly fell off the ladder.

Bob Hawke, the Prime Minister of Australia came on an official visit to UK. The City gave a Banquet for him and his party at the Mansion House. They were told that the dress would be 'white tie and tails'. Apparently they said that being of Labour persuasion they never wore such dress. Before he became Prime Minister Bob Hawke was president of the Australian equivalent of the Trades Union Congress in UK. As is usual in such circumstances they were informed that other guests would be so attired but that if they felt strongly about it they could dress as they pleased. If they had turned up in boiler suits they would not have been refused admission. In the event they decided to bite the bullet and go to Moss Bros. Hawke was quite a handsome man with silvery grey hair, known in Australia as 'The Silver Bodgie'. During the reception before the dinner the mirrors in the Salon were working overtime as Bob and his mates preened themselves. They all seemed to be adjusting their ties a great deal. Perhaps The Chancellor of the Exchequer and his minions who make such a point of turning up at the Dinner for the Bankers and Merchants of the City in their 'working' clothes might take a lesson and go home take a bath and change.

At a lunch held in the Mansion House for disabled athletes Wyn and I had seated between us that queen of disabled athletes, Tani Gray. Her greatest feats were still ahead of her, but she is a fantastic character. She is bubbly, funny and clearly a very determined lady. We were very impressed and had a very enjoyable lunch. She told us that she lived in the northeast and that she would be getting a taxi to Kings Cross to catch a train home. We insisted on giving her a lift in our Sheriff's Rolls Royce. At the station all the porters seemed to know her. She said that she travelled quite a bit and that they always came to her assistance. I wish that we had thought to get her to visit the school for the disabled run by the City Corporation, The Lord Mayor Treloar College. She would have been a tremendous inspiration.

For the lunches at the Old Bailey we purchased Mercier champagne for the guests. In one of the cases there were labels on the necks of the bottles drawing attention to a competition that was being run by Mercier and Citroen. The competition was to fill in the last line of a limerick. Wyn put her name and address on one of the labels. Then she asked me to fill in the last line of the limerick. I know that it started off 'There was a young man called Guy'. I cannot remember the rest of the limerick but my last line was 'Quelle sparkling vitesse was his cry'. A couple of months later Wyn had a call telling her that she had won a Citroen BX19 GTI. Mademoiselle Mercier came over to present her with the car and a jeroboam of champagne. A couple of months after that she won a set of Jaguar luggage in a competition where the first prize was a Jaguar car. I had been hoping that she would win the car, as her luck seemed to be in.

Preparing for the Mayoralty

When my year as Sheriff finished I returned to my Aldermanic duties. At the time I was Senior Warden of the Worshipful Company of Engineers. The week after I finished my Shrieval duties I was at the Company's Annual Banquet in the Mansion House. As Senior Warden, it was my duty to make a speech and propose the toast to the Guests. I was seated at the end of one of the tables. A loving cup filled with a red wine punch had been placed in front of me in preparation for the loving cup ceremony. Such a ceremony is a feature of all Livery Company dinners. In the ceremony the cup is passed along the table so that each person may stand and drink the health of the person next to him or her. Whilst the toast is being drunk the person on the other side of the drinker stands to guard the drinker's back. It is said that the rapid spread of the plague in London in 1665 when many thousands of the City's population died was partly because of the Loving Cups being passed around at Livery Company dinners. At the appropriate moment I was due to start a loving cup from my end of the table.

Before this however we had to stand for the singing of the Grace after the meal. I think that the end of the tablecloth must have been under my feet. At any rate when I stood up, the Loving Cup toppled soaking me with the scarlet-coloured punch. There I stood with white bow tie, stiff white shirt and waistcoat, looking as though I had been stabbed. In about fifteen minutes I was due to give my speech. I called over one of the Lord Mayor's footmen and asked him to go and ask the Lord Mayor if I could borrow a tie and shirt. Fortunately we took the same size. I nipped up to the Lord Mayor's dressing room and changed. I could hear how the proceedings were going and in spite of the usual problems of tying a bow tie I returned in time to perform my allotted task. One of our personal guests Alderman Bryan Toye had asked Wyn where I had gone. Wyn was aware what I was doing but she said as a joke, 'I think he has gone home.' Bryan was extremely worried.

'Murphy's Law' states that on any occasion anything that can go wrong will go wrong. My experience of this law came when I was Master of the Worshipful Company of Engineers. We were having a Livery Dinner at the Goldsmiths' Hall, one of the most elegant and sumptuously decorated of Livery Halls in the City. Its chandeliers can be used either with electric bulbs or with real candles. If you want the real candles you have to pay an extra hire charge, but it is worth it. The Company has of course a fabulous collection of gold and silver some of which is put on display when there is an event in the hall. There is a story told about a Master of the Company who arranged for his daughter's wedding reception to be held in the hall. Some of the Company's treasures were on display. An awe-struck guest from their home village was heard to comment that the couple had received some marvellous wedding-presents.

As the time for going into the Engineer's dinner approached, Bryan Gibson, the Learned Clerk of the Company, asked if we could go in. I knew that one of the principal guests had not yet arrived. So I asked Bryan to hold on for a little while. Later he came back and said that the caterers were becoming agitated. They felt that the food would be spoiled. I told him that we should give the guest two more minutes. Almost immediately he arrived full of apologies. His driver had taken him to the wrong hall. First crisis over.

The dinner proceeded without incident and we reached the stage where the Loyal Toasts are drunk. Here the Master rises without a glass in his hand and calls 'The Queen'. The band strikes up and plays 'God Save The Queen'. Usually this is sung with great gusto. At the appropriate moment I stood up and exclaimed in a loud voice 'The Queen'. There was dead silence. I waited to give the band a chance to play, then I picked up my glass and said again, 'The Queen' and raised my glass to drink. The band started up. The next toast is to the Royal Family. At that time the Toast was, 'Queen Elizabeth the Queen Mother, Prince Philip the Duke of Edinburgh, the Prince and Princess of Wales, (the Princess of Wales was dropped after the divorce and, of course, the Queen Mother is now no longer with us) and the other members of the Royal Family'. I did this and waited for the band to strike up the shortened version of the National Anthem. I waited and I waited but nothing happened. I thought 'This time for sure they are not going to play'. So I said, 'The Royal Family', and raised my glass to drink. The band struck up.

After the Loyal Toasts the coffee was served. While I was drinking my coffee the Company Beadle, Stephen Grundy, who was acting as Master of Ceremonies came to me and said, 'The Dean has had a nose-bleed. He does not think that he can speak.' He was referring to the late Very Reverend Peter Moore, the Dean of St Albans Abbey. Peter, a very gentle man, was due to reply to the toast to the guests and propose a toast to the Worshipful Company of Engineers. I followed Stephen out of the room to where Peter was sitting in an anteroom. His face was grey and his handkerchief was soaked in blood. He was most apologetic. I told him with more confidence than I felt not to worry, as I would sort it out. I gave him a clean handkerchief and returned to the hall. I spoke to Sir Denis Rooke who is a Past-Master of the Company, I told him what had happened and asked him to say a few words and to propose a toast to the Company. He agreed to do so. I then proceeded to alter my speech to take account of the fact that the Dean was not now speaking. Just then the Beadle appeared and said that the Dean was feeling much better and would be happy to give his speech and propose the toast. All the bits that I had scored out were now back in. I thanked Sir Denis and told him that he was not now required to speak. Peter made an excellent and very witty speech.

It was now my turn. I stood up and put my speech on the lectern. The speech was going well and I was recovering my confidence when, horror of horrors, the speech slipped off the lectern and landed underneath the table. I slotted in one of my standard jokes. While the audience were laughing I bent down and retrieved my speech. Fortunately Wyn was in the habit of punching a hole in the pages and keeping them together with a tag. I carried on as though nothing had happened. After the dinner was over I was speaking to one of the guests. I said what a terrible evening it had been. How Murphy's Law had been working overtime. He said that he had not noticed any hitches and that he doubted whether anyone else had either.

For many Livery Company Masters the Company Banquet with the Lord Mayor as the chief guest is the highlight of their year as Master. Some of them become very anxious in case anything goes wrong. When I was Lord Mayor and the Master at a Livery Banquet seemed to be particularly nervous I would relate these happenings to him. The fact that I had had to cope with such incidents seemed to help him overcome his nervousness. One Master's wife after listening as I told the stories of my disasters to her husband said in a voice full of disbelief, 'And they still let you be Lord Mayor after all that.'

I was very fortunate to persuade my friend Charles Winter CBE who was Chief Executive of the Royal Bank of Scotland to speak at one of my dinners. Charles was a very good banker and a very nice person. He had a wonderful sense of humour. A Scottish banking paper referred to him as 'Mister Nice Guy', an unusual description of a banker. Sadly he died a few years ago. He was a much sought-after speaker at dinners in Scotland. One of his stories was about the Scottish banker who was thrown out of a performance of 'The Merchant of Venice' at the Barbican because he insisted on giving Shylock a standing ovation. It was the sort of story that flashed round the financial organisations in the City. Charles considered himself to be the worst golfer in Scotland. As the Royal Bank had taken a share in the Spanish bank Banco Santander, Charles was a director of that bank. The president of Banco Santander is the father-in-law of the great Spanish golfer Severiano Ballesteros. When Charles was due to go to Spain for a board meeting, the president of the bank rang him and said that 'Seve' was at home that week and would Charles like to go over a day early and have a round of golf with him. Charles turned the offer down. Almost any other golfer in the world would have jumped at the chance to play with one of the world's great golfers. Charles said that he would have been too embarrassed.

The Court of Aldermen has to agree on the candidate who will be supported as Lord Mayor when the two names are relayed to the

Court of Aldermen by the Recorder on Michaelmas Day. This decision is made at the meeting of the Privileges Committee in May in the year before you are due to take office, to give the prospective Lord Mayor time to prepare for his year of office. Except in unusual circumstances the choice will fall on the Alderman next in seniority to 'The Senior Alderman below the Chair'. The Senior Alderman below the Chair is due to assume office in that year.

Almost immediately after a Lord Mayor has assumed office and you have become the 'Senior Alderman Below the Chair', the Pageant Master phones. The gist of the conversation is that if you are going to be Lord Mayor next year you had better start thinking about the Lord Mayor's Show. Letters are expected to go out to prospective participants early in January. Most City institutions and companies are happy to provide support for an employee becoming Lord Mayor. As I did not have such backing this meant that the burden of preparing such letters fell on Wyn. Since she had finished all the courses that she wished to take Wyn was looking after all the secretarial and administrative arrangements connected with my Arbitrations.

Douglas and his wife Ianthe were staying with us over Christmas in 1991 so we decided to have a discussion of the various matters that would have to be dealt with in the run-up to the Mayoralty. The discussion lasted all afternoon and evening. At the end of it we had twenty-six A4 pages of things to do. These ranged from 'Deciding on the theme for the Lord Mayor's Show' to 'Getting our teeth seen to'. Douglas was particularly responsible for the latter. He reasoned that it would be a real nuisance to be out of action because of toothache during a mayoral year. I think that the thought was provoked by reading that Douglas Jardine captain of the England cricket team during the controversial 'Body-line' tour of Australia, had insisted that all the members of the squad should have their teeth seen to before they embarked for Australia. He did not want any of his players to be unavailable during the tour because of toothache. When we had drawn up the formidable list Douglas said that we had had the kind of brainstorming session that IBM would have if they were starting out to design a new computer. From then on it was all go.

Over the next ten months or so items were ticked off as they were accomplished.

The theme for the show and my year of office was 'The City and Industry in Partnership'. In accordance with the Pageant Master John Reid's advice, Wyn prepared letters to be sent to a large number of financial institutions and industrial organisations inviting them to take part in the Show. I hoped that during the year by stressing the need for closer co-operation between the financial and industrial communities the economic performance of the country would be improved. I do believe that the need for long-term financing of industrial projects became a matter for realisation.

In order to cover the expenses of the Show, it is necessary to get at least sixty paying participants. If this number is not achieved the Lord Mayor has to meet the shortfall. Bands and Military units do not pay. Charities do not pay unless they come in with a commercial sponsor. In all there are usually about 140 items in the Show.

Unfortunately, in April 1992 John Reid died suddenly. He had been responsible for over twenty shows. His son Dominic stepped into the breach and took over the organisation of the Lord Mayor's Show. Dominic had worked with his father for a number of years and the transfer of duties was carried out without a hitch. In memory of John we named a new lane in the City 'Pageant Master Court'. Dominic had a close rapport with the BBC. Between him and the producers they set out to rejuvenate the broadcasting of the Show.

During the year Douglas arranged a series of dinner-parties at his home. He invited bankers and industrialists. We discussed the problems facing British industry such as the cost of raising capital. An interesting comment was made by Godfried Bruder, a German banker who had lived in the UK for a long time. He believed that German banks tried to give the impression that they were providing a service for their customers whereas British banks gave the impression that they were doing them a favour by allowing them to be customers. This may be a slight exaggeration but some of the industrialists especially those from outside London said that going to see the bank manager was a bit like going to see the headmaster in his study.

As a result of the discussions and a meeting with Kenneth Adams, Industrial Fellow of the Comino Foundation, it was agreed that one of my Charities would be The Foundation for Manufacturing and Industry to which I would give half of the money raised by my charitable activities. The Comino Foundation agreed to give £50,000 a year for three years. All Lord Mayors have at least one nominated charity for their year. Very often charities will contact the senior alderman below the chair to see if he will nominate them. My second charity was RedR. RedR The Register of Engineers for Disaster Relief is the charity, which arranges for engineers to be sent to anywhere where there has been a disaster. Such disasters, whether natural or man-made seem to be increasing all the time. RedR has members all over the world performing vital tasks such as setting up refugee camps in Rwanda, or constructing roads in Kosovo.

When RedR was set up its first assignment was setting up camps for Vietnamese boat people in Malaysia. I was a member of the Red Crescent Society in Malaysia at the time and remember it well. The RedR volunteers are usually called in by the aid agencies such as the Red Cross, Oxfam or Save the Children. HRH the Princess Royal in her role as President of Save the Children was so impressed with the work of RedR that she agreed to become the President. Her work in the field of aid is very impressive indeed.

It was quite amusing when after I had become Lord Mayor and the Private Secretary rang up RedR to say that I had nominated them as one of my charities. They explained that they did not have much money and did not feel that they could contribute to the Lord Mayor's charity even if he was an engineer. They were surprised and delighted to find that they were to be recipients of what turned out to be half of £500,000.

As it happened, HRH the Princess Royal was to become the Master of the Worshipful Company of Loriners my mother Livery Company, during 1992. The Master of the Lord Mayor's mother company has a right to become a member of the Lord Mayor and Sheriffs' Committee and to take part in the Lord Mayor's Show. The

Committee under the Chairmanship of my Deputy in the Ward Joyce Nash was charged with organising the Lord Mayor's Banquet. I checked with the City Police as to the security situation. Their view was that with so many military bands and units in the Show the level of security was already of the highest order. Adding in a member of the Royal Family would not add anything to that level of security.

I asked the Princess Royal if she would participate in the Show and become a member of the Lord Mayor and Sheriffs' Committee. She said that she would be delighted. In bygone days, it had been the custom for the Monarch to take part in the Lord Mayor's in the first year of the Monarch's reign. The last Monarch to do so had been Queen Victoria in 1837. So the Princess Royal was the first member of the Royal Family to take part in the Lord Mayor's Show since 1837.

Elected Lord Mayor of London

The Mansion House had been closed for refurbishment and was due to be reopened on the 1st September 1993. The date was chosen so that the actual moving could be done during the August recess. This meant that many of the functions, which would normally have taken place in the Mansion House, took place in the Guildhall.

The City Corporation had purchased a former City merchant's house in Ironmonger Lane, not far from the Guildhall. It had been refurbished to make a very comfortable residence and office for the Lord Mayor during the period that the Mansion House was closed. This meant that Wyn and I would be the first occupants of the newly refurbished Mansion House. It also meant that sadly Sir Brian and Lady Jenkins did not have the opportunity to stay in the Mansion House. Later we invited them to stay overnight so that they would not have missed out completely.

Bill Row, the Director of Building and Services was doing a marvellous job on the restoration work. He told me that when they were stripping the paintwork they found that over the period since the building had been constructed, in some places forty five coats of paint had been applied. That meant a repainting approximately once every five years. I bet Bill two dozen golf balls that the job would not be finished on time. I suppose it is what is called a win-win situation. If I won I would not have to pay out the golf balls. If I lost I would be happy to pay out.

A prospective Lord Mayor has to buy a number of presents to be given during his year of office. These are of differing value. You are advised as to the likely number of gifts of each value that you will require. We had crystal quaichs (Scottish drinking cups), pewter tankards, prints of an old map of the ward of Aldersgate originally made for one of my predecessors in 1757, mugs with my name and coat of arms for the children's' party, coasters with my coat of arms, and Wyn had perfume sprays shaped rather like a fountain-pen. The year seemed to fly past. Sir Brian and Lady Jenkins were most helpful with their advice. Wyn, the family and all the friends whose aid we enlisted, performed magnificently. In addition to everything else Wyn had to get her wardrobe together. Although in the City of London unlike most other cities the Lady Mayoress has no official position, she is expected to play an important part in the Lord Mayor's year. Indeed it was considered essential that the Lord Mayor's wife should be suitable to be a Lady Mayoress. Hence the Senior Alderman's request to meet Wyn. For a long time bachelors and divorcees were not considered suitable to be Lord Mayor.

I have a great affection for Edinburgh and I had invited the Lord Provost and Lady Provost of Edinburgh to take part in the Lord Mayor's Show and to be guests at the Lord Mayor's Banquet. I knew that it was likely that there would be a new Lord Provost in place before the date of the Show but the invitation had been put in the Lord Provost's Diary. After the Local Government elections the two major parties could not agree on who should be the Lord Provost. Out of the blue one of the Scottish Nationalists on the Edinburgh City Council, Norman Irons, found himself elected as a compromise candidate. I have to confess that I was slightly worried. I had visions of him with a banner on the side of his carriage in the Show, saying something like 'Independence for Scotland'. I need not have worried. Norman and his wife Anne are a delightful couple. They charmed everyone that they met and did a tremendous amount to enhance the prestige of the City of Edinburgh. I was very pleased that I had invited them to take part in my Show. Norman was later honoured by Her Majesty with a CBE.

There were lists of names required for all sorts of events. Starting with the Show both going out and coming back. Because of the way that the dates fell we would not be attending the Albert Hall for the Remembrance Service. This usually occurs in the evening of the day of the Lord Mayor's Show. We decided to have a private dinner in Ironmonger Lane for members of the family and those of our guests who had come from overseas. There was a list for that. We had thought that we would have a buffet but the head steward, Peter Drury, did not approve of the idea. A proper sit-down dinner it had to be.

Then there was the Banquet itself. The Lord Mayor's Banquet is given in honour of the out-going Lord Mayor. It is held in the Guildhall. There is room for about 730 people. The Lord Mayor pays for half of the cost and the Sheriffs pay for a quarter each. Initially out of the 730 places the Lord Mayor is allocated sixty four and the Sheriffs thirty two each. (thirty two is the number of people who sit on one of the sprigs that run at right angles to the top table.) The remainder of the places are for official guests such as the Prime Minister, members of the Cabinet, members of the Court of Aldermen and members of the Common Council. Invitations to the Lord Mayor's Banquet are very much sought-after. It is a very splendid occasion. However if there are drop-outs from the official guest-list the places are allocated to the Lord Mayor and the Sheriffs in the same ratio as the original allocation. So you have to have a back-up list to be used as and when places become available. In the event I believe that I had a hundred personal guests and the Sheriffs had fifty each.

On Michaelmas Day 30th September 1992 I was elected to be the Lord Mayor for the year ensuing. This election takes place at a Common Hall held in the Great Hall of Guildhall. Common Hall is a meeting, which all Liverymen who have been Liverymen for more than twelve months are entitled to attend. The twelve months stipulation was I believe designed to prevent anyone from packing the meeting with new Liverymen so as to be elected Lord Mayor. The Clerk of each Livery Company has to submit a list of all qualified Liverymen to the Town Clerk and the beadles of the Livery Companies stand at the appropriate gate at the Guildhall to ensure that no one who is not entitled to be there can gain admission.

In practice of the 20,000 or so Liverymen approximately 1,200 turn up. They are crowded into the front part of the assembly and a few rows of seats are made available for tourists and other visitors. In the past there have been occasions when fighting has broken out between supporters of rival candidates for the Mayoralty. Today the whole atmosphere is very gentlemanly. The names of all the Aldermen who have served in the office of Sheriff but have not yet been Lord Mayor are read out in order of seniority. Seniority is determined by the date of election to the Court of Aldermen. The question is put in the form 'All those who would have Alderman 'X' as Lord Mayor for the year ensuing, please signify'. When the first name is read out, the Liverymen call out 'All! All!' When it comes to the next name they call 'Next year!' These are the two names that are placed before the whole Court of Aldermen who then choose which one is to be Lord Mayor for the year ensuing. When other names are called the Liverymen call 'Some other time!' Having spent a year as Sheriff I had some idea what I was undertaking. Nevertheless when it actually comes down to it, you become again aware of the weight of history. You know that your name will be added to those of all your predecessors that are listed on the windows around the Great Hall.

It is all done in a gentlemanly fashion but on one occasion Tommy Tucker, the Mace Bearer and Common Cryer, whose task it was to call for the vote on any resolutions to be put at Common Hall called out, 'Those in favour of the revolution, please signify.' He never lived it down. He was subsequently known to some as 'Colonel Trotsky.' In case it slipped out again he changed from saying 'resolution' to 'motion'.

In the evening of the day of the election Wyn and I were at a reception at the Chinese Embassy. There was quite a crowd there and we became separated. Later I found her talking to a member of the Embassy staff who was looking rather puzzled. Afterwards I asked Wyn what she had been talking about that had him so puzzled. She said that she had been telling him that I had my Election that morning. I roared with laughter. 'Don't you know that most Chinese have difficulty distinguishing between 'L' and 'R'?' He must have thought that you were boasting. I had now moved from being 'The Senior Alderman below the Chair' to 'Lord Mayor-Elect'.

On the 5th October 1992 it was gazetted that Her Majesty had been pleased to honour me as a Knight Grand Cross of the Most Excellent Order of the British Empire. (GBE). That was the day of the 'Presentation Ceremony'. This was the ceremony at the House of Lords where Her Majesty the Queen, through the Lord Chancellor, duly approved the choice of the citizens of London of

Alderman Francis McWilliams to be the Lord Mayor for the year ensuing. At the ceremony attended by the whole of the Court of Aldermen and a few of the Lord Mayor-Elect's relatives the Recorder of London, who is the senior resident judge at the Old Bailey, makes a speech to introduce the Lord Mayor Elect. The Lord Chancellor makes a speech conveying Her Majesty's approval. Toasts are drunk from a Loving Cup passed round those present. The Loving Cup contains a most excellent punch, the recipe for which the Lord Chancellor's staff keeps a closely guarded secret. The date set for me to go to Buckingham Palace to be knighted was 10th November.

The preparations for the Lord Mayor's banquet were speeding up. There was a wine tasting together with a trial of suggestions for the meal. We tried five different champagnes. I think that everyone with one exception chose the same one. For each course of the meal there were three or four suggestions. A small portion of each suggestion was provided. There was no consensus regarding the pudding and Wyn eventually suggested that Dick Morley, who was in charge of the catering, should ring up the 'Open Arms' in Dirleton in East Lothian and get the recipe for cranachan. This he did and produced the Ring and Brymer version, which he called 'Edinburgh Fog'. Three wines were tried for each course. It was all most enjoyable. Later at a function called 'The Lighting-up Dinner' the whole meal was tried out and details of the music and the fanfares for the banquet were agreed. The Lighting-up Dinner was brought into the preparations many years ago after a Lord Mayor and his Lady Mayoress were nearly severely burned when the torches used for lighting the hall fell off the wall behind them. The ostensible reason for the dinner was to check the lighting arrangements. I of course had a couple of pipers up on the balcony. I like pipers but I think that indoors there should be a little distance between the musicians and the audience. Everything was falling into place. Most of the items on the list of things to do had been scored off. The whole family was getting more excited as each day passed.

Then it happened!

Disaster strikes

On the 28th October 1992 Wyn drove into London from St. Albans. Among other things she wanted to buy a pair of gloves to match a green jacket that she had bought. I was going to a dinner of the Smeatonian Society of Engineers at the Institution of Civil Engineers in Great George Street Westminster in the evening. I came into London by train. We had arranged that she would park her car at the Guildhall and we would meet up there and have a cup of tea before she returned to St Albans by train. I was to drive her car to the dinner then back to St Albans afterwards. For many years now I have driven myself to and from dinners. The reason is that if I do so I drink very little. I waited in the Guildhall until I had to leave for the dinner. The car was in the car park at the Guildhall but there was no sign of Wyn. I was uneasy. It was not like Wyn to be so late.

I was having my one drink at the reception before the dinner. I looked across the room and saw Sir William Barlow pointing me out to one of the waitresses. She came over and told me that there was a phone-call for me. I felt that there was something seriously wrong and rushed out to take the call. It was Michael's wife Rowena who had returned home from Malaysia before Michael and was staying with us in St Albans. She said that she had had a call from the police to say that Wyn had been in an accident. The only information that she had was that she was in St Mary's Hospital Paddington and that they had done a brain scan and had found no damage. Now I tell Wyn that the message that I got was that they had done a brain scan and had found nothing.

In her efforts to locate me Rowena had contacted the Lord Mayor's office. They had told her to let them know when she had found me. By some clever detective work, Rowena had located me. The result was that immediately after I had put the phone down after talking to Rowena the phone rang again. It was Air Vice-Marshal Michael Dicken, the Lord Mayor's Private Secretary. He told me that I was to stay where I was. The City of London Police had sent someone to pick me up and take me to the hospital. I walked out of the door and there was a Police car waiting for me. We drove at high speed with flashing lights to the hospital.

When I entered the hospital I had no idea what to expect. Wyn was lying on a trolley. Round her nostrils and her ears there were traces of encrusted blood. She looked so pale and helpless and was deeply unconscious. They were about to take her to the intensive care unit. I followed them up. I was terrified as they hooked her up to monitoring machines and drips of various kinds. There she was with machines bleeping and drips dripping. It was like an episode of the TV series 'Casualty'. Only this was for real. When they had finished they brought a chair. I, dressed in a dinner jacket feeling absolutely useless, sat beside the bed holding Wyn's hand willing her to wake up. Finally I was persuaded to leave. They did not expect her to regain consciousness for some time. The police driver was still waiting for me. I had forgotten all about him. It was two o'clock in the morning but he offered to drive me to St Albans. I asked him to take me to where I had left Wyn's car. The next day I couldn't remember driving home. Early next morning I was back at the hospital. They assured me that Wyn was stable and that it was only a matter of time before she would wake up. I stayed there all day. I was there when they changed some of the drips. She started to cry a bit. This seemed to please the medical staff. They said that it was a sign that she was regaining consciousness. By the next day word had got round the City that Wyn had been in an accident. A report of the accident also appeared in the newspapers. Messages and flowers started to arrive. Before long Wyn's bed was surrounded by baskets and bouquets. On the third day I was there when they were changing the drips. Wyn screamed in agony. I could not stand it and had to leave the ward.

By the fourth day she was showing signs of restlessness and seemed to be nearing consciousness. Father Robert Plourde, our priest from St Albans, came as soon as he heard. He prayed beside her bed. The late Rev. Eric Evans, Dean of St Paul's Cathedral, also came to pray for Wyn's recovery. I believe that both in St Albans and in St Paul's prayers were said for her every day until Wyn came out of hospital. Mr D W Dowlen, the Master of the Worshipful

Company of Gardeners, Wyn's Livery Company, told me later that prayers were also said for her at the start of their Court meeting. He said that some of the members were in tears when they heard of Wyn's accident.

Douglas, Ianthe, and Rowena were a great support. I do not know how I would have coped without them. Rowena had phoned Michael in Malaysia. He was due home the following week but wanted to fly home straightaway. We told him to carry on with the arrangements that he had already made. On the fourth day while I was sitting by Wyn's bed to my great relief she finally opened her eyes. The nurse who was nearby said, 'Ask her a mundane question to see how she responds.' I asked Wyn if she knew the name of the Prime Minister. She seemed to think that it was a silly sort of question and she muttered 'John Major'. I then asked her what kind of computer she had. A bit irritably she replied 'an Amstrad' and promptly went back to sleep. The nurse was delighted. She said that it confirmed that Wyn had suffered no brain damage.

Later when they were changing her drips Wyn screamed in pain again and called out, 'Don't let them do this to me.' I'm afraid that I was almost sick on the ward. When Wyn had settled down again I told her that Her Majesty's Private Secretary and the Prime Minister's Private Secretary had both phoned the hospital to find out how she was. She asked why they were interested in her. She clearly had little recollection of who I was or who she was. I tell her that she expressed considerable disappointment when she discovered that I was her husband because she had been hoping that one of the handsome young doctors was her husband.

I was due to go to a meeting in the Guildhall on the following day. Douglas felt that it would be a good thing to attend because it would reassure people in the City that Wyn was recovering. As she was now out of danger Wyn was removed to a private room. They brought enough flowers to fill the room. The rest they put round the hospital. Douglas reminded me to collect the cards attached to the flowers so that I could thank those who had sent them. For the rest of her stay in hospital, flowers continued to arrive daily. We had a system that when a new basket arrived we would remove one of the existing baskets. I think that nearly every ward in the hospital had flowers that had originally come to Wyn. Also as the news got round we received many lovely letters.

When Michael arrived home he and Rowena brought grandson Christopher aged three and a half to see Wyn. It so happened that Wyn had been told that she should get out of bed and take a short walk along the corridor. Christopher led her along the corridor and back to the room. The following morning, he got up early and told his parents that he had to go to the hospital because 'Grandpa said that I was to take Grandma for a walk'.

As is common with such accidents where the victim is concussed Wyn cannot remember anything immediately before the accident. She can remember what happened before she left St. Albans but nothing thereafter. The police could find no witnesses who could say exactly what had happened. It appears that the motorcycle, a 1000cc Kawasaki, had come across Oxford Street and knocked Wyn over. According to the police sergeant, the young man who had been riding the motorcycle was very distressed. I told the sergeant to let the lad know that Wyn was recovering. Now the only things that she can remember about her stay in hospital are my questions about the Prime Minister and her computer and Christopher taking her for a walk. She has a partial impairment to her hearing but apart from that has fortunately suffered no after-effects from the accident. Later as Lady Mayoress she returned to the hospital to thank the nurses and to give them souvenirs of her stay.

The Lord Mayor's Show and The Lord Mayor's Banquet

People who attend functions and ceremonies in the City of London are often amazed at the way everything seems to go like clockwork. The secret is of course planning and rehearsal. Everyone involved in an event receives in advance a copy of the programme for the occasion. They are summoned by the City's Remembrancer Adrian Barnes to appear at a given time to carry out the practice for the event. The action will be carried out as many times as are needed to get it right. The whole ceremony will be timed to within about 10 seconds.

Standing at the entrance to the Guildhall, awaiting the arrival of a member of the Royal family or a visiting Head of State is a bit like a count down for a NASA rocket-launch. There will be a two-minute warning. One minute. Then 30 seconds. Adrian stands about 6 feet 6 inches tall. When he is formally dressed complete with wig and gown he looks even taller. He and his staff have great expertise in all aspects of organising highly complicated and sensitive events. Food, wine, music and flowers—they know it all. Even more importantly they know all about protocol. This is especially important when dealing with foreign Heads of State. At 05.30 hours, on the morning of the Wednesday before the Lord Mayor's Show there is a rehearsal. The present Golden Coach was built in 1757. It has been refurbished several times since. It is difficult to know how much of it is original and how much is of later addition but I believe that the last refurbishment was in 1952. The coach is brought out of the Museum of London, where it is stored in temperature and humidity controlled conditions. Normally the Lady Mayoress gets a chance to ride in the coach at the rehearsal but Wyn, to her great disappointment, was, of course, still in St Mary's hospital.

Christopher came with me to the rehearsal. Somehow the news that he was coming leaked to the press. The result was that there were lovely photographs of Christopher on the steps of the coach, Christopher leaning out of the window of the coach and Christopher patting the huge dray horses that are provided by Whitbread's to pull the coach. The horses used to be stabled at the brewery in Chiswell Street, which has now been closed. I presume that they are now kept at the Whitbread farm in Kent where they used to grow the hops. Although we were sad that Wyn was not there to share it, Christopher and I enjoyed the morning. We went from the Guildhall to St. Paul's Cathedral. The rehearsal concluded with a huge traditional English breakfast at the Hall of the Worshipful Company of Butchers.

Wyn had continued to make good progress and after the Breakfast some ten days after the accident I was allowed to take her home. It was quite an astonishing recovery. I took Wyn back to St Albans where Father Robert was waiting for us. Never were prayers of thanksgiving said with more fervour.

The Installation Lunch given by the existing Lord Mayor, Sir Brian Jenkins, for me as his successor took place on Friday 13th November. The date did not bother me. Wyn's accident had already taken care of the bad luck associated with such a date. Some members of my family were in accordance with custom invited. Poor Wyn was in the Ironmonger Lane house in bed. The members of the Lord Mayor and Sheriffs Committee including the Master of the Worshipful Company of Loriners, HRH the Princess Royal, also attended the lunch. Douglas and Michael and my brother John and the representatives of the Sheriffs Roger Cork and Tony Moss were also members of the Committee. After the lunch they all left for the Guildhall where they were to escort the Lord Mayor-Elect into the Silent Ceremony.

The Silent Ceremony when the Lord Mayor-Elect takes up office is very moving and very impressive. The Ceremony takes place in semi-darkness in the Guildhall. Apart from the new Lord Mayor being sworn in everything else is done in silence. The various symbols of office are presented to the new incumbent who signifies acceptance by touching the Sword, the Mace and the Purse. The Mace, which is probably of 15th century origin, consists of a rock crystal shaft with gold mountings and a gold head, which is decorated with pearls and jewels. The Chamberlain, Bernard Harty, told me that he became worried about presenting the Mace on a cushion in case it fell off and was broken. He had it valued eight or nine years ago at over a million pounds. Apart from the Silent Ceremony, the only other time that the Mace is brought out is when the Lord Mayor carries it at the Coronation of a monarch.

The Lord Mayor also signs a document running to twenty three pages acknowledging receipt of the Ceremonial Gowns and all the gold and silver plate normally stored at the Mansion House. This includes Loving Cups, Vases, Trays, Table Ornaments and all the knives, forks, and spoons. I did not have the chance to count them. The weights of the various items are given in ounces. The Lord Mayor also accepts receipt of the Mayoral badge which is described as follows: 'A Diamond Badge, representing the Rose, Shamrocks and Thistle with an onyx in the centre; engraved with the City Arms and surrounded by a Garter and the City Motto in rose diamonds; the number of diamonds exclusive of those in the Motto is 254. Collar of SS with fourteen pairs of enamelled red and white roses in fine gold'. The Badge is said to weigh 36ozs. The Collar was given to the City by the will of Sir John Alen who had been Lord Mayor in 1525-26 and 1535-36. There is no record of when it was made. It has been suggested that it belonged to Sir Thomas More and that Sir John Alen purchased it from Henry the Eighth who had confiscated it when Sir Thomas More was executed. There are two duplicates of the Collar and the Badge.

When travelling outside the City the Lord Mayor wears one of the duplicates. Sir Brian Jenkins said that when he visited South Africa, the diamond merchants there could tell at 30 paces that he was wearing a copy of the real badge.

During the ceremony I changed from being 'The Lord Mayor-Elect', to being 'The Lord Mayor'. My predecessor Sir Brian Jenkins became 'The Late Lord Mayor'. When the Silent Ceremony was over the Late Lord Mayor and his Lady Mayoress Anne returned to Ironmonger Lane with me. Wyn was already there. Rowena and Christopher had brought her there from St Albans. We all had tea together then in accordance with custom the Private Secretary came and announced that the staff were waiting to say farewell to Brian and Anne. They took their leave at the end of a highly successful year of office. Wyn weak and thin as a needle, and I, weary with worry, took over as the 665th Lord Mayor and Lady Mayoress of the City of London.

I suppose that, because most of my recent predecessors were considerably younger than I was their children were also younger than ours. In our case Douglas and Ianthe, and Michael and Rowena, were able to play a meaningful supporting role in the Mayoral activities. Douglas's help in the run-up to the Mayoral year had been invaluable. His management approach to the many tasks to be performed had enabled Wyn and I to deal with them in a logical manner without becoming too fussed. Our 'up' days and 'down' days philosophy which had evolved from the time that we bought our first house also helped to avoid us becoming upset when things did not turn out exactly as planned.

The original purpose of the Lord Mayor's Show was to enable the citizens of London to see the new Lord Mayor as he made his way to be presented to the Barons of the Exchequer at Westminster to be sworn in. Certainly there has been a Show of some sort since the 14th century. Initially the Lord Mayor and the Court of Aldermen rode on horseback. Later the Pageant went by river. There were magnificent barges owned by the City Corporation and the Livery Companies. That is why the various vehicles in the Lord Mayor's Show are called 'floats'.

The day of the Show arrived. Father Robert and I went across to St Lawrence Jewry where he said a Mass in thanksgiving for Wyn's recovery and to pray for a successful year.

The Princess Royal had made it clear to everyone that she was in the Show as Master of the Worshipful Company of Loriners. Accordingly she was to be treated as the Master of the Lord Mayor's mother Company. She was, as usual, dedicated to carrying out her duties. She did not want any mix-up as a member of the Royal Family. Before the Show there is a very personal ceremony that takes place in the Crypt of the Guildhall. The various organisations with which the Lord Mayor and Sheriffs are involved present them with Scrolls or with mementoes. I was very fortunate. The Master Loriner, the Princess Royal presented me with a pair of spurs mounted on a wooden plinth. This was designed by the late Past-master Dr. James White. The Master Engineer John Bartlett presented me with a replica of the Ironbridge that spans the Severn Gorge in Shropshire. Ironbridge represents the beginnings of the Industrial Revolution in Britain. The memento was particularly appropriate in view of the theme for my year of 'The City and Industry in Partnership'. The Master Arbitrator Ron Mildred presented me with a lovely silver Armada dish. The Master Plaisterer the late Fred Warren presented me with a beautiful Tantalus containing three crystal decanters, which can be locked in so that 'the servants cannot get at the liquor.' Wyn would normally have been in the show in a carriage with the outgoing Lady Mayoress and her daughter. This was in the circumstances impossible, so she watched the Show on television in Ironmonger Lane. Originally the idea had been that in the carriage Wyn would have been accompanied on the outward journey by Ianthe and on the return journey by Rowena. Now the two girls made both journeys. The programme indicated that the Lady Mayoress would be accompanied by a daughter-in-law each way. The girls said that they could hear people asking which of them was the Lady Mayoress.

The programme for the Lord Mayor's Show is an important item. The proceeds from its sale are applied to the Lord Mayor's Charities. We were very fortunate that a good friend of Douglas, Nigel Bance, agreed to produce it. The result was superb. The cover was colourful and imaginatively depicted my theme. Apart from giving details of the order of the floats it contained a number of interesting articles, among which was a well-researched piece on the history of my ward of Aldersgate written by my friend Bill Linton. I was delighted with the programme and Nigel's innovative approach and connections made sure that it made a real contribution to the Charities. You need a lot of help. Wyn and I were fortunate to have Douglas and Ianthe, Michael and Rowena, and many friends.

One of the items in the Show was The Donkey Society, which was celebrating its 25th Anniversary. There were about twenty lovely donkeys ridden by children. We had been warned that horses do not like donkeys so we had to ensure that horses and donkeys were kept well away from each other. The most spectacular float in the Show was that put in by my Malaysian friends. Malaysian Airlines and the Malaysian Tourist Board sponsored the float. Over three thousand orchids were flown in from Malaysia. There were Malaysian dancers and musicians on the float. It was magnificent. At the end of the Show they gave away the orchids. I believe that people were leaving with their arms full of beautiful exotic flowers. By common consent the Show was extremely successful.

The BBC coverage of the Show was good and they had brought in some new ideas. However, a few days after the Show I received a letter from a lady who is an 'Agony Aunt' in a newspaper. She said that she had watched the Show on television and, because of all its military units, it appeared to her to be like an October Revolution Parade in Moscow's Red Square. Nothing could have been further from the truth. The Show had been a happy fun occasion. At first I was incensed. I did however write her a polite letter inviting her to come and discuss the matter. She did not reply. Subsequently I looked at a video of the BBC transmission. I could see what she meant. The BBC, although they had given the Show good coverage, seemed to be reluctant to show the floats sponsored by commercial organisations unless they were connected with a Charity. This resulted in an over-emphasis of the military bands and units of the armed forces. They missed quite a lot of the fun and jollity of the event.

For me and I suspect for many of those watching the broadcast of the Show the most moving part of the proceedings was the arrival of the Lord Mayor on the steps of St Paul's Cathedral. When I arrived the Choir sang an anthem. The delightful Dean the late Eric Evans was there to greet me. After he had enquired about Wyn I knelt and he laid his hands on my head. He prayed that I would be granted the wisdom to carry out the task ahead and presented me with a copy of the Bible with the wish that it would provide me with the guidance that I would need.

The outward procession on reaching the Law Courts in the Strand takes a break. Here the participants are fed. This is one of the Show expenses. The WVS undertakes the feeding. They provide food and hot drinks for some 4000 people. Some years it has been bitterly cold and hot drinks have been an absolute necessity. In 1992 it was not too bad but it rained a little towards the end.

The Lord Mayor, the Members of the Court of Aldermen and a small number of relatives of the Lord Mayor make their way to the Courtroom of the Lord Chief Justice. There the Recorder of London introduces the new Lord Mayor to the Lord Chief Justice and the two other judges on the bench. The Lord Chief Justice then makes a speech welcoming the new Lord Mayor. The speeches that are made are always very clever and amusing. In my case the Lord Chief Justice referred to my careers as an Engineer and then in the law as a barrister and Arbitrator.

He said that my first career was spent building sewers and my second suing builders!

In front of the Lord Chief Justice the Lord Mayor signs a document swearing allegiance to the Monarch. After a similar visit to the courtroom of the Master of the Rolls there is time for a sandwich and a quick drink before the return procession to the Mansion House for lunch. In my case the lunch was in the Guildhall.

Wyn having watched the BBC broadcast of the Show came in a wheelchair to the Guildhall. We had lunch with the Princess Royal. She appeared to have enjoyed taking part in the Show. Referring to the proximity of Wyn's accident to my taking office the Princess said, 'I suppose the timing could have been worse but not much.' The Lord Mayor has to go round greeting the many guests. Everyone was pleased to see Wyn and she was surrounded with well-wishers. It was Michael who saw that it was wearing her out and wheeled her back to Ironmonger Lane.

During the lunch Owen Kelly the Commissioner of the City of London Police told me that on the Friday night, the evening before the Show, a lorry loaded with explosives had been brought into the City. The security was so tight that the driver had been afraid to stop. The lorry had been followed up to Hampstead where the driver and his mate abandoned the lorry. They were subsequently arrested. It was a near miss. I could have had a disaster on my hands right at the start of my Mayoralty. There was not much time between the end of

Sir Francis and Lady McWilliams, St Andrew's Night 1971
with two pipers from British Caledonian Airways Pipe Band

The wedding
of engineer
V Mahalingham
and his wife
Vimala

Receiving the sword at the first ceremony for installation as a Dato'

Her Majesty Queen Elizabeth the Queen Mother arrives for the Reception for Far East Prisoners

Sir Francis McWilliams dressed for his appearance at the Privy Council

Sir Francis and Lady McWilliams on the left, with Their Royal Highnesses The Sultan and Tengu Ampuan Selangor (centre), and other Royal Dato's and their wives, 1973

The Mayoral Party for the Lord Mayor's Banquet

Back row: Father Robert, Col John Ansell, Very Rev Peter Moore,
Col Tommy Tucker, Col Mark Carnegie-Brown
Seated: Alderman & Sheriff Roger Cork, Barbara Cork, Sir Francis, Lady Winifred,
Jennifer Moss, Sheriff Tony Moss

The Lord Mayor's Staff at Ironmonger Lane

The Lord Provost Of Edinburgh's Team
verus
The Lord Mayor Of London's Team

Group photograph taken at the breakfast organised
by Eric Milligan for former pupils of Holy Cross Academy

the lunch and the beginning of the fireworks display. Before the fireworks I had to visit the funfair that was set up in Paternoster Square. I am not a great lover of rides that go round about and up and down and usually finish up by being sick. I had to show willing for the sake of the press so I took a short ride on one of the roundabouts and I managed to retain my lunch.

The fireworks display on the Thames was sponsored by a firm DTW Advertising and Marketing and was staged by Standard Brock Fireworks. It was magnificent. I started it off by firing a Verey pistol. The fireworks were on a barge anchored in the middle of the river and we watched the display from HQS Wellington. Wellington is in fact the Livery Hall of the Honourable Company of Master Mariners. It is moored at Temple Steps on the Embankment.

It was then back to Ironmonger Lane for the dinner that we had arranged for the family and our overseas guests. Poor Wyn was so exhausted that she had to retire to bed and missed a very enjoyable party. When it was over my sister Isobel, well into her seventies, decided that she wanted to fulfil a lifetime's ambition to visit Ronnie Scott's Jazz Club. She persuaded Douglas and Ianthe, my nephew Michael Harris from Australia, and Sarah O'Malley from Ireland, to go with her. Apparently she got back to the hotel at four o' clock in the morning.

Next morning there was a Remembrance Day service at St Paul's. I took the salute at a March-past of War veterans.

Monday morning started with a rehearsal for the Banquet to be held that evening. Announcements, fanfares and processions were rehearsed and timed so that everyone knew where they should be at any particular time.

The Lady Mayoress is expected to appear at most of the functions in the Lord Mayor's Diary suitably dressed. This requires a considerable number of evening dresses, cocktail dresses and daytime suits. It is inadvisable to pop along to a major store to buy anything off the peg. You may find yourself in a receiving line, greeting someone wearing the same dress. That would be most embarrassing. Wyn had some lovely clothes made. Of course the most beautiful was the gown for the Lord Mayor's Banquet with a cream-coloured brocade skirt and separate wine-coloured velvet top, specially designed by a lady who lived near St Albans. To me, it looked exactly right for the occasion. She looked gorgeous. The dressmaker was invited to come along to the Guildhall on the evening of the Lord Mayor's Banquet to see her handiwork. Wyn had lost a stone and a half in weight as a result of the accident and unfortunately there was not time to alter the dress. For the Banquet it had to be pinned at the waist. Wyn said that it was a good job that her mother was not there to see it. She would have been mortified. Michael Evans, Wyn's hairdresser from St Albans, was also invited. After doing Wyn's hair he stayed on to attend the Banquet.

In the afternoon we all got dressed up for a photographic session. We were very pleased with the photographs especially those taken with the boys, Ianthe and Rowena, and Christopher. It was then back to the Ironmonger Lane for a quick cup of tea.

The Lord Mayor has two special robes. One is the black and gold for the big occasions such as the official Banquets. The other, crimson with ermine trimmings similar to the robes of an Earl, is worn when Her Majesty the Queen or another Head of State is being entertained on a 'State' occasion. For the Lord Mayor's Banquet it was the black and gold robe.

Suitably dressed I returned to the Guildhall. I stood on the dais in the Old Library and greeted the special guests. Members of the Lord Mayor and Sheriffs' Committee escorted them up. Because she felt that her presence might cause protocol difficulties, Her Royal Highness the Princess Royal reluctantly decided not to attend the Lord Mayor's Banquet where the Prime Minister was the guest of honour. When the time for his arrival drew near we formed a procession and I left the dais to go and greet the Prime Minister. We had agreed that Wyn would not have to stand beside me to greet the arriving guests. She came along later to come in with the Prime Minister, John Major, while I escorted the Prime Minister's wife Norma. After photographs, Wyn then returned to Ironmonger Lane and came back to the Guildhall for the speeches.

When Wyn appeared, the applause was deafening. I was told afterwards, that many of the Members of the Common Council and their wives were in tears. They were so relieved to see her. Wyn was I believe a particularly popular Lady Mayoress. Her accident had been a great shock to the Members. After the other guests were seated, with the guest of honour, and Mrs Major, the Sheriffs, Alderman Roger Cork and his late wife Barbara and Tony Moss and his wife Jennifer, I processed into the Great Hall of Guildhall. The meal that we had chosen was excellent. The wines also went down well. Wyn arrived back at the Guildhall in her wheelchair and slipped in beside John Major. The order of the speeches remains the same each year. After the toasts to Her Majesty the Queen and the Royal family there comes the moment of truth. If he gets it right the new Lord Mayor will set his year of office going with a momentum that will carry forward. If he gets it wrong it is very difficult to get back on track. Fortunately most Lord Mayors get it more or less right. I remembered the advice given to me by one of my predecessors as Chieftain of the Selangor St. Andrew's Society. He said 'Remember that the audience wants you to do well. They are on your side.'

The lights in the Guildhall dimmed. The signal was given. The drummers of the Household cavalry resplendent in their cloth-of-gold tabards gave a loud attention-grabbing roll on their drums. This was followed immediately by a fanfare by four equally resplendent trumpeters and an echo fanfare by another four who were picked out by a spotlight as they stood on the gallery between the figures of the mythical giants Gog and Magog.

Bernard Sullivan MBE, the doyen of City toast-masters with a panache that comes from officiating at hundreds of great Banquets, imperiously commanded, 'Pray silence for the Right Honourable the Lord Mayor, Sir Francis McWilliams Knight Grand Cross Of the Most Excellent Order of the British Empire, Fellow of the Royal Academy of Engineering, Doctor of Civil Laws!' I was on. The buzz of conversation ceased. There was an expectant hush. I rose to my feet and in accordance with City custom there was a burst of enthusiastic applause. The enthusiasm was helped by the presence at the Banquet of some of my relatives and friends from around the world. Australia, Malaysia, Canada, Ireland, United States and Continental Europe were all represented. There was also a 'Tartan Army' of my Scottish relatives. I smiled as I looked round the glittering assembly. There were tiaras, stars, medals and sashes in great profusion and colourful national costumes worn by my friends from Malaysia. The magnificent gold and silver table decorations glowing in the candlelight and superb floral displays of Malaysian orchids, added to the atmosphere of opulence and splendour.

I started by thanking everyone for the way that they had received Wyn and for all the messages of sympathy that we had received. This drew a great burst of sympathetic applause. I had been afraid that my voice would shake with emotion at that point and had to make a conscious effort to control it. Once I had that bit out of the way I carried on quite confidently. I had expected to be very nervous. I am sure that the emotion of the first bit left me with little room to be nervous.

The Banquet was a great success. My brother and sisters could not believe that their 'Wee Brother' was capable of standing up in front of the 'Great and the Good' of the country and acquitting himself so well. I suppose that I was just as surprised. After the Banquet the Prime Minister and Mrs Major, the Lord Chancellor and Lady MacKay and a number of other guests were invited back to Ironmonger Lane for a nightcap. They all seemed to have enjoyed the evening. I found the Majors to be a very nice couple. I was however disappointed that the Prime Minister did not appear to have the kind of vision that I expected. He seemed to be too concerned with short-term matters. Perhaps I expected too much. Certainly out of office he has appeared to be more statesmanlike than he appeared in office. We found the other principal guests were very easy to get on with, especially the Lord Chancellor James Mackay and his wife Beth.

Starting the Mayoral Year

One of my predecessors Sir Anthony Jolliffe GBE once said, 'After six weeks as Lord Mayor you have to keep telling yourself that you are not, repeat not, Lord God Almighty. Everyone treats you as though you were.' In the City the Lord Mayor outranks everyone apart from Her Majesty the Queen herself. Only Her Majesty walks on the Lord Mayor's right in a procession in the City. Everyone else walks on his left. Outside the City he ranks after Earls. When the Monarch dies the Lord Mayor is summoned to the Privy Council to sign the Proclamation of the Successor. Indeed, the name of Robert Lee, who was Lord Mayor at the time, heads the proclamation when James VI of Scotland was proclaimed as James I of the combined kingdoms. It is no wonder that occasionally a Lord Mayor becomes a bit pompous.

Wyn and I had our first contact with a Lord Mayor and Sheriffs in Malaysia when we were invited to a reception at the British High Commissioner's residence. We both formed the impression that they were all extremely pompous. I suppose that the clothes do not help. Velvet suits and lace ruffles can give the appearance of pomposity. The newspapers often refer to the Aldermen and the Lord Mayor as 'Wearing Funny Clothes' or 'Wearing Silly Clothes'. I have to confess that I never felt self-conscious about wearing them. I found that people like the Lord Mayor to look like a Lord Mayor. Provided that he does not come across as a pompous twit, they are happy.

The staff at Ironmonger Lane had moved over from the Mansion House when it closed. Their objective was to make the Lord Mayor's busy life as smooth as possible. They were especially attentive to Wyn. Her memories of the Show, the lunch afterwards, and the banquet are blurred. Fortunately we have a video of the Show and recordings of the speeches at the banquet. One of our Aldermen was John Chalstrey who was a surgeon at St Bartholomew's Hospital. He was very attentive to Wyn. He made sure that his colleagues in the various specialities examined her. As a result of their treatment Wyn was soon raring to get involved in everything. She very quickly told the staff that they were to stop telling people that she could not attend functions with me. She also wanted to get started on a programme of her own.

Lord Mayor's lives have become busier and busier in recent years. We have become more active in promoting initiatives, which we believe affect the future of the Financial City. A favourite way of such promotion is 'the Business Breakfast'. We found that the easiest way of getting together high-powered businessmen and women for a discussion was to invite them to breakfast. Breakfasts at Ironmonger Lane were the real thing with bacon, eggs, mushrooms, kidneys etc. I held such breakfasts throughout my year of office. On trips abroad the Lord Mayor acts as an ambassador for the Financial City. Where possible business people are included in the party and destinations for overseas visits are decided after consultation with the business community, the Foreign Office and other interested parties. For diplomatic purposes, the Lord Mayor, when he travels overseas, ranks as a Cabinet Minister. In most places a visit to the Head of State is obligatory. The City as one of the world's great financial centres lives or dies on the strength of its communications. One of the reasons for the location of London was that it was the site of the first bridge across the Thames. Later it became the junction of a number of routes. Our engineer's department did a computer study, which showed that The Mansion House is the most accessible point in London by means of public transport. There was no suggestion, however that the Lord Mayor should abandon the stretched Rolls Royce for the Number 10 bus.

In modern terms 'Communications', in addition to the convenience for people getting to and from work means telecommunications. This embraces telephones, the Internet and all the rapidly growing aspects of e-commerce. We had numerous discussions regarding transport policy with those who had influence in the industry. Here I was very fortunate that, as well as my own engineering understanding of the technical aspects of the subject, Douglas has a deep knowledge and understanding of the economic aspects of transportation.

The City was foremost in promoting the advantages of the Jubilee Line Extension and Crossrail. It is not surprising that the City supported Ken Livingstone, the Mayor of London, in his desire to improve the performance of London Transport. For the City, it is not a matter of convenience; it is a matter of survival in the face of increasing competition from New York, Tokyo and Europe. Commuter routes and the Underground System are for the City top priority. One of the messages that we had to keep hammering home was that, if financial business leaves the City, it would most likely end up in either New York or Tokyo. Other Europeans seem to think that they can move it to Paris or Frankfurt.

I saw my role as ambassador for the Financial City. During my year as Lord Mayor I became more and more convinced that there was a need for a voice to speak for the whole of London. I have however never been convinced that the case had been made for the system that has been adopted. Since no Government of any complexion in this country would wish to have a challenging, powerful figure on their doorstep after the fashion of Mr. Chirac in Paris or Mr. Guiliani in New York, the power of the Mayor for London was bound to be circumscribed. It did not seem to make sense to go through all the problems of taking the choice of the voice for London away from the boroughs, which are the basis of Local Government in London. It would have made more sense to ask the boroughs to elect from among their members delegates to an electoral college. They could then have elected one of their number to be the voice for the whole of London. The system adopted gave the impression that the Mayor with his vast electorate was to be a very powerful figure. Central Government however wishes to continue to exercise control. But Mayor Livingstone, as he showed when he was Chairman of the GLC, is a past master at using public funds to bolster his own ego and to upset Central Government. There has been talk of Court cases by the Mayor against the Government. The Financial City is extremely worried that such disputes will delay much-needed improvements to the transport system. When I was in office we had hoped that when a revaluation was done for the purposes of the Uniform Business Rate there would be scope to put in place a transport levy to upgrade the Underground System. Unfortunately when the revaluation came, they reduced the values but put up the rate. In any case the Treasury considered that the scheme would be 'hypothecation', one of the dirtiest words in the Treasury's vocabulary. All it means is raising a tax for a specific purpose. In effect the Uniform Business Rate is already hypothecated revenue.

In the year before I took office I had lost seven pounds in weight by cutting out toast at breakfast. Unsurprisingly within six weeks of the start of my Mayoralty I had put it back on. I decided to cut out bread and potatoes. The day I decided to do this we were guests of the Lord Mayor of Westminster for lunch. The menu included the most delicious looking 'Rosti' potatoes that I have seen. As they came round the table I was trying to decide whether it would do any harm if I postponed my new regime until the following day. I decided that if I could resist this delicious cooking it would be much easier to resist more ordinary potatoes in the future. Throughout the rest of the year I stuck to my plan. By the end of the year in spite of eating puddings and after-dinner sweets I did not put on another ounce. In this I was fortunate. One of my predecessors started his year of office wearing a sixteen and a half inch collar and finished with an eighteen-inch collar.

The Lord Mayor's life is busy. If there is no breakfast meeting the day starts with the briefing regarding the day's events. After that it is all go. The greatest number of events that I attended in one day was twelve. That was the day that I made six speeches. The speechwriter, Wing Commander Robbie Robinson, would prepare the drafts of the speeches and I would add the personal touches. Robbie loved puns. I gave him strict orders not to put them into my speeches but I believe that towards the end of my year he managed to slip one in. I did not notice it.

When I was not opening things, inaugurating events, or meeting members of the Royal family, visiting the City, I was lunching with the City institutions such as Lloyd's or the Baltic Exchange. There were also lunches with the Ward Clubs. We also tried to make the foreign banks feel at home with us. There are over 150 of them in the City. I visited a number of them. At one bank our host decided to show us their foreign exchange operation. He said, 'I'll buy 20 million US dollars worth of yen.' He then placed the order on his screen. Almost immediately the message came back that he had purchased some phenomenal amount of yen. I hope that he had a need for them.

I visited one of the Japanese banks with Tony Moss who was the Lay Sheriff. We were having lunch and the conversation was all about golf. Both the Chairman and the Chief Executive were keen golfers. Tony suggested that I tell one of the golf stories that I was in the habit of including in my speeches at Livery Dinners when I knew that the Master was a keen golfer. I told Tony that he had heard them often enough to know them off by heart. He made a brave try but the one he chose, to be really credible requires a Scottish accent and also a British sense of humour. I know this because I had told it to an American and finished up explaining what it was about. Although the Japanese laughed heartily I was doubtful if they really appreciated it. One of the offices that the Lord Mayor holds is Chancellor of City University. When I was installed they conferred on me an Honorary Degree of Doctor of Civil Law. Later I received an Honorary Doctorate of Engineering from Kingston University.

My old Alma Mater the University of Edinburgh made me a Doctor Honoris Causa. I was also elected a Fellow of the City and Guilds Institute and a Member of the Guildhall School of Music and Drama. Giving Degree Certificates at University Convocations was for me an enjoyable duty. The pride of the parents in their children's achievement reminded me of my own parents' pride when they came to see me receive my certificate in the McEwan Hall in Edinburgh and the pride that Wyn and I felt in our own sons' achievements. I decided that in order to make it more meaningful for the recipients, I would try to address them by name as they came forward. Thus I would say, 'Well done! George or Jane or Ganesh.' At one of the ceremonies an academic sitting close by said, 'Nobody has ever done that before. How did you do it?' I told him that while I was handing over one certificate I was listening to the announcement of the next one. It worked quite well except for some of the more exotic foreign names. I found Nigerian names to be the most difficult.

School prize-givings were also interesting. Some of the children would look you straight in the eye and say, 'Thank you sir.' Others would shuffle up, grab the prize, and shuffle off without looking at you at all. Teachers should ensure that their pupils have enough confidence in themselves to look people in the eye on such occasions. In one school the senior boys had voted to have the model Naomi Campbell give away the prizes. The school decided that their funds would not run to it. Lord Mayors come free. I am sure that the boys would have sacrificed other activities to have the lovely Miss Campbell instead of a boring Lord Mayor.

One day the Secretary of the Institution of Civil Engineers, Roger Dobson, phoned me. He said that the previous evening the Council of the Institution had decided to elect me an Honorary Fellow. For the first time in many years I blushed. I said that I thought that such an honour was only for those engineers who were regarded as being very distinguished in the profession or were non-engineers who had performed great service to the profession. Roger assured me that my fellow engineers felt that I had brought honour to the profession of civil engineer by taking on the prestigious office of Lord Mayor of London. When I finally retired from the Court of Aldermen and no longer needed my Shrieval chain and badge I gave it to the Institution on permanent loan. It is exhibited at the Institution in Great George Street. I hope that it will inspire other engineers to play a role in public affairs and thus enhance the standing of engineers in the community. If any of my descendants ever becomes a Sheriff of the City of London he or she will be able to borrow it back.

Another of the titles held by the Lord Mayor is Admiral of the Port of London. The Commanders of foreign ships arriving in London usually called on the Lord Mayor and invited him to pay a visit to their ships. Knowing the delicate nature of my intestinal organs I always declined visits afloat.

The first great function of my year was at the Guildhall, hosting a luncheon to celebrate the Fortieth Anniversary of Her Majesty the

Queen's Accession to the Throne. This was the famous 'Annus Horribilis' lunch. It was on 24th November 1992, shortly after the fire at Windsor Castle. In the morning before the lunch the Palace phoned to ask if I would mind if the speeches were made before the start of the meal. Her Majesty had a throat infection and it was thought that she would be more comfortable if she could get the speeches out of the way. I of course had no objection. For this occasion I wore the scarlet robe with the ermine at the top. Members of the House of Lords wear a similar robe on formal occasions. I felt that it made me look as though I was ten foot tall. I waited with Wyn and the Sheriffs and their ladies for the Royal Guests at the entrance to the Guildhall. It was a beautiful day and pale autumnal sun was shining on us as we waited. The first thing the Duke of Edinburgh said as he alighted from the car was, 'You look magnificent standing there.'

The question of what to give Her Majesty as a present had caused much discussion. It was considered that we should try to make it something personal to her. What do you give to someone who can have anything that they want? Eventually after some delicate questioning, it was agreed that we should have a painting done of Her Majesty's favourite horses. This turned out extremely well. After the usual formalities of signing the guest-book and introducing the Sheriffs and their ladies, Wyn and I escorted Her Majesty and the Duke into the Old Library. The painting was handed over and Her Majesty was delighted. We then processed into the Great Hall of The Guildhall. The other guests were already seated. Bernard Sullivan was officiating as usual on these State occasions. Immediately after the Grace he got things under way by calling for silence for the Right Honourable the Lord Mayor. I am sure that the guests were a bit puzzled. To me it felt a bit strange starting off speaking after the Grace instead of after the Coffee. We had decided that as this was Her Majesty's day my speech would be quite short. I did however tell her about the garden that I had created in Malacca to celebrate her Coronation nearly forty years before.

The Queen was wearing dark green and what with the throat infection and the smoke from the fire at Windsor Castle Her

Majesty's voice had a terrible croak. The result of the combination was that the television coverage made it appear that it was a very dull and drab occasion. Her Majesty was I think slightly nervous. She was well aware that she was departing from tradition by making such a personal speech. We were all certainly aware that it was apart from the historical standpoint a very special occasion. It showed Her Majesty revealing her inner thoughts in a way that had not been done before. On many subsequent occasions a clip of the lunch has been shown on television. It always looks quite sombre.

In fact it was a very happy occasion. Once the speeches were out of the way Her Majesty relaxed. She was in great form. She is one of those people whose face lights up when she smiles. Her eyes sparkle. She is very adept at telling photographers when to take pictures and from where to take them. John Major who was on the other side of me was also enjoying a spell away from the cares of office. Wyn was seated between the HRH the Duke of Edinburgh and Lord Wakeham. She said afterwards that it had been a laugh a minute. Wyn had been talking to the Duke about the Princess Royal being in the Lord Mayor's Show. He said that he had been Master of a Livery Company but that he had never been invited to take part in the Show. He thought that he would have enjoyed it. Wyn explained that the Princess Royal was Master of my mother Livery Company and had thus a right to take part in the Show. Her Majesty and the Duke both said how much they had enjoyed the Lunch. I heard later from a friend who had attended a meeting at Buckingham Palace that same afternoon that the Duke had said what a great party it had been.

The letter, which I received from the Queen's Private Secretary, Robert Fellowes, afterwards was most complimentary. He said that both Her Majesty and the Duke were extremely pleased to see Wyn present and that Her Majesty was very happy with the painting that we presented to her, particularly with the efforts that we had taken to ensure that it was a gift which was personal to her. I have a print of the painting and I like it also.

Because the Princess Royal was Master of my mother Livery Company, the Loriners, we attended a dinner for the members of the Court of the Company at Buckingham Palace. I found her to be very good company. She has been to so many places and has been given so much information, that I have not yet found a topic that she is not able to discuss knowledgeably. She is particularly good on rugby football as her son played flanker for Scottish schoolboys and she is Patron of the Scottish Rugby Union. The amusing thing about the dinner at Buckingham Palace was that when Wyn and I arrived we found our Head Steward Peter Drury moonlighting at the Palace.

One of the most evocative evenings of my Mayoralty was the Installation Dinner of the Worshipful Company of Loriners. It would normally have been held in the Mansion House at my invitation but because of the closure it was held in the Guildhall. Her Royal Highness was handing over as Master to Leon Jessel. I was being installed as Junior Warden. Leon, who is Jewish, had as a youth escaped from Germany before the War. His family had been in the leather business. He found his way to Walsall, which was and still is a centre of the leather business. I believe that as a German he was interned for a while after war was declared. After the war he prospered and was awarded an MBE for his public work. Here he was in the splendid Great Hall of the Guildhall taking over from a Member of the Royal Family as Master of a Livery Company of the City of London. We are often being told that we live in a class-ridden society. Where else in the world could a Member of the Royal Family be succeeded in a prestigious office by a Jewish refugee? I felt very proud to be British.

Another outstanding evening, from a personal point of view was the Mass celebrated in St. Thomas More's cell in the Tower of London. Father Robert had arranged with the Resident Governor Major-General Christopher Tyler to say the Mass on the Feast of the Saint, the 7th of February. When we came to the Lord's Prayer, we sang it in Latin. As we sang 'Pater noster qui es in coelis' (Our Father Who art in Heaven) it was not difficult to imagine Thomas More himself doing the same thing as he prepared to meet his death. I felt that it was almost as though we were present at the execution. It is difficult to believe in these more enlightened days that someone who came to hear of the Mass wrote to the Queen to complain about it. Our first major outside event was the evening at

Buckingham Palace when Her Majesty entertains the members of the Diplomatic Corps. We had attended this large reception when I was Sheriff. On that occasion we had been rather lost among the crowd. As Lord Mayor it was considerably different. We were right up among the Great and the Good. I was chatting with the Prime Minister and the Foreign Secretary Douglas Hurd about the appointment of Chris Patten as Governor of Hong Kong. At the time I thought that it was an excellent idea. The combination of a tough politician who had the confidence of the Government seemed to me to be what was needed in the run-up to the handover of the colony to the Chinese. Certainly in the short-term it was a disaster. Whether he achieved anything of long-term value is extremely doubtful. He apparently would not listen to those who had spent their lives in Hong Kong and were used to dealing with the Chinese. He insisted on holding elections and generally upsetting the Chinese government. The Chinese attitude was that the British had held the Colony for a hundred years and had felt no need to have elections but that when it came to the time for the handover elections were apparently essential. The Chinese regarded it as an attempt to embarrass them. They were very angry indeed.

Shortly after my chat with the Prime Minister, Wyn and I were ushered into the White Drawing Room. This seemed to be the Holy of Holies. Assembled there were the Prime Minister and Mrs Major, the Lord Chancellor and Lady MacKay and others of Cabinet rank. Once we were all there a door opened. In came Her Majesty and the Duke of Edinburgh, followed by the Prince and Princess of Wales and other members of the Royal Family. Everyone circulated chatting sociably. Wyn was sitting talking to some of the other ladies when Her Majesty arrived at the group. They all stood up. Her Majesty said to Wyn, 'You should not be standing.' Wyn did as she was told and sat down. Her Majesty drew up a chair and sat down beside her.

At one stage I was seated on a sofa having a long chat with the Princess of Wales. As usual we found plenty to talk about and she was her normal charming self. I did not get the impression that there was anything wrong. The next morning it was announced that the

Prince and she were separating. In the evening after the announcement I was attending a function with the Prince of Wales. He did not appear to be affected by the furore that had greeted the announcement.

The Corporation of the City of London has a fund called 'City's Cash'. It consists of the income from money which has been invested in property and shares over many years. In the past rich merchants would leave legacies to the City. Over the years it has been invested by some very shrewd officers of the City. In recent times Bernard Harty, the City Chamberlain, has been particularly successful in handling the investments. The result is that City's Cash is in a very healthy state. This money is kept separate from the Rate-payers Funds. It is used for a variety of purposes. The large subsidies to the London Symphony Orchestra, The Royal Shakespeare Company and the Guildhall School of Music and Drama put the City up among the major patrons of the arts in the country. Subsidies to schools connected with the City also come from City's Cash. The cost of running the Mansion House and some of the costs of the Mayoralty also come from the same source.

From time to time the City is asked to host receptions or banquets for deserving organisations or visiting dignitaries. Again City's Cash provides the funds for these. We were asked to hold a reception for the Far East Prisoners of War Associations. The members of these Associations are either people who were imprisoned in the Far East by the Japanese during the Second World War or the spouses of former prisoners who had died in the prison camps. The Corporation and I were happy to host the Reception. Queen Elizabeth the Queen Mother was the guest of honour. Members of the Associations had come from all over the country and as I made my speech of welcome in the Great Hall of Guildhall I could see handkerchiefs coming out. Some of the men present were meeting each other for the first time since they were released from the prison camps. Some of the widows were meeting men who had known their husbands and had seen them die, often in very difficult circumstances. It was clearly going to be an emotional evening.

The President made his speech. It was the first time ever that any official body had held a function to recognise the special suffering that this group had endured. When they had been released from the camps in the Far East, most of them were emaciated skeletons. Some of them weighed less than five stone. Grown men! Because of malnutrition young men looked old. They had clearly been unfit to travel and had been kept in the Far East until they were fit to return home. By the time that they arrived in UK celebrations for the end of the war were over. People were getting on with their lives. Few were interested in what had gone on so far away. Compensation for their suffering was dealt with in a cavalier fashion. They received a pittance. No wonder they felt forgotten. Later an attempt was made to rectify the situation but it seems to have been too little and too late.

The guests were ranged down the length of the Great Hall. There was a passage cleared down the centre defined by movable posts holding purple velvet ropes. The idea was that I would lead Her Majesty down the passage so that she could meet the guests who were standing about six deep behind the rope. Everyone wanted to shake her hand and she was quite happy to allow them to do so. I was terrified. People were leaning over from several rows back. I was afraid that Her Majesty would be buried under a pile of bodies. I walked backwards with my arms spread trying to protect her. She moved serenely along smiling and shaking hands with anyone that she could reach. I almost collapsed with relief when we at last reached the end of the hall.

At these events Members of the Court of Aldermen and Common Councilmen act as hosts. I was told that at the end, many of the guests when thanking the hosts were in tears. At last someone had brought them together and recognised them as a special case. The many letters of thanks, which I received, were very moving. The City of London, so often derided as being only interested in finance, had proved once again that it understands what real people think and feel.

Before you become Lord Mayor you are asked about your allergies and your likes and dislikes with regard to food. Fortunately neither Wyn nor I have any food allergies but I do not like tomatoes, liver or vinegar. Somewhere this information is stored away and if I attend an official function at the Guildhall or the Mansion House, I am not served anything containing any of these. A lady guest at Guildhall was very impressed by the attention paid to details of guests' needs. At a function she was attending she said that she was suffering from a back complaint and asked if it would be possible to get a cushion to put behind her. This presented no problem. Some weeks later she was again attending a Banquet in Guildhall. When she reached her place at table there was a cushion on her chair.

The Lord Mayor's Children's' Christmas Party is a very happy occasion. Children and grandchildren of people with a close connection with the City are invited to attend in fancy dress. Rowena produced a most delightful drawing for the invitations. Because the Mansion House was closed our party was held in the Guildhall. There were clowns and magic shows and at the end the children each received a mug as a present from the Lord Mayor. We had ordered 700 mugs and at the end of the year there were only five left.

Mindful of my narrow escape in not becoming a name at Lloyds I asked a friend, the late Edmund Hambly, to give his acclaimed Cambridge lecture on Risk Assessment to representatives of Lloyds. We held the lecture in the Guildhall. There was a large turnout and after the lecture the questions kept coming until I eventually had to call a halt. David Rowlands, the Chairman who had worked so hard to find a reasonable solution to the problems of Lloyds, commented somewhat ruefully afterwards, 'It's a pity this did not happen five years ago.' David was later the recipient of a well-deserved knighthood.

It is said of the Pope that he has little power but a lot of influence. The Lord Mayor of London has no power but he or she has a little influence. Early on in my mayoralty the question of insurance of buildings against terrorist attack was raised by the Chamberlain. Of course the City itself had a serious interest in this, as it owns a large number of properties in the City. There was however a much wider issue which had arisen as a result of the IRA bomb, which had exploded in St Mary Axe the previous year. In Belfast the Government held property insured against by terrorists above a threshold of, I believe, £220. Since the IRA had obviously decided that the City was a target the cost of insuring property against terrorist attack had become prohibitive where cover could be obtained. Two of the major re-insurers had announced that they would not cover terrorist damage. Some of the major insurance companies had said that as from the 1st January 1993 terrorist cover would not be obtainable. The President of the Board of Trade, Michael Heseltine, had said that the Government did not wish to be involved. Things were getting pretty desperate. The biggest insurance market in the world could have found itself without insurance cover. Eventually after I had been to see the Minister and explained the nature of the problem we managed to reach an agreement on a scheme, which was satisfactory to all concerned. One newspaper under the headline 'Heseltine gives way on bomb cover' hailed it as a major triumph for the new Lord Mayor.

One day Mr Justice Saville phoned me and asked me to write to the Lord Chancellor's office explaining the importance of the Commercial Court to the future of the City as a world financial centre. He explained that delays in getting cases to Court were increasing and an extra Judge was required to try to cut down on the delays. I was very happy to take the matter up and having a degree of knowledge in the matter I was able to make out a convincing case. I was very pleased when it was agreed that a further Judge should be appointed.

These were two of the occasions when the Lord Mayor was called upon to exercise his role as leader of the Financial City and to do so successfully.

Because I was seen to be actively and successfully promoting causes, which were important to the Financial City, the *Evening Standard* was even moved to say in an article about me, 'I think that the present Lord Mayor of London Francis McWilliams will turn out to be one of the greatest Lord Mayors in the Corporation's history.' I do not know whether I fulfilled the *Evening Standard*'s hopes for me. In any case Sir Anthony Joliffe's advice was important to prevent me from becoming bigheaded. We had a young man called Nigel Szembel who was employed by the City Corporation's Public Relations Department attached to the Mansion House. Nigel was highly suspicious of the Press and said that they had a penchant for building people up then knocking them down. I have to confess that throughout my year of office the Press were very kind to me. Nigel also had a dry sense of humour. One day we were in Guildhall Yard when a bullion van with a large police escort trundled along Gresham Street. Obviously it was full of gold and bound for the Bank of England. Without a flicker of a smile he said, 'They must be paving the streets today.'

I was only partially successful in my attempt to persuade the Secretary of State for Health, Virginia Bottomley, to desist from her efforts to kill off St Bartholomew's Hospital (Barts). She had had a report prepared by a Professor Tomlinson, a Professor of Medicine from somewhere in the North-east of England. His report came to the conclusion that there were too many hospital beds in London and that Barts was one of the hospitals that should have its facilities reduced. It was clear that if the proposals were carried out Barts would eventually close. I read the report and came to the conclusion that it was flawed in its approach. Among other matters, the calculation of the number of beds required appeared to ignore the large number of persons who came into London to work. It also ignored the large population from London's East End for whom Barts was 'Their Hospital'. They had been born there and would probably die there. It had been thus for hundreds of years.

So a campaign was started to save the City's only hospital. We believed that as part of our infrastructure as a major Financial Centre we needed to have a first class hospital. Initially the Barts campaigners seemed to be saying, 'We are the oldest public hospital in the country. We have centuries of tradition in serving the public. You should not close us.' We pointed out to them that in the past we in the City had tried to use that type of defence when we were threatened with extinction and it had not been very effective. We had changed our approach to pointing out what we actually achieved in terms of the economy of the nation. We pointed to the billions of pounds, which were added to the country's invisible earnings because of the activities carried out in the City. We found this approach much more effective. We suggested that Barts should use the same approach and point out the fields in which they were acknowledged world leaders. We advised them that the approach should be, 'These are the things that we do well. We deserve to remain open because we perform a very useful function.'

Traditionally ministers will always see the Lord Mayor so it was agreed that I would go to see the Secretary of State. Before I went I was briefed by our friends at Barts. They had an impressive story to tell. They were acknowledged leaders in a number of fields. I started by agreeing with the Secretary of State that the National Health Service in London needed a thorough overhaul. Where I disagreed with her was that I did not believe that the Tomlinson Report was a suitable basis for such a project. As an example I pointed out that in quite a number of hospitals the Accident and Emergency Departments were being used as a substitute for local General Practitioners.

This resulted in lengthy waiting times and overcrowding. Clearly this should be tackled. I laid before the Secretary of State our concerns. In spite of the seriousness of the situation it was quite clear that she was not really interested in what I had to say. It appeared that she had made up her mind. I came away very disappointed. The ambassador of one oil-rich Middle Eastern country told me that his country was interested in buying Barts. That was not what I considered to be in the best interests of the City and the country. We did not give up. By enlisting the support of a number of members of Parliament and we believed as a result of the Prime Minister's intervention we managed to get a reprieve for some of the important departments at Barts. It is now experiencing a revival of its fortunes in specialist areas.

Another disappointment was the location of the European Central Bank. My immediate predecessor Sir Brian Jenkins had worked extremely hard in lobbying for the Bank to be located in London. Clearly the logical place for it was where the greatest banking expertise was available. Undoubtedly that was London. After Eddie George had taken over from Robin Leigh-Pemberton as

Governor of the Bank of England, I was invited to go with Eddie to see the Chancellor of the Exchequer who was now Kenneth Clarke. When we arrived at the Treasury, Eddie said to the receptionist that Sir Francis McWilliams and Mr Eddie George wished to see the Chancellor of the Exchequer. She asked where we were from. I thought that it was understandable that she did not know who I was but I thought that she would have known the name of the Governor of the Bank of England. The reason that we had been invited to meet the Chancellor was that the Government had decided that they were not intending to press for the European Central Bank, as they did not consider that it would be successful. After the amount of work that had been put in this was a great disappointment.

Shipping is a very important business in the City. Apart from buying and selling ships, chartering ships and arranging cargoes are every-day activities for large numbers of people. A large part of the insurance business in the City has to do with insuring ships and cargoes. Settling of Maritime Disputes either in the Commercial Courts or by arbitration is part of that business. The shrinking of the numbers of ships sailing under the British flag is a great cause for concern among shipping people. 'Flagging Out' is done for a variety of reasons. Some of these reasons are connected with health and safety regulations. Most responsible ship-owners can live with these regulations.

Their other problem is the system of taxation. They have tried to point out to the Government that if the system were revised it would in the long-term benefit both the ship-owners and the Government. The Treasury have now, I believe, at last managed to get the message. Shipping people were pretty paranoid about the whole thing. I was invited to speak at the Institute of Chartered Shipbrokers' Dinner in the Grosvenor House Hotel. The shipping publication Lloyd's List International said that the two Speakers at the Dinner would be 'The strikingly contrasting Lord Mayor of London Sir Francis McWilliams and the ever-pugnacious Labour transport spokesman John Prescott'. It made it sound quite interesting.

The evening did not get off to the best of starts. I arrived in good time and John Prescott arrived just afterwards. The President and Secretary of the Institute wished to have a photograph taken of the four of us together. The photographer lined us up and when he looked through his lens he asked John Prescott if he would like to move his hands. Somewhat aggressively he replied that he would put his hands where he liked. So one of the photographs probably shows John Prescott in the line as though he was in 'the wall' protecting his most precious parts when David Beckham is about to unleash one of his most venomous free kicks.

One of the problems about the Grosvenor House is the size of the dining room. It is huge. Although they can hear the speakers without difficulty, people on the periphery can feel slightly detached from the main body. Even the best speakers speak at length at their peril. I had decided that I would give about ten minutes outlining the importance of the shipping industry to the City. I thought that if he played his cards right John Prescott could sit down to thunderous applause or even a standing ovation. As an opposition spokesman he did not have to promise anything. All he had to do was show that he understood what the problem was. He started off well. This was the part of his speech that had been typed by someone else. Unfortunately the speech had been added to in his own handwriting. It went on and on and on. From where I was sitting I could see what was happening. The people on the outskirts started talking among themselves and the people closer in began to have difficulty hearing the speaker. They too started talking among themselves. It was like watching the tide coming higher and higher up the beach. The noise was getting louder and louder. Eventually the toastmaster had to bang his gavel to ask for silence so that the speaker could continue. Mr Prescott was not best pleased but it was his own fault.

When the President of Ukraine and Mrs Kravchuk came to London, it was classed as an official visit and we had a dinner for them at Guildhall. The President seemed to have brought with him all the members of his government. I wondered who was running the country whilst they were all in London. He told me that one of the great problems that he had was the inefficiency of the transport system. This resulted in the large potato crop standing rotting in rail-way sidings instead of reaching the markets. The day after the President's visit I had a visit from a group of Ukrainian children. They were from Chernobyl and had been brought over by a British Charity for a holiday away from the radiation, which has blighted that city.

Supporting education

There is an annual dinner given by the Lord Mayor to the Masters of the City Livery Companies. The purpose of the Dinner is really for the Lord Mayor to thank the Livery Companies firstly for electing him Lord Mayor and secondly for the very generous way in which they support his chosen charities. It also helps to repay the hospitality that the various companies extend to the Lord Mayor and the Sheriffs. The Guest Speakers on this occasion are the Master Mercer and the Master Grocer. The Mercers are the number one company and the Grocers are the number two. We were particularly fortunate that both the Master Mercer, Henry Palmer, and the Master Grocer, Sir John Smiley, and their wives were very good company. Most of the Livery Companies take a great interest in education. They provide members of boards of governors, scholarships and prizes to schools and universities. At the dinner I took this as my theme and I suggested that the City could not remain an island of prosperity in a sea of deprivation. I also suggested that many of the Companies supported schools which had originally been set up to provide education for the under-privileged. Through the effluction of time they were now providing education for the privileged. I urged them to take a look at the schools in the boroughs surrounding the City. These are some of the poorest areas in the country. The *Evening Standard* seemed extremely pleased with this initiative .The next day there was an editorial on the subject and as a result of my speech I was invited by the Leathersellers Company to visit the Prendergast school in Lewisham with which they had a strong on-going relationship. I was happy to do so with Wyn, Alderman and Sheriff Roger Cork and his wife the late Barbara Cork.

Predergast is a Girls' School. The Leathersellers had provided prizes and other financial support and had recently given the school an I. T. Laboratory. Two of their Liverymen were on the Board of Governors. The Headmistress was an exceptional lady. She said that whilst they were extremely grateful for all the financial help, the greatest contribution that the Company made to the school was the two Governors whose input was invaluable. We discussed the difficulties caused by the deprived backgrounds of some of her pupils. Her view was that no matter where they came from the school added value to their lives. If I had been an Ofsted Inspector I would have been most impressed by the positive approach and the atmosphere in the school. We were each allocated two girls to take us round the school. The Headmistress warned us not to be surprised if we were shown the toilets. She said that the girls were very proud of these and regarded them as the cleanest toilets in Lewisham. We discussed 'League Tables' and how such tables failed to show the value, which schools add to the lives of children brought up in extremely difficult circumstances. She quoted as examples two of the girls in the school who had particularly difficult lives. They were fifteen years old and had had to grow up very fast. She confidently predicted that they would both get five GCSEs.

Later in my Mayoralty two Members of the Common Council Tom Willmot and Hugh Barnes-Yallowley asked to come to see me. They had heard my speech at the Livery Dinner and suggested that as had been done in the past the Lord Mayor should call together representatives of the Livery and suggest to them that something should be done about inner-city schools. They also suggested that advice should be sought from Dr. Nick Carey the Director General of the City and Guilds Institute.

The City and Guilds Institute is the largest provider of qualifications in Commerce and Industry in Britain and possibly the world. Most people would be surprised to learn that it was founded in the year 1878 after the Lord Mayor of the day called together representatives of sixteen of the City Livery Companies to see what could be done to prevent Britain from falling behind other industrialised countries. It was decided that an institute should be set up to provide for education in technical and commercial subjects and to provide certificates showing the standard reached. In 1900 the Institute received a Royal Charter which stated that the purpose of the Institute was 'for the advancement, dissemination, propagation, promotion, culture and application of all such branches of Science and the Fine Arts as benefit commerce and industry in general and productive and technical industries in particular'. The Institute continues to carry out its original objectives successfully. Today it is an enormous charity with an annual turnover of over £40 million.

Many private schools have charitable status. From time to time opponents of private education propose that such charitable status should be removed. What such people fail to realise is that unless care is taken to exclude them, organisations such as City and Guilds could also lose their charitable status at the same time.

I invited the Livery Companies to send representatives to a meeting in the Mansion House. In some cases the Master himself attended, in others the Clerks came. In the case of two Companies, the Mercers and the Clothworkers their Clerks Michael Wakeford OBE and Michael Harris provided the administrative backup. Their support was crucial. Happily Dr Carey from City and Guilds saw that our aims coincided with the philosophy of the Institute and he also came to the meeting. We had representatives from 98 of the 100 Livery Companies at the meeting. Considerable enthusiasm was shown and under the leadership of Francis Baden-Powell of the Mercers and the late Alan Benjamin of the Information Technologists, 'Logvec' was formed. This is an acronym for 'London October Group Vocational Education Committee'. On a number of occasions attempts have been made to change the name but each time the view has been expressed that it is so awful that people remember it.

The most successful of the activities of Logvec is the programme for the adoption of schools. At the last count over fifty inner-city schools have a connection with a Livery Company. Other activities include the promotion of NVQs in various trades and Special Projects suggested by the distinguished speakers at our Annual General Meeting. The City and Guilds Institute has been most supportive throughout the life of Logvec. At one time I suggested that Logvec take over a failing inner-city school and run it on the lines of the City's other schools. I had discussed it with the Mayor of the borough concerned. He was very enthusiastic. The idea was to show that inner-city schools could be run successfully. We also hoped that it would set a standard that other schools would try to reach but the Minister said that the school was not needed, as there were sufficient school places in the area. The school was closed. I believe that a great opportunity was missed

Logvec continues to thrive. There are a number of heartening stories of the help, which has enabled failing schools to react to the interest shown by Livery companies and to come off the danger list. The mere fact that someone from outside has shown an interest helps to raise morale among teachers and pupils.

Apart from the City of London Boys School and the City of London Girls School that are largely day-schools, the City Corporation is closely linked with the City of London Freeman's School, King Edward's School Witley and Christ's Hospital which are boarding schools. A feature of all of these schools is the number of scholarships and the amount of help available so that parents of limited means can send their children to them. I believe that at Christ's Hospital nearly 75% of the pupils are subsidised in one way or another. For me it was always a pleasure to attend the Speech days and Prize-givings at the City Schools. All of them have high academic standards. The aim however, is to turn out well-rounded human beings who set themselves significant goals but care about those less fortunate than themselves.

The visit to Christ's Hospital is particularly daunting. 'The Senior Grecian' is the title of the Head Boy or Girl. When I visited, the Senior Grecian was a delightful girl called Harriet Richmond. She sat between Wyn and myself at lunch and we found her to be very bright with a cheerful and caring attitude. It was easy to see why she had been elected Senior Grecian. We all got on extremely well. It is one of the Senior Grecian's tasks to make the first speech, which is a report on what has happened in the School over the past year. Harriet spoke beautifully for twenty minutes without looking at a note. I was a bit ashamed of my ten or fifteen minutes of written speech after her. Later I congratulated Harriet on her performance and asked her how she did it. She confessed that there was someone hidden away ready to prompt if she slipped up but was happy that on this occasion no prompting had been needed. She then said that she had been very nervous at the start but that she looked down from the stage at Wyn and me and pretended that she was talking to us as we had been talking over lunch. Her nervousness had disappeared. A high proportion of the pupils from Christ's Hospital go on Voluntary Overseas Service during a Gap year. There is a strong sense of social responsibility throughout the school.

I visited Christ's Hospital a second time for the end of year Beating of the Retreat by the School Band. Christ's Hospital Band is quite famous and it is also very good. It often plays at the lunch interval at Lord's Cricket Ground on the first day during a Test Match. By tradition the Band leads the Lord Mayor's Show. The school uniform has not changed since the school was opened in the 16th century. The thick long black gowns and yellow woollen stockings must be quite hot in the summer. It is certainly not 'cool' in any sense of the word. Not surprisingly many of the pupils are not very keen on the uniform when they first arrive at the school. The Beating of the Retreat is the last occasion that those members of the band who are leaving school will wear the uniform. After the parade some of them become very emotional when they change out of uniform for the last time to go home. Tears are not unknown.

Sir William Treloar, who was Lord Mayor 1906-07, set up his 'Little Cripples' Fund'. The purpose of the fund was to build a hospital in the country for children suffering from non-pulmonary tuberculosis. The fund-raising was a great success and the hospital was built near Alton, which lies between Guildford and Winchester. Later, Colleges were added to provide education and eventually the Hospital was taken into the National Health Service. The Treloar Foundation is now concerned with providing education for 290 physically handicapped young people between the ages of eight and nineteen for whom a mainstream school is not satisfactory. One of the aims is to promote in the pupils as high a level of independence as is possible in the light of their disabilities. When I visited the College I was extremely impressed with the atmosphere. All too often people suffering from physical handicaps are patronised and treated as though they were also sub-normal mentally. At Treloar the atmosphere is happy and caring and the level of competitiveness is astonishing. One wheelchair-bound young lady told me her story.

Her parents had insisted that she should attend a mainstream school. She said that for the first year she was a curiosity. In the second year she was a nuisance. In the third year she was ignored. At Treloar she was treated as a real person. I later spoke to a Michael Cassidy about it. Michael had been a pupil at Treloar College for three years after being disabled by polio. He said that those three years were among the happiest years of his life. Lord Mayor Treloar would be proud of the College if he were alive today.

In alternate years the City would host a Banquet for the Judges and the Bishops. In my year it was a Judges' year. I would have loved to have had a Bishops' year. Throughout my life I must have sat through thousands of sermons. Here would have been the chance to get my own back. A captive audience of Bishops! I am sure that I would have enjoyed it.

The Bishopsgate bomb

On Saturday 24th April 1993 a huge bomb exploded in Bishopsgate in the heart of the City. The explosion occurred whilst Wyn and I were on the way to visit Michael and Rowena who had just bought a house in Tenterden in Kent. When we arrived we were told that we had to return to the City because a large bomb had been exploded. We turned round and by the time we reached the City the wheels were already turning. Sadly, there was one fatality, Edward Henty, a press photographer and the son of friends of Anne Marten, who was secretary of my Lord Mayor's charity. He had heard about the suspicious lorry which had been discovered parked in Bishopsgate and had dodged round the police cordon to try to get a picture. I suppose that it was foolhardy but I imagine that he felt that he was doing his job even if it involved risk. Those who had been injured had been taken to Barts Hospital. That was our first port of call. Next we went to visit the Corporation's housing estate at Middlesex Street. The residents were largely elderly and this was the second time in twelve months that they had suffered an explosion. We asked our Social Services Department to make sure that they visited those who were obviously severely shocked. Later in the year Wyn and I attended a reception in Middlesex Street. They all seemed to have recovered well.

The bomb in Bishopsgate was a major test of the City's capacity to deal with disaster. The previous year there had been an IRA bomb in St. Mary's Axe in the City and the Baltic Exchange, the worldwide centre for all matters to do with shipping, shipping cargo and shipping insurance had been destroyed. The Baltic had recovered and was again trading successfully. It was clear that the IRA had come to the conclusion that attacking the financial heart of Britain was a most cost-effective way of using their resources. Their objective was to cause serious commercial damage. They had attacked the City on a Saturday when it was quiet. Loss of life would be minimal. I do not believe that this was for humanitarian reasons. Rather it was because it was easier to bring a lorry into the City at weekends when a lot of construction work takes place.

We believed that our task was to maintain confidence in our ability to recover from the attack quickly and efficiently. We had learned much from the previous attack and I believe that we succeeded. We wanted no photo opportunities for Government Ministers and no sympathy visits from members of the Royal family. At press conferences, which I shared with Michael Cassidy, the Chairman of our Policy Committee, we put across the message that we knew what we were doing and recovery would be swift. I received some lovely letters from children in Scotland, including my old primary school St. John's in Portobello and another school in Ayrshire. In my reply to them I stressed that it was important for all of us that evil should not triumph over good.

After visiting Bart's it was down to work. I had visited Liverpool Street Station. It was a mess and there seemed to be mountains of glass all over the place. I believed that we could not say that we were back in action if the station was closed. When I got back to the office I tried to phone the stationmaster. He was obviously busy and I could not reach him so I rang Sir Robert Reid, the chairman of British Rail who was a friend. He said that he would phone me back. About an hour later he rang to say that the stationmaster had said that I was not to worry. Everything would be cleared up by Monday morning. Then it was over to the Guildhall where the Corporation's staff were performing miracles in relocating offices. Fortunately at the time there was a surplus of space. Estate agents had been called in and the space which they had available was allocated to those in need. Wyn and I were engaged in the issue of permits to those who could be allowed into the cordoned off area to recover documents. In some areas they were only allowed in with an escort. One group in a Japanese bank seemed to have disappeared. They were later found working at their desks by candlelight. Where space was allocated we had to arrange for the connection of telephones and other services.

On the Sunday evening there was a reception for the Board of the European Bank for Reconstruction and Development, (EBRD). It was held at the Natural History Museum. I circulated vigorously spreading our message. I was pleased to find that we were definitely winning. The foreign bankers had confidence in us. On the Monday evening the City Corporation gave a reception for the directors of the EBRD. This was followed by a dinner given by the Chancellor of the Exchequer. Both of these events were held in the City. The positive reaction to the confidence that we portrayed was very gratifying. The crunch would come on Monday. I hardly slept that Sunday night. Our credibility was on the line. As soon as it was light enough I was up. The first stop was Liverpool Street Station. It was spotless. All the glass had been cleared away and the empty platforms awaited silently for the arrival of the first city workers. To Ironmonger Lane for breakfast then back to Liverpool Street. I was nearly bursting with pride as I watched everyone streaming through the station. There we were handing out maps and telling people that if they normally worked within the area shown on the map and had not already been told where they were working they should go to the Guildhall. There they would be told where to go. It was a great feat of organisation and it worked. Having spent thirty years of my life organising civil engineering and building works it seemed natural to be involved in such an operation. The adrenaline really flowed.

In a strange way, the massive attack had enhanced the City's reputation among the foreign banking community. Their view was that nowhere else in the world, after an attack of such magnitude, would the head of the local government proclaim so confidently that it would be 'business as usual' within 48 hours and actually mean it.

There is only one word to describe Colin Snowden, the City Engineer. Brilliant! It was as though his whole career had been building towards this crisis. How well he responded. The award of an OBE was a fitting recognition of his energy and skill in mitigating the effects of the massive explosion. He had contractors clearing mountains of broken glass from the streets. He had others making the streets safe from huge panes of glass hanging precariously from tall buildings. The glass falling from that height could easily slice you in two from head to toe. I visited one Livery Hall where they had shards of glass sticking like daggers into the wood panelling. Colin did not go home from the Saturday until Tuesday. He was not terribly amused when he was criticised by the City Corporation's public relations department. He appeared on television wearing a donkey jacket instead of a suit when he was representing The City of London!

Perhaps my main claim to fame as Lord Mayor of London is that in the aftermath of the Bishopsgate bomb being an engineer I was able to appear on television looking comfortable in a hard hat even when wearing a priceless diamond badge of office, a tail coat and striped trousers!

Later that week I went with Michael Cassidy and Owen Kelly to Downing Street for a discussion with the Prime Minister and the Home Secretary who at the time was Kenneth Clarke. They seemed very happy to leave matters in our hands. I did however appear on television with the Home Secretary saying what I thought of the people who had carried out the bombing. I was not in the least complimentary. At our Press conferences the message was always the same, 'We know what we are doing and we can keep the City working'. I had discussed with Michael and Owen the possibility of offering a reward for information. We agreed that we would try to raise £1 million. I spent one day phoning round the banks and other financial institutions in the City. By mid-afternoon I had ten pledges of £100,000. Unfortunately none of it was ever needed. I hoped that I was performing better than my predecessor as Alderman for the Ward of Aldersgate Sir Thomas Bludworth did in the Great Fire.

We held many working breakfasts. We invited American bankers, Japanese bankers and representatives of foreign and British firms doing business in the City. The message that we received was that they were happy with what we had done but that they would like to see some increase in the security in the City. The Crisis Management Group held discussions about future actions to be taken to enhance security. We had a list of people who were immediately to be called in any emergency. We were already increasing the number of the cctv cameras. It is probably difficult to believe in these days when cctv cameras seem to be everywhere but when we came to put one on the boundary between the City and Islington, Islington Council insisted that it be sited in such a way that it could not 'spy on residents of Islington'. It was from the breakfast discussions that the idea for the so-called 'ring of steel' was evolved. The idea was that access to the City would be restricted to certain streets. At the boundaries there would be police checkpoints, a system that was in use in Belfast City-centre. Our road traffic department did computer simulations that indicated that the system would not cause congestion either in the City itself or in the surrounding boroughs.

The system of restricted access was put in place one weekend in July. The idea was that with people starting to take their holidays, traffic would be lighter than usual. Wyn and I had gone off to St Albans late on the Friday night. Preparations for the checkpoints were already being made. We drove back on the Sunday evening. Everything was supposed to be in place. I chose a somewhat unusual route into the City. There was a gaping hole in the system. I immediately phoned Owen Kelly and told him about it. At first he could not believe it. Everything had been checked and double-checked. Fortunately the gap was easily closed by moving the checkpoint about 30 yards. Soon afterwards the *Evening Standard* published the most amusing cartoon by Jak that is reproduced on the cover. I purchased the original. About this time I issued an appeal for City workers to come forward to serve as Special Constables. As a result of the restriction of access the already low incidence of street crime dropped even lower.

An interesting post-script came with a visit from a group of school children from outside London. I asked them if they had any questions. The smallest girl in the group said, 'Lord Mayor do the bombs worry you?' I asked her how she had heard about the bombs. She replied, 'My daddy has a window-cleaning business and nearly all the windows that he usually cleans have been broken.' I repeated the message, which had become a sort of mantra, that we must not allow the terrorists to succeed.

Visiting foreign dignitaries

So that we could keep the confidence of the City my programme continued as normal. On Tuesday 27th April President Mario Soares of Portugal arrived and I went with the Sheriffs to Victoria station to meet him. There I met Her Majesty, members of the Royal Family and members of the Cabinet. All were anxious to know how we were coping. I was able to assure them that everything was under control. On his arrival we were introduced to the President. That evening Wyn and I went to the Banquet at Buckingham Palace. I was wearing the insignia of the Order of Grande Oficial da Ordem do Infante Dom Henrique that had been sent to me that afternoon. I had already received the Order du Merite of Senegal and the Order of Independence (Class III) of United Arab Emirates as a result of State visits when I was Sheriff. These, together with my GBE, Knight of St. John, Knight of St. Gregory (from the Pope) and my Malaysian decorations, mean that I have quite a variety of stars and medals to choose from when I dress up in white tie and tails to attend a formal function. I call it my 'Christmas tree outfit'.

After dinner I was chatting with the Duchess of Gloucester when the President came over. He said that he had been very impressed with the style of the Banquet. HRH said that he would probably find the ceremonial at the Guildhall even more impressive. On the Wednesday evening Wyn and I were hosts at the Banquet in the Guildhall. We had the whole works. I wore the crimson robe with the ermine. We had the Pikemen lined up. There was an address of welcome in the Old Library read by the Recorder of London. It was then placed in a Silver Casket and presented to the President. As he left after the Banquet the President said that the only place that he had seen comparable style and ceremonial was in the Vatican.

There had however as far as I was concerned been a near disaster. I had not realised that the President was going to make his speech at the banquet in Portuguese and that translations of the speech had been placed on the guests' chairs. After we had processed into the Great Hall I had the scarlet gown removed as I stood in front of my seat. The translation of the President's speech, which had been on the seat, must have been wafted away. At any rate when the President spoke I had not the faintest idea what he was saying and I did not know that there had been translations provided. I was due to make a short reply to the speech and all I could do was get up and say a few more words about the long and close friendship between Britain and Portugal and wish everyone a safe journey home.

During the year, the Lord Mayor of London receives visits from many foreign dignitaries. Many of these are the Mayors of Cities around the world. Almost the first question that they all ask is whether they can be twinned with London. We always reply that we are flattered to be asked but that we have a policy of not being twinned with anyone. The reason is simple. If we twinned with one, others would take offence if we refused them. Even if we restricted ourselves to Capital Cities that would amount to hundreds. Shanghai aims to be the Financial Capital of China. I had a visit from two delegations from Shanghai. One was led by the Mayor Mr Huang Ju.

The second was quite a large delegation and was led by the Deputy-Mayor Mr Zhao Qizheng. We were told that he was an important political figure. He was in charge of the very large industrial development at Pudong, which is across the river from the City of Shanghai. Because of my experience in the field of development we had a lot to talk about. The Deputy-Mayor did not speak English. He had a very nice young lady interpreter Xu Bing. I had been airing my limited Cantonese and Mandarin. The Deputy-Mayor asked the interpreter something. She started to giggle. She found it funny because he had asked her in Mandarin if I knew the Cantonese word for something. Here she was asking me in English for the Cantonese translation of a Mandarin expression. Fortunately it was within my somewhat limited vocabulary and she was able to relay it back. Later we had a visit from a group of people who worked in Financial Services in Shanghai. I believe that good relationships were established between them and firms in the City.

I do not know the collective noun for a group of Mayors. We had decided that the collective word for a group of Aldermen is an 'Aggravation'. The topic came up because we were about to have a visit from representatives of seven Australian Cities. Over the years many Lord Mayors of London had visited Australia but no Australian Lord Mayors had been entertained by us. Most of the suggestions for a collective such as a Madness or Madhouse, a Maladministration or because they were Australian, a Marsupium were decidedly uncomplimentary or unwieldy. We decided that the correct word should be a Magisterium but it was too pompous. We decided to forget about a collective noun and call it the 'Mayoral Party'.

We had the Lord Mayors of Adelaide, Brisbane, Darwin, Hobart, Melbourne, Perth, and an Alderman representing Sydney. The Official Visit lasted from 16th June to 18th June but they started to arrive earlier and the Remembrancer's Department made arrangements for them to visit places of interest such as the Bank of England and the Docklands Development. At a Breakfast Meeting in the Savoy where we had arranged for them to stay, we explained what the City Corporation did. Like most people who hear about it, they were fascinated by the variety of roles played by the City of London in addition to its obvious Local Government role. Its custodianship of Epping Forest, Hampstead Heath, and other open spaces for the benefit of all Londoners; the entertainment of Foreign Heads of State; the role of the Lord Mayor as ambassador for the Financial City; the involvement in Education; the Livery Companies and the City's Role in the history of Britain. There is so much to tell that we were only able to give them a flavour of the City Story.

Among the many events was a large Lunch in the Guildhall where the guest speaker was a very impressive lady, Alderman Doone Kennedy who was Lord Mayor of Hobart. The highlight of the visit was the day at Lord's Cricket Ground for the first day of the Test Match between England and Australia. Our guests had reason to be pleased as Michael Slater played a beautiful innings and the Australians were in a strong position at the end of the day.

We also had a visit from the Lord Mayor of Dublin, Gay Mitchell and his Lady Mayoress. This was a visit of considerable political significance. Sir Christopher Collett had paid a visit to Dublin in 1989 when he was Lord Mayor. This was by way of a return visit. We really pulled out all the stops. It turned out to be a very happy visit. Gay and his wife Norma were a charming couple and enjoyed everything that they did. They were wonderful guests. We had a superb Lunch in the Guildhall and it was said that it was the first time that the National Anthem and the Irish National Anthem had been played at the same function in the Guildhall. Some time after my year of office was finished Wyn and I visited Gay in Dublin. By this time he was a Minister in the Prime Minister's office. He made us most welcome.

My friend HRH the Sultan of Selangor came to visit twice whilst I was Lord Mayor. On the first occasion he came to dinner in the house we were occupying in Ironmonger Lane. By the time he came on the second visit we were in the Mansion House. After dinner we showed him round. He was clearly impressed. He said how proud he was that one of his Royal Dato's was the holder of such an important office as Lord Mayor of London. Jokingly he then suggested that I return to Malaysia and become Mayor of Kuala Lumpur. He then added, 'I don't think that Dr Mahathir would let you live in a palace like this.'

The City of London tries to keep a good relationship with other Cities and Boroughs in Britain. Accordingly visits are arranged with other Local Authorities from time to time. In connection with Her Majesty's Fortieth Anniversary celebrations Chester had been designated as a City and the Mayor had been designated as a Lord Mayor. He had invited the other Lord Mayors in England and the Lord Provosts in Scotland to a weekend of discussions. Everyone deferred to the Lord Mayor of London, my being non-party political helped. The Lord Provosts of Aberdeen and Dundee were very left wing. They were very affable with me but they found it difficult to believe that Lord Mayors eschewed party politics whilst in office. Of course the Lord Provosts hold office for four years while Lord Mayors only serve for one year. I found it amazing how pompous some people could become in a year as a Lord Mayor.

I also visited Cardiff, Sheffield and Leicester. Most people will by now have forgotten the tragedy that struck the town of Hungerford in August 1987. It was a forerunner of what happened in Dunblane in 1996. A man went berserk with a gun and shot a number of people. Someone suggested that the people of Hungerford might appreciate a visit from the Lord Mayor of London to show our sympathy for them. They made us extremely welcome and were very pleased that we came to share their annual Hocktide celebration.

Because of my Scottish connections I was invited to speak at various Scottish events in London and in Edinburgh. At the Burns' Night at the Caledonian Club in London Wyn and I met the late John Smith, leader of the Labour Party. We both liked him and found him to be very good company. He was also very sharp. I believe that he would have made a good Prime Minister. When he died it was a great loss to the political life of the country.

During one of my visits to Edinburgh Eric Milligan, who at that time was Convenor (Chairman) of Lothian Region Council, held a breakfast in my honour. He invited distinguished former pupils of my old school, Holy Cross Academy. Among them were a Cardinal, a Bishop and one of Scotland's most successful entrepreneurs, Sir Tom Farmer. There were also two senior members of the Scottish civil service. Also attending the breakfast was John Gibson who writes for the *Edinburgh Evening Standard*. He had taken a great interest in the lad from Portobello who had become Lord Mayor of London. On the assumption that his readers would also be interested he had written quite a lot about my activities during the year. My sister Patricia said that when she wanted to know what I had been doing she would read John Gibson's column. I asked John whether it was he who had invented the name 'Jock Whittington'. His reply was, 'No but I wish that I had.' Eric and his charming wife Janice came to have dinner with us in London. They are now in the middle of a second highly successful term as Lord and Lady Provost of Edinburgh.

The Lord Mayor on his travels

The Overseas Visits Committee as well as having City Corporation representatives, also has representatives from the Foreign and Commonwealth Office, British Invisibles, the City Financial and the Confederation for British Industry. The Committee discussed and made recommendations as to where the Lord Mayor should visit. The planning starts before the Lord Mayor actually takes office.

Our first trip overseas was scheduled to take place over Easter 1993. We were to take in Pakistan and Nepal with an overnight stop in Delhi between the two. We landed in Karachi, which reminded me of Kuala Lumpur before independence in 1957, but is considerably larger. The Civic party consisted of Wyn and me, Sheriff Tony Moss and his wife Jennifer, and Colonel Tommy Tucker one of the Mansion House Household Officers who was in charge of the arrangements for the visit. Also with us were representatives of the Financial City who were either doing business in Pakistan or were hoping to do so. In the party was a representative of one of the largest shipbrokers in the City.

We were entertained to a large dinner in the garden of the Deputy High Commissioner's residence. Carpets had been laid on the ground and the tables set up on them. Apparently this was standard practice. What struck me was the fact that there seemed to be representatives of dozens of different political parties present. When I mentioned this to the Deputy High Commissioner he said that this was a feature of the Pakistan Parliament. Some political Parties consisted of one person. I met various government and quasi-government officials. Wyn had a separate programme. After a couple of days our shipbroker returned to the hotel elated. He had sold two ships for breaking. He said that he had first to ensure that they understood that he worked for a ship-'broker' not a rival ship-'breaker'. Pakistan is apparently the centre for world ship breaking. They have a long flat stretch of beach where ships are driven at high speed up the beach at high tide and then cut up.

Everywhere we went we had a motorcycle escort. When we moved to Lahore and I called on the Mayor, he had a guard of honour composed of the famous Spahis for me to inspect. They all had very neatly trimmed black moustaches. My grey moustache looked most unkempt and straggly compared with theirs. We then moved on to the capital, Islamabad. Here I was reminded of my early days of developing Petaling Jaya. The scheme of development seemed to be the same. I had been invited to meet the President and my CV had been sent on to those people that I was to meet so The President knew of my Malaysian connection. Almost the first thing that he asked was how it was that Malaysia, which had achieved independence ten years after Pakistan, was so far ahead in terms of economic development. I explained that in Malaysia the political party, which had negotiated for independence, had remained in power continuously since independence. I also explained that Rural Development had been pursued in parallel with the drive to attract industrial investment. These policies had remained in place for thirty six years. The result had been stability. Since Pakistan had become independent it had lurched from democratic rule to military rule and back a number of times. He appeared to understand the need for stability but, unfortunately, not continuity because within a couple of days he sacked the Prime Minister Nawaz Shariff in controversial circumstances.

Pakistan's dispute with India over Kashmir is a topic that comes up often in conversation. When they discovered that my profession was an arbitrator some of the politicians asked whether I would be willing to arbitrate in that dispute. I told them that I would be very happy to do so provided that both parties agreed to abide by my decision. In the present climate there would be very little chance of getting such an agreement.

It had been arranged that the City would make a donation to the St Thomas's Church in Islamabad. Tommy Tucker and I were the only ones fit enough to go to the Good Friday Service at the church. Everyone else was suffering from stomach upsets. Tommy thought that it was as a compliment to him that they had named the church after him. At times Christians in Pakistan have a hard time. The

Church of England, Church of Scotland, the Methodists and the Lutherans had combined together and after a number of setbacks, had managed to build their church. At the service their pleasure to see us was very touching. There was a lady with a magnificent voice who sang a Negro spiritual 'Were You There?' It was very moving. Among those hoping to do business was a representative of a large fund manager. They had been trying to set up an office in Pakistan for nearly two years. Because he was in our party, he had managed to get to see the Minister concerned with his application. We had been in Islamabad two days when he arrived back at the hotel waving the permit that he needed. He said that they had even invited him to dictate the terms of the permit.

Another member of our party was a young man Mukhtar Hussain, whose parents had come from Pakistan. He apparently had a large number of relatives living near Islamabad. He worked for the well-known city merchant-bankers Samuel Montagu. The day before we were due to leave he was out meeting business contacts and meeting relatives. He arrived back at the hotel after the rest of us had gone to bed. Tommy Tucker had asked us to have our luggage brought down to the lobby so that it could be sent off early to the airport. He left a message for Mukhtar asking him to do the same. When Mukhtar returned he got ready for bed and called the porter to put his luggage with everyone else's. The next morning the luggage went off to the airport. As we waited in the lobby before going off to the airport there was no sign of Mukhtar. He had sent his suit off with the rest of his luggage and now had no trousers. We had to leave but Tommy left a car to wait for Mukhtar. Just before the plane took off he arrived wearing a very tight pair of jeans. He had bought them off one of the waiters in the hotel for US$20.00. Fortunately, once he had caught the plane Mukhtar could see the funny side of it.

In Delhi we spent the night at the Ambassador's residence where the Ambassador's wife had left Easter Eggs for us in our rooms. The journey to and from the airport was made in a rather ancient Daimler. It was apparently armour-plated. What it weighed was anybody's guess. Sitting in it as it laboured up a hill belching out clouds of smoke was a unique experience.

Flying into Kathmandu is also a unique experience of a spectacularly different kind. The airport is hemmed in by towering mountains on all sides. You wonder how the pilot is going to get over them and stop on what appears to be a very small runway. It is a bit like going into the old Hong Kong Airport where the pilot seemed to be threading his way in through a narrow gap between a forest of skyscrapers.

The Mayor of Kathmandu, P L Singh, and his deputy, Nabinra Raj Joshi, had only recently been elected when we arrived. They were at the airport to meet us, where there were little girls to garland us with flowers. Also present were the leaders of the thirty two wards. Each leader had a posy of flowers to present to me. I waited until I had eight posies then handed them over to Tommy Tucker. I then received another eight. This happened four times. On the drive from the airport I was in one car with the Mayor, and Wyn was in another with the Deputy. Both men had been in jail as dissidents. They did not appear to have suffered whilst incarcerated. In fact from the way they told it they appeared to have rather enjoyed it. On the evening of our arrival the Mayor gave a dinner in our honour. At the reception before the meal he and I set off round the room so that he could introduce me again to the ward leaders. When we had been round the room I enquired what had happened to the leader of ward 10. The Mayor was completely surprised. He told me that that particular leader had an important family matter to attend to and had asked to be excused. He asked me how I knew that he was not present. I suppose that I had been ticking the numbers off in my head as we went and had ended up one short.

The Jesuits have a church in Khatmandu. When we attended Mass there Wyn and I were pleased to see that other Christians were allowed to take Communion. In most other places this is not permitted. The visit was a great success. The Mayor was particularly pleased that he, one of the newest Mayors in the world had been visited by the holder one of the oldest offices of Mayor in the world. I was very sad to see that what appeared to be extremely precious fertile land around Kathmandu was being built over. I believe that they will come to regret it. On our last day in Nepal we were taken on a drive up among the mountains. The views of the massive peaks were quite amazing. Unfortunately for the only day in my year as Lord Mayor I had an upset stomach. Lunch was a curry. It made me green to even look at it. I told Tommy Tucker that I could have happily killed him as he passed me saying that it was a wonderful curry and he was going for a second helping.

The Overseas visits Committee had decided that it was time for a Lord Mayor to visit Morocco. It was arranged that our trip would be made in a private British Aerospace jet plane. Sheriff Tony Moss and his wife Jennifer came with us. BAE wished to take the plane to Morocco to demonstrate it to the Moroccan Air Force and Royal Air Maroc. The arrangement was that we would pay BAE the equivalent of the commercial airfares for our trip. The plane was very well equipped. It flew at 41,000 feet and was very smooth. The seats were like very comfortable armchairs, which could be swivelled around. Wyn remarked that she now knew what she would really like for Christmas. In the event BAE were able to demonstrate the plane to the entire top 'brass' of both the Air Force and the civilian airline. They said that if they had not come with us they would have been fobbed off with junior staff. They reckoned that they had a very good chance of selling two of the planes. The Merchant Bankers that we had with us also arranged at least one financial deal. They were, of course, ready to arrange the finance for the planes if they were sold. BAE were so pleased with the result of the visit that they decided not to charge us for the flights.

The British Ambassador in Morocco and the Bank of England had sent us very detailed and accurate briefings about all the people that we were scheduled to meet. Most of the people that we met spoke French and Arabic. It was decided that when I spoke to the Rabat Chamber of Commerce I would speak in French. I had a twenty-minute speech. Afterwards I was talking to one of the members. He was English but he had lived in Morocco for many years and spoke fluent French. He said that he had been expecting me to speak in English. Halfway through my speech he suddenly realised that I was speaking in French. He inferred that it was because my French accent was so good and he understood all that I said. I have a suspicion that it was because my French sounded like English. I had discussion meetings with the Prime Minister and various Ministers. My meeting with a former Finance Minister was especially interesting. He was very friendly. He spoke little English and my French was not up to financial discussion but we got along very well together.

After the capital Rabat we went to Casablanca. Having seen the film 'Casablanca', we expected to be impressed. I believe that Casablanca is twinned with Manchester. There did not appear to be anything intriguing or romantic about it. It does however, have the second largest Mosque in the world. When we visited it, it was nearing completion. It is a splendid example of modern Islamic architecture. It also has some superb examples of craftsmanship in its wooden panels. It is designed to hold 20,000 worshipers. It is enormous.

After Casablanca we visited Marrakech. Wyn and Jennifer went to the hotel where Winston Churchill used to stay when he went to Morocco on his painting trips. They have a room dedicated to Winston.

In June we visited Poland. The party included Douglas Woodward the Chief Commoner and his wife Ann. We also had with us Jonathan Charkham an official of the Bank of England. On our visit I met Lech Walesa as well as various Ministers. Lech Walesa was a very interesting man. He was clearly very worried about what was happening in Ukraine and Russia. In Warsaw we saw some very sensitive restoration work that was being carried out in the centre of the city. After Warsaw we made the trip to Poznan by road. On the way we stopped to have lunch at the famous Walewice Stud Farm with its beautiful Arab Horses. In Poznan the large Industrial Fair takes place. We attended the opening ceremony of the 1993 Trade Fair and visited all the British Exhibitors. It was interesting that throughout the period of Communist rule the Fair had continued to be successfully held. We visited the Cigielski engineering works. They had been engaged in the construction of railway carriages.

They told me that they had had to cut their labour force by more than half because their main customer the Soviet Union was no longer buying goods. They said that this had happened practically overnight. I asked whether they had tendered for the carriages for the Eurostar. The managing director told me that when those tenders were being called they were working at full capacity on Soviet orders and had not been able to tender. I later sent him the address of a Malaysian company with whom I thought he could do business.

Everyone on the Overseas Visits committee had agreed that, for me, a visit to the Far East was a must. It was arranged that I would visit Malaysia, Singapore, Brunei and the Philippines. One of the wonderful things about travelling as Lord Mayor is that luggage and passports are taken care of while you have coffee in the VIP lounge. You then drive up to the plane just before take-off. When you return the car is waiting for you at the foot of the aircraft steps. It beats Business class by a mile. On two occasions I flew in the British Airways plane named 'the City of London'. On our trip to the Far East the pilot Captain Christopher Hodgkinson was about to be installed as the Master of the Guild of Air Pilots and Navigators which is number 81 in the list of Livery Companies.

Our party for our Far Eastern trip comprised Wyn and me, Alderman and Sheriff Roger Cork and his wife Barbara and Colonel John Ansell, the Household Officer in charge of the arrangements. The main focus of the trip was to be the Financial City's expertise in arranging the privatisation of government-owned bodies. Several of the countries that we were visiting had privatisation programmes. When we arrived in Kuala Lumpur we were staying with the High Commissioner Duncan Slater CMG. The house is immediately adjacent to the Royal Selangor Golf Club. It was designed by my friend Dato Hisham Albakri who with his wife Valerie had come over to attend the Lord Mayor's Banquet.

As usual for such visits there had been press handouts before we arrived. The *New Straits Times* had had a five-page supplement. The details they gave of me ensured that when I visited the Mayor of Kuala Lumpur there was a large turnout of the press. They were intrigued by this engineer who had lived in Malaysia for twenty three years and had returned to UK to become Lord Mayor of London. The Press conference initially followed the usual routine on such occasions. They wanted to know what was the purpose of my visit and what I hoped to achieve. Then someone asked in the Malay language whether I spoke Malay. Without thinking I replied that I spoke a little. From then on nearly the whole interview was in the Malay language. They really enjoyed testing to see how much I did know. The fact that I was able to throw in a few vernacular idiomatic expressions pleased them enormously. Afterwards Duncan said that they had never had a press conference like it before. The local newspapers ran stories about the Lord Mayor of London who was a fluent speaker of the National Language.

I called on the Prime Minister Dr. Mahathir. Dr Mahathir gets a bad Press in UK but he has done a very good job for Malaysia. I have known him for many years and we have always got on well together. He was sacked from a Ministerial post by Tengku Abdul Rahman after the racial riots in 1969 for publishing a book. The book was banned in Malaysia but I managed to get a copy. It was considered that it was liable to cause racial tension at a very sensitive time. Some of the things it said I disagreed with but others were what I had been saying for years. Dr. Mahathir refers to me as 'The Malaysian Lord Mayor of London'. He reckoned that good publicity for Malaysia was largely due to my efforts.

It was said of Dr. Mahathir that he was the first Malaysian Prime Minister who did not receive his university education in UK and that he did not have the same affinity towards the British as his predecessors. However I have heard him make a speech where he has praised the work of the British in Malaya and the legacy left by them at Independence. He is a very interesting personality. On two occasions he has introduced anti-British policies: at one point he operated a 'Look East' policy and the second time he introduced a policy of not allowing British firms to tender for government work in Malaysia. Ostensibly on both occasions the cause of the problem was the attitude of the British press towards Malaysia. The first occasion was the way that the press treated the take-over by Malaysians of

Guthries, a large mainly British-owned company operating in Malaysia. The take-over was portrayed as nationalisation by the back door. It was nothing of the sort. The second occasion was over the Pergau Dam. *The Sunday Times* included in an article on the Dam an insinuation of corruption 'at the highest level'. Although the story was quite ridiculous Dr. Mahathir took the matter very personally. I am sure that when he read the article there was steam coming out of his ears. Eventually, Rupert Murdoch, who chaired the company that ran the paper, decided that Andrew Neil the editor of *The Sunday Times* should be sacrificed. Afterwards everything went back to normal.

Because my younger son Michael is a director of the consulting firm, which designed the Pergau dam, I was able to go and see it for myself during my visit to Malaysia. The accusations regarding the dam were that it was not an economic scheme and that it was environmentally unfriendly. I think that the truth was that the Ministry of Overseas Development did not like to see a very large part of their budget being used to give a 'soft' loan for the project. Like the Dinorwic pump-storage scheme in Wales, Pergau was designed to come into use at peak loads. It was a sort of insurance against future shutdowns. For both schemes, although they are of major importance, it is very easy to produce calculations that show that the figures do not add up. In the case of Pergau its importance was proved when before it came on stream Malaysia was suffering from shut downs at peak times. Most people would agree that hydropower is the most environmentally friendly way of producing electricity. However any such scheme must involve the use of land and the people living there have to be moved. At Pergau the amount of land being used was minimal. It was not virgin jungle as was alleged. It was scrubby secondary land. The number of people who had to be moved was, I understood, thirty families. They were given land elsewhere. The whole campaign was based on false premises and should never have been started. It certainly cost British companies considerable opportunities.

Dr. Mahathir's aim is that by the year 2020 Malaysia should be a knowledge-based industrial country. He has moved the Federal

Capital to a new town called Putra Jaya and nearby there is another new area called Cyber Jaya.

As part of my Malaysian visit I went to Petaling Jaya where I had spent ten happy years. Wyn visited the Convent school that she had helped to start. She also visited St. Anne's Kindergarten that was the first one that she owned. Everywhere we were welcomed very warmly. It was most gratifying. We called on His Majesty the Yang DiPertuan Agong. He was Raja Azlan Shah the Sultan of Perak. We had played golf together in the past. During the audience we discussed his forth-coming State Visit to UK. This visit was due to take place in the last week of my Mayoralty. I think that everyone had agreed that it was appropriate that it should take place during my year of office. I asked his Majesty if he would be speaking in the Malay language at our Banquet. He replied that if any Malay was to be spoken on that occasion it should be spoken by me. After I had introduced Roger and Barbara as we were leaving, his Majesty said, 'We'll see you in half-an-hour.' We had arranged to play golf on a new course that had been built just outside Kuala Lumpur. In fact it is the course, which lies in the area in which we used to watch the bombing of terrorists all those years ago. Wyn came along and she and the wife of the Mayor of Kuala Lumpur had fun taking it in turns to drive along in a golf-buggy. Apart from the personal aspects of our visit I believe that it resulted in a considerable amount of Malaysian investment in UK. Companies such as Lotus Cars and LEC who make refrigerators, are now owned by Malaysian companies.

I think that Duncan Slater enjoyed our visit. I am sure that he met a lot of the ordinary people of Malaysia that he would not otherwise have met. We certainly enjoyed it.

We moved on to Singapore. For a Socialist Lee Kuan Yew had enthusiastically embraced Mrs Thatcher's property-owning democracy ideas. With the booming economy the Singapore Housing Authority was selling homes as fast as they could build them. We were taken to meet some of the people who were buying their homes. They appeared to be very happy with them. Singapore was also embracing new technology in a big way. We visited a kindergarten at a Mosque. They had one room with about twenty computers on desks around the walls. In a kindergarten! At the Singapore Monetary Authority we met Teh Kok Peng, one of Douglas's friends from Oxford. He was by then a very senior officer of that body.

Next stop was Sarawak, famous as the home of the Brooke family the 'White Rajahs' who ruled it until 1940. Sarawak lies on the Western side of the island of Borneo. Borneo is divided into four parts; Sabah and Sarawak, which are both part of Malaysia; the Indonesian region called Kalimantan; and Brunei, which is an independent Sultanate. In the 1960s there was a long-running dispute between Malaysia and Indonesia about the borders of Sabah and Sarawak and Kalimantan. It was called 'Confrontation' or as the Indonesians called it 'Confrontasi'. British troops were heavily involved. One evening Wyn and I were at a function in the Sultan of Selangor's palace. Wyn was sitting next to Tun Razak, who at that time was Deputy Prime Minister. Tun Razak was called away to take a phone-call. When he returned he seemed quite excited. He said to Wyn, 'You are the first person to be told, confrontation is now over.' Both Sabah and Sarawak have large areas of forest. In spite of legislation designed to protect these tropical rain forests one of their great problems is illegal logging. The loggers have been getting away with it for years and see no reason to stop. The tropical rain forest is being seriously depleted.

In Sarawak we visited an orang utan rehabilitation centre. 'Orang Utan' in the Malay language means 'Jungle Person'. In the past, people in rural areas kept baby orang utans as pets. Often these had been orphaned when the mother had been illegally killed. Baby orang utans grow up to quite a large size. Some are enormous. They were then killed or abandoned in the jungle. Because they had been reared by humans they could not fend for themselves in the jungle and died. The Government had outlawed the practice of keeping orang utans as pets. Anyone who had one had to surrender it to the government. Such animals were taken to the rehabilitation centre with a view to reintroducing them gradually into the jungle. They were meeting with mixed success. Some of the animals had been so long associated with humans that there was little chance of getting them back into their natural habitat. Others when released would start off by staying away for a day or two at a time and then would gradually leave completely. This usually happened when the animal had found a mate in the jungle. The young zoologist in charge was very enthusiastic and people were bringing her other animals to look after. She showed us a large bird with a broken wing. I think that it was a sea eagle. She said that someone had found it on the golf course. Quite without thinking I said, 'Someone got a birdie.' Stupidly, I then tried to explain what I meant. I could hear myself getting deeper and deeper into the mire as I tried to explain a golfing term to someone who quite obviously knew nothing about golf. In the background John Ansell and Roger were killing themselves laughing. At a Cultural Evening that we attended in Sarawak we were invited to go up on to the stage to try to perform the dances that we had seen. Poor Barbara went over on her ankle and cracked a bone in her foot.

We then moved on to oil-rich Brunei Darussalam. The first time that I visited Brunei was in 1965. Then the only hotel in Bandar Seri Bagawan the capital was a very seedy place with single unshaded light bulbs in the corridors and rooms and paint peeling off the walls. There were flies everywhere. It was straight out of Somerset Maugham. I had arrived on the Thursday afternoon when every-thing shuts down. They operate a sort of double weekend. They close on the Thursday in preparation for the Islamic day of prayer on the Friday. They then close on the Saturday for the weekend. That time I had people to call on including the present Sultan's father. I was bringing a message from my friend the Sultan of Selangor to him. I had to wait around doing nothing until the Monday. I had finished the book I had brought with me and could not even buy a new one. It was a very long weekend.

There is great respect for Winston Churchill in Brunei. There is a Churchill Museum where among the other items, is a bronze statue of Winston. It is one of three cast about the same time. One is at Westminster; one is in the Guildhall and the third in Brunei. I did not know about the Museum on my first visit to Brunei. It certainly would have relieved the boredom.

On this visit it was different. We were staying at the new Sheraton Hotel. From the minute we arrived until we left we were kept pretty busy. Brunei is quite small but is seriously rich. The people of Brunei are Malays. At one time there was talk of Brunei becoming part of Malaysia, but I suspect that they found it better to hold on to their independence and their oil revenues. Every Brunei citizen is entitled to a non-contributory old-age pension. I visited a housing site where the houses were being built for civil servants to purchase. Low interest loans were available. The amount of the loan varied according to the salary of the civil servant. The relationship with Britain is very cordial. The army to all intents and purposes is a battalion of Ghurkas supplied by us. As we had found in Pakistan everywhere we went we had two motorcycle outriders. In Brunei anyone on the road at the same time was moved to the side for us to pass.

I found His Majesty the Sultan very easy to talk to. We had a meaningful discussion regarding the suitability of the UK as a place for investment. This was important when talking with one of the richest men in the world. The conversation was held in the Malay language. Initially we spoke through and interpreter but when the Sultan found out that I spoke the language he was very happy to converse directly. As I was leaving the interpreter laughingly said, 'If we have more visitors like you I will be out of a job.'

In the meantime Wyn was visiting His Majesty's two wives. According to Islamic teaching a man can have up to four wives but he must not favour one above the others. The Sultan of Brunei adheres to this doctrine. The wives have separate palaces. When he travels they both go along. Wyn found that when the wives heard that she had lived in Malaysia and spoke the language they were more than happy to speak to her without the intervention of an interpreter. Wyn said that she had also been shown the Royal Stables where 300 polo ponies were kept in air-conditioned comfort. His Majesty had a team of professional polo players who came from Argentina.

In the evening we were entertained at a dinner that was nominally hosted by the famous or infamous Prince Jefri at Istana Edinburgh. Apart from being Minister of Finance, Prince Jefri was Chairman of Royal Brunei Airlines, Chairman of Brunei Shell Petroleum and head of the Jasra Group, which was the Royal Family's private company. Not long after our visit it was discovered that Prince Jefri had lost billions of dollars belonging to the State of Brunei. There were all sorts of stories about him. One was that he sent seven of his friends Mercedes Benz cars to celebrate his birthday. He was reported to own 2000 cars himself. I presume that he kept them at various places around the world because 2000 cars would just about fill all the roads in Brunei. In fact Prince Jefri did not arrive at the dinner. With his apologies he sent Wyn a lovely piece of Kain Songket. That is the brightly coloured Malay cloth with silver thread woven through it. The dinner was actually hosted by Yang Amat Mulia Pengiran Haji Bahrin, the Minister of Law. He was most hospitable, remembering me from my first big arbitration, which was related to the construction of the Port at Muara in Brunei. At the time he had not long been qualified and had come over to Singapore where we had held our first meeting. After an excellent dinner the Pengiran took us to see the floodlit golf course. Not only were the fairways floodlit but also the trees had fairy lights woven through the branches. Since there was no one playing I asked whether they turned off the lights. The answer was that the lights were kept on all night. The golf course had its own power station. The overall impression is that in Brunei money does not matter in the way that ordinary people think about it.

A flight on a Royal Brunei Airlines is a real eye-opener. The toilets on the plane are quite opulent. The toilet-seats are like armchairs and the fittings are all gold plated. At least I presume that they are plated. Being Brunei they might be solid gold.

The first impression of Manila is how congested it is. The traffic was horrendous. I was interviewed for radio and television a number of times. The main concern seemed to be that British companies were not investing in the Philippines. I visited the port at Subic Bay. It is a marvellous natural deep-water harbour strategically located for the whole of Asia. It was first used for trading by the Spaniards. The Americans had developed it as a naval base during the Vietnam War. When the time came to renegotiate the terms of lease for its future use by the Americans, some hard bargaining took place. Eventually an agreement was hammered out. When the agreement was put before the Philippine Senate they refused to ratify it. They thought that they could squeeze more out of the Americans. The Americans walked away. The Filipinos had either forgotten or ignored the fact that with the conclusion of the Vietnam War the Americans had no great need for the base. The effect on the local economy was devastating. It was estimated that over eighty thousand jobs were lost. Forty thousand in the naval base itself and forty thousand outside. Now they were left with a large number of houses, industrial buildings, offices and even a golf course. Given its location it was ideally suited to be developed as an industrial site. The local people who had previously been employed on the base were voluntarily keeping the area tidy by cutting the grass and clearing the weeds from the golf course. They were also guarding the houses against vandalism. When I returned home I was talking to a friend about the possibilities as an industrial site. He said that they were looking at it. Eventually they did put up a factory at Subic Bay. I believe that eventually the whole site was filled.

Wyn was taken to see an orphanage for 'street children'. Many of these children were the result of liaisons between members of the American armed forces and local women. Their plight was dreadful. Some of them had spent their early years living on the rubbish tips. Although in the orphanage they could do little more than provide basic food and shelter it was a hundred times better than they had experienced before. When Wyn told me about the orphanage, I remembered reading about how, the City of London had, around the year 1610 begun sending its 'street children' to Virginia. A descendant of one of these 'street children' provided a large sum of money to start the Peabody Trust that provides low-cost housing in London.

The flight from Manila to Subic Bay had been interesting. The plane was a small single-engined monoplane. We and our luggage were weighed together. While the engine was warming up the pilot was sitting in his seat having a smoke. When take-off time came he threw the remains of his cigarette out of the window, slid it shut and off we went. We did not fly very high, in fact we rather hedge hopped. We had a lovely view of the ground from the plane.

Last months as Lord Mayor

Most Lord Mayors take a longer trip abroad during August but we had to be back for the beginning of the Edinburgh Festival. We returned from Manila on 13th August and left for Edinburgh the following day. In Scotland I had visited Glasgow and of course I visited Edinburgh several times. One of these occasions was when I was invited to speak at the Centenary Celebration of the Edinburgh Merchants' Golf Club. My nephew Gordon Hunter is a member of the Committee. At a Committee meeting they were discussing who they could get to speak. The suggested speakers were all too expensive. Eventually Gordon suggested the Lord Mayor of London. There were howls of derision. 'Why on earth would the Lord Mayor of London agree to speak at our function?' was the question. 'Because he is my uncle,' was the reply. We managed to find a weekend when I was free and I was happy to oblige.

Norman Irons, the Lord Provost, had invited us to the Edinburgh Festival, which starts in August every year. I arranged to take a team of golfers to play against the Lord Provost's team. Through my brother-in-law Bill Hunter who was a member we arranged for the match to be played at the Royal Burgess Golf Club that is one of the oldest golf clubs in Scotland. We also arranged for members of the team to play at Luffness where Bill is also a member. They also played at Muirfield. My team consisted of members of Livery Companies. The Lord Provost's team was captained by the Captain of the Royal Burgess, Peter Collins, and half of them were members of Royal Burgess. I think our team managed to half one match and lost all the rest. But everyone had a wonderful time.

We arranged to have a Livery Dinner at the Marine Hotel in North Berwick where the team would be based. When we were arranging for the dinner the hotel manager asked how many we expected to attend. I said that I thought that we would probably have about 100. We notified all the Livery Companies about the Dinner. Mark Carnegie-Brown, who was the Household Officer in charge of the arrangements, was nearly overwhelmed with applications. He contacted the hotel regarding the maximum number. He told them that he had 350 applications. They said that they had never had as many as that for a dinner before but that they could cater for that number. Later applicants went on a waiting list. In the event 350 sat down to a dinner for Liverymen of the City of London in Scotland. One of our guest speakers was the Lord Provost. In his speech Norman referred to the fact that he had been born in Glasgow. Immediately he said it the fire alarm went off and we had to evacuate the hotel. It was a false alarm. In my speech I said that perhaps the Lord Provost of Edinburgh saying that he had been born in Glasgow had been inflammatory enough to set off the alarm.

The Lord Provost entertained us very generously. The match had been arranged to coincide with the start of the Festival. We were all invited to the Festival Parade, the Opening Concert and I took the salute at the Tattoo. The whole trip was enjoyed enormously by us all. People keep asking when we can do it again.

The Remembrancer called me one day to say that Sir Patrick Wright and Alex Allen wished to come to see me. Sir Patrick was Head of the Civil Service and Alex was in charge of the Prime Minister's private office. The meeting was set up. The news was not good. The Prime Minister had decided that there should be an end to what were described as 'automatic honours'. It was considered that the GBE, which Lord Mayors had been awarded since the early sixties, was such an automatic honour. Previously both the Sheriffs had been knighted. The Lord Mayor was therefore a Knight when he took up his office. He then received a Baronetcy, which is hereditary. When in 1964 the Government stopped awarding hereditary honours the title of Knight Grand Cross of the Most Excellent Order of the British Empire (GBE) was substituted.

The Prime Minister had said that the only people who would in future receive automatic honours would be High Court judges. I asked why there was to be this exception. I was told that the Prime Minister felt that judges trying cases that involved the Government should not feel that an honour was in jeopardy if they found against the Government. My snort of derision could have been heard in

Westminster. I said that most of the judges that I knew were not so venal as to allow their judgements to be influenced by the thought of a knighthood.

I argued that to get to be Lord Mayor one had to devote at least twelve years to the service of the City. This service included sitting as a Magistrate and giving up a considerable amount of time to civic duties. In the case of the City such duties were unpaid. I also pointed out that the Knighthood was one of the tools for performing the task of Lord Mayor. People at home and abroad expected that the first citizen of one of the most important Financial Centres in the world should be a person of distinction. In Britain a knighthood was a mark of such distinction.

It appeared that the Prime Minister had made up his mind and would not be moved. I suggested that I should go to see the Prime Minister and try to make him see the force of my arguments. The Civil Servants counselled against it.

One of the Aldermen, Sir Peter Levene, (now Lord Levene) was a government adviser. He was asked to find out whether it would be worthwhile for me to seek a meeting with the Prime Minister. He came back with the advice that it might do more harm than good. It would probably upset him. Perhaps this is why I have such negative feelings about John Major. I believe that when you make important decisions you should try to get as much information as there is available. In this instance it appeared that the message I was getting was that the Prime Minister did not want further information in case he discovered that he was making a mistake. I had no personal axe to grind. I already had my GBE.

I decided to try another tack. I arranged to see Her Majesty's Private Secretary, Robert Fellowes, the Lord Chancellor Lord Mackay and the Permanent Secretary at the Foreign Office, the late Lord Gillmore who was an old friend. I explained the problem to each of them. I had been hoping that in view of the close relationship which existed between the City and the Monarch she might see her way to award an incoming Lord Mayor an honour such as a Knight Commander of the Victorian Order (KCVO). Robert told me that knowing what I was coming to see him about he had already consulted Her Majesty. While sympathetic Her Majesty felt that the Prime Minister had made a political decision and that it would be wrong for her to be seen to be going against it. Although the Lord Mayor is the Chief Magistrate of the City the Lord Chancellor felt that there was nothing he could do to change the Prime Minister's mind. David Gillmore was quite gloomy. He said that he had to placate countries that were used to having a knight as ambassador. When they received a 'mister' they took it as an affront. In the end I was frustrated. I believed that the Civil Servants would soon get their automatic honours back and the only persons to lose out would be my successors. My immediate successor Paul Newall did receive a knighthood in the Birthday honours in June of his year of office.

We had a few days off at Praewood House before returning to the City on 31st August. Everything had been moved to the Mansion House. We had a quick look round when we arrived. The bed was enormous and stood about four feet high. I thought that Wyn would have to get a springboard. She could then do a running leap and bounce up on to the bed like one of those gymnasts in the Olympics. Eventually they had a step made so that she could get into bed more easily. Nobody had thought to tell the people who issue permits for overnight working in the City that we were coming back into the Mansion House. No sooner had we climbed into bed than an air-compressor with a drill attached opened up below our window. I rang the police to see if they could find out how long they were expecting to be working. Back came the reply, 'They say that they have a permit to work all night.' They stopped eventually but it took considerable persuasion.

Designed by George Dance and first occupied by the Lord Mayor when it was completed in 1753 the Mansion House is like a palace. What was the main entrance facing Poultry with its two separate flights of stone steps is now only used when the Lord Mayor returns at the end of the Lord Mayor's Show. For other functions the entrance on Bucklersbury is used.

The main public rooms are on the first floor. The Lord Mayor's office, which is in what is known as the Venetian Parlour, has a very ornate ceiling with intricately moulded plasterwork. There is then the Salon where the Lord Mayor receives guests at formal functions. Dinners are held in the magnificent Egyptian Hall with its spectacular gilded columns and beautiful curved ceiling. The gilded niches around the hall contain classical marble statues. The hall can seat 340 people for a dinner. Occasionally by using the high-level galleries that run round the upper levels, nearly 400 have been seated. These galleries are where an orchestra usually plays during a dinner. On the same floor as the Egyptian Hall there are also two parlours that are used for receptions. The Samuel Collection of paintings by 16th and 17th Dutch masters is hung on this floor. These superb paintings were donated to the City Corporation by the late Lord Samuel to be displayed in the Mansion House. The most well known of the paintings is 'The Lute-Player' by Frans Hals.

The private apartments are up above. Apart from the bedroom and dressing rooms for the Lord Mayor and the Lady Mayoress there are a private sitting room and a private dining room. There are also the two 'State bedrooms' for the use of the Lord Mayor's important guests. There is a ballroom. It has not as far as I know been used for a ball for many years. I believe that the grandchildren of one Lord Mayor found that it made an excellent roller-skating rink. There are also other spare bedrooms. The accommodation is very comfortable.

Susan Jeffries has written a superb book giving an enormous amount of detail about the refurbishment of the Mansion House. For anyone interested in the refurbishment of classical buildings it is well worth reading. The City Corporation never does anything by halves.

Everything has been restored as close to the original as was humanly possible. Because the City Corporation rarely throws anything away, they were able to look up the original sketches and receipts for the furniture. Some of the wooden arms of settees and chairs had at some time been gilded. The gilding was removed. There were comments that some of the materials used were garish in their colours. I pointed out that fashions had changed in the last 250 years and that in another 250 years the colours would have faded a bit. The morning after we moved in we had a ceremony where the Chief Commoner Douglas Woodward handed over to me a giant key. The Mansion House was back in use. I gladly paid my two dozen golf balls to Bill Row for our bet about him finishing the work on time. The Rector of the Parish in which the Mansion House is located is Rev. Dr. Chad Varah. We invited him to come and bless the refurbished Mansion House. He was happy to do so and when he came he prayed for all who would live and work there.

One of the most enjoyable perks of being Lord Mayor is the facility to have private lunches and dinners in the Mansion House. Of course due to the closure of the Mansion House for most of the year our lunches and dinners were held in the Ironmonger Lane house. Nevertheless people seemed to be very pleased to be invited. Having persuaded Michael Heseltine of the justice of our cause with regard to terrorist insurance we felt that we should invite him to dinner. As he came through the door of 11 Ironmonger Lane he exclaimed, 'I do not believe it! This is where I came to start work in my first job as a trainee accountant with Peat Marwick's.' I think that he said that it was in January 1954.

Another who came to dinner in Ironmonger Lane was the presenter of 'Desert Island Discs', Sue Lawley. She was greatly taken by the delightful paintings by Tissot that hung in the entrance hall. When we told her that they would not be going with us to the Mansion House, she suggested that she would organise a petition to get the Corporation to let us take them with us. We did not think that was a good idea but the thought was nice.

I used such lunches and dinners to promote my charities and to repay hospitality that I had received. They were also useful to obtain information about the countries that we were going to visit. We invited ambassadors and people who were doing business in those countries. On one occasion I invited George Graham, the then manager of Arsenal FC, to dinner. I knew that Tony Clarke, the then chairman of the Labour Party was a life-long Arsenal supporter so I invited him and his wife at the same time. He was a fellow parishioner of Father Robert's in St Albans. Now he is a member of the

House of Lords. I met Tony not long ago and he said that it was one of the most enjoyable dinners of his life.

A series of lunches are arranged where members of the Court of Aldermen and the Court of Common Council are invited in groups. The lunches are very informal. They are called 'en famille' lunches. Wyn and I held five of them and enjoyed them all. They are extremely useful in cementing the relationship between the Lord Mayor and the Members of the Common Council.

I had launched my Charities in the Guildhall. I suppose that if you are appealing on behalf of either Cancer relief or Children's' Charities they already have staff available who are engaged in fund-raising. People can easily relate to such Charities. Neither of my Charities was in that position. Douglas made available to me on a part-time basis his PA, Anne Marten. Anne, who was born in Malaysia of Chinese parents, is married to a former British diplomat Tim. She entered into the role of fund-raiser with enormous enthusiasm. She was very good at it. I had asked an extremely able and energetic man John Wilson, who was Chairman of the London Electricity Board, to be Chairman of my Charity Committee. He readily agreed and did an excellent job. John Williams had been most helpful to me over the years from when we first met when he was Secretary of Aldersgate Ward Club. He agreed to be Treasurer of the Committee.

Some Lord Mayors have a large number of charity events with the result that the City sometimes suffers from 'Charity fatigue'. To a large extent you can be hitting the same people time after time. We decided to restrict ourselves to the normal appeal to the Livery Companies and to have four major events. The City Corporation treats its staff well. In return the staff are extremely loyal and helpful. They organised two events for the Lord Mayor's Charity: 'City Dip', a swimming event, and a Karate exhibition. When I told my fellow Lord Mayors and Lord Provosts of this co-operation from the staff during our discussions in Chester they could scarcely believe it. For the majority of them the relationship with the Town Hall staff appeared to be barely concealed hostility. I found this extremely sad. Perhaps the reason for our good relationship is that the Corporation's staff are members of the Staff Association and outside unions have found it very difficult to get a foothold. We like to feel that the Corporation of London is in the forefront of local government employers.

The first of the four major events was a Malaysian Evening in the Guildhall. This was generously sponsored by the consortium of firms that were constructing the new Kuala Lumpur airport. A friend, Sir Robin Biggam, was the Chairman of the consortium, which consisted of Balfour Beatty, Trafalgar House, Jardine Matheson, GEC and Marubeni of Japan. They flew in cooks for Malaysian food, musicians and dancers: and hundreds of orchids to decorate the Guildhall. We had a fabulous evening. The Charity got off to a good start.

Ianthe took charge of the three dinners that we were organising once the Mansion House was reopened. We thought that it would be a good opportunity for members of the Livery to be able to see the results of the refurbishment. We held the dinners on three consecutive evenings. One night was sponsored by Unipart whose Chairman was another friend, John Neill. Another was sponsored by British Airways. The third had the wines sponsored by the Lowndes Lambert Group. The dinners were all sold out and were a great success. Everyone enjoyed seeing the results of the £14 million that had been spent on the refurbishment. When we reached the end of my Mayoralty the total amount in the Charity fund was £495,000. Our fund-raiser, Anne was determined that we would reach the nice round figure of £500,000. She phoned John Zochonis (now Sir John) in Manchester. He had been a very generous supporter. She told him the position and he found the final £5,000 from one of his Charitable Trusts.

Living in a palace can be strange but the design of the Mansion House is such that it is not overpowering. The private rooms were no larger than those in a number of houses that we had lived in. The huge public rooms could easily be thought of as being in some other building. Nevertheless we enjoyed living there. Private dinner parties took on a new dimension. When Wyn and I had decided to celebrate our 43rd Wedding Anniversary with a dinner and dance, Douglas and Ianthe joined in to celebrate their 14th Anniversary. All the staff at the Mansion House joined in to make the party a success. John Ansell found an excellent band to play Scottish Dance music. The leader also acted rather like the 'caller' for American Square Dancing. He talked us through the more complicated dances. By far the best dancers were His Excellency the Malaysian High Commissioner Dato' Kamaruddin and his wife Datin Jamayiah. They had both learned Scottish dancing at school in Malaysia. In such a setting as the Mansion House the party had to be a success but it really was something special.

Life as Lord Mayor is not entirely about dinners and speeches. If you are lucky you can be invited to major sporting events. The problem with going to such events as a VIP is that it spoils you from going as an ordinary person ever again. I was fortunate to be able go to Twickenham, Murrayfield and Wimbledon. Having lunch beforehand and then sitting in exceptionally good seats to watch the matches is an experience to be savoured. At Wimbledon we had lunch with some of the former great tennis players, then we watched some tennis from the Royal Box. After we had tea, we watched some more tennis. Then we had a drink and watched more tennis. It was a very good way to go to Wimbledon.

Lord Mayors also spend quite a lot of time in church. St. Paul's Cathedral is the official City church and when Aldermen attend City functions at St. Paul's they are seated up beyond the choir. When the Lord Mayor greets the Queen at St. Paul's he carries the City sword. I did not have such an occasion at St. Paul's during my year of office, but we went to Westminster Abbey for a Commonwealth Day service. It was very ecumenical with prayers said by representatives of a number of different religions. Roger Cork (now Sir Roger) was the Sheriff with me that day. We were seated so that Roger was immediately behind the choir. Roger's singing is on a par with mine. At one point in the service the choir moved to a different location to join up with another choir. I remarked to Roger that the choir had to move because of his singing. He got his revenge by presenting me on my birthday with a tape recording of him singing 'Happy Birthday' deliberately off key. It must be the worst recording ever made. With it came a beautiful knitted doll of a Scottish piper, which Barbara had managed to find.

The new Sheriffs, Alderman John Chalstrey and Jeremy Gotch, had been elected and installed. The out-going Sheriffs and their wives, Roger and Barbara Cork, and Tony and Jennifer Moss, had been a great support to Wyn and me. They were especially helpful to Wyn in the early days of my Mayoralty when Wyn was recovering from the accident. Barbara was marvellous. For a number of years she had suffered from cancer. Even after a bout of chemotherapy, which must have left her feeling awful, she would arrive for a function beautifully turned out and behaving as though she did not have a care in the world. If it can be said of anyone that they showed courage in their illness, it was Barbara. Sadly she died before Roger became Lord Mayor. Wyn and I agreed that with her caring nature and natural cheerfulness Barbara would have been an outstanding Lady Mayoress.

On the day after the new Sheriffs are installed the Lord Mayor for the ensuing year is elected. At the same time it is customary for a resolution to be passed by the Liverymen congratulating the Lord Mayor on his year of office. For me this happened on the 29th of September 1993. The terms of the Resolution are later transcribed into a beautifully illuminated address that is framed and presented to the Late Lord Mayor. The Resolution presented to me was:

In a meeting or assembly of the Mayor, Aldermen and Liverymen of the City of London in Common Hall assembled at the Guildhall on Wednesday the 29th day of September, 1993.

RESOLVED UNANIMOUSLY:-

That the Liverymen of the City of London in Common Hall assembled have very much pleasure in conveying to the

Right Honourable The Lord Mayor
SIR FRANCIS McWILLIAMS GBE BSc, FEng, DCL

their warmest congratulations on the distinguished manner in which he has discharged the exacting duties of his high office.

The year of office of Sir Francis has been a formidable success. His Lord Mayor's Show had the distinction of including Her Royal

Highness the Princess Royal as Master of the Worshipful Company of Loriners, the Lord Mayor's mother company. Later in the year, a Luncheon was given to mark the Fortieth Anniversary of Her Majesty the Queen's accession, thereby extending the Corporation's long-standing and valued relationship with the Royal Family.

Sir Francis McWilliams took as his theme **"The City and Industry in Partnership"** for which his long experience as a civil engineer, barrister and arbitrator equipped him so well. He has followed this theme both at home and abroad with great success. In April he visited, together with a team of businessmen, Islamabad, Karachi, Lahore and Nepal, extending the goodwill of the City and promoting business activity. In May he was in Rabat, Casablanca and Tangiers and June saw him in Warsaw and Poznan.

At the end of July and the beginning of August, his travels, to promote British companies and inward investment, together with the support of specific business and corresponding interests representing the construction and engineering sector, took him to Kuala Lumpur, Pergau, Langkawi, Kuching, Singapore, Brunei and Manila.

Sir Francis has also been very active in visiting cities in Great Britain with visits to Glasgow, Leicester, Edinburgh, Cardiff and Sheffield. Closer to home his leadership was appreciated when the City was, again, called upon to show its strength in overcoming the effects of terrorist activity. He has effectively used his skills in the campaign to retain St. Bartholemew's Hospital, the needs of Inner City education and the move to increase the number of High Court Judges. His charity appeal on behalf of the Register of Engineers for Disaster relief, or RedR as it is known, and the setting up of a Foundation for Manufacturing and Industry, has received considerable support from City institutions and matches his theme for the year.

These are just a few of his achievements in a year when the Livery have admired the tremendous energy, enthusiasm and commitment with which the Lord Mayor has promoted the financial, business and civic City during his outstanding year of office. They recall with pleasure the numerous events of the Mayoralty at all of which Sir Francis has most worthily upheld the traditions of the City.

We recall also the accident suffered by the Lady Mayoress prior to the start of the Mayoralty and everyone of us here today has the greatest admiration and respect for her bravery and resolution in fully supporting Sir Francis, during her recovery and throughout the year. Indeed the support of all the members of his family has been recognised by the Livery. It is appropriate, when the year has been marked by family involvement to close with the words of the Lady Mayoress when she said of Sir Francis that " His life and career are characterised by passions; for family, international understanding, practical professionalism, a love of the new and a great respect for tradition.

Also at the Election of his successor, although he still has some time to go before he hands over, it is the custom for the Lord Mayor to give a farewell speech to the Livery. In the speech the Lord Mayor thanks everyone who has helped him during his Mayoralty. The staffs at Mansion House and Guildhall deserve great praise for the way they set out to make each Lord Mayor's Year memorable. No matter how difficult the Lord Mayor and Lady Mayoress are, they remain dedicated to that task and their discretion is absolute. Then there are those who have helped with the Lord Mayor's Charity and the Chaplains. Certainly in my case my family had been of enormous help. I had got through this part successfully when I turned to thank Wyn. I had not got far when I had a flashback of Wyn lying unconscious on the trolley in the hospital with blood encrusting her nostrils and her ears. I nearly cracked up. Fortunately, I had mentioned her bravery after the accident and there was a burst of applause which gave me a little time to recover. However, I was shaking and finished off the speech very quickly. I was still shaking when I got back to the Mansion House. Michael Dicken the Lord Mayor's Private Secretary was as far as I know the only person who knew how close I had been to making an ass of myself. Poor Wyn was never adequately thanked in public for her wonderful support.

The Visits Committee had suggested a visit was due to Argentina. The dates set aside were four days in late October. I queried whether it was worth while travelling all that way for a short visit . Previous Lord Mayors who had gone to South America had visited several countries. Word came back that they were particularly keen for a visit. Our Ambassador in Buenos Aires was visiting London and came to see me to convince me of the importance that he attached to the visit. We again flew in the plane called 'The City of London'. When we were about to land in Buenos Aires, Wyn and I were invited into the cockpit by the pilot. As we were making our approach to the runway there was a plane taxiing along it. I did not believe that such a thing could happen. As he aborted the landing the pilot said that in all his years of flying this was the first time that he had seen such an incident.

After such a shaky start the visit went well. I did a number of television and radio interviews. At the end of each interview the interviewer would say, 'Lord Mayor, what do you think about the situation with regard to the Malvinas?' I was prepared for such a question and had decided on a stock answer. In each case I replied, 'I am sure that the present difficulties will not interfere with the deep friendship which so obviously exists between the people of Britain and the people of Argentina.' Each interviewer smiled and thanked me. Everybody was happy.

One of the fascinating things about Argentina is the number of people that you meet whose grandfathers and great-grandfathers came to Argentina to build the railways. We met some of them first when we went to the 'Hurlingham Club' for a lunch. The Club is used for golf and polo and is situated on the outskirts of Buenos Aires. I accepted an invitation to play a quick nine holes. We had some free time before the main dinner of our trip, which was to take place at the prestigious Jockey Club that evening. It rained a bit but I enjoyed the golf. I enquired as to what had happened to people of British extraction during the Falklands War. I expected to hear that they had been interned or restricted in some way. It appears that life continued pretty much as usual. They said that they kept a low profile and no one bothered them.

We had with us representatives of British companies who were interested in some large projects in Argentina. I am sure that this was the purpose of the exercise. Someone like the Lord Mayor who is non-political can be useful in obtaining entry to ministerial offices when there is a degree of political tension. I was welcomed wherever I went. On the second day we visited a number of ministries. What I found most interesting was that three of the ministers who I met were engineers. I doubt whether there have been many ministers in any British Government who were engineers. There is a saying that when you are in business you buy in your own language and sell in your customers' language. I was delighted to find that our businessmen could converse with the ministers that we met in fluent Spanish. They seemed to make good progress.

Towards the end of my Mayoral Year Wyn and I went to meet The Princess of Wales who was attending a Charity function in the City. Wyn said that we were coming to the end of our year. Rather poignantly the Princess replied, 'How lucky for you. I have to go on like this all the time.' What a sad reflection on what should have been a fairytale life. Time was rapidly running out on my Mayoralty but we had one more visit to make. We had been invited to visit Tyldesley. The invitation had come about in a strange fashion. Apparently the *Manchester Evening News* arranged to rent a train and sponsor a day out in London for their readers. The trip was to coincide with my Lord Mayor's Show. The idea was that after seeing the Show the participants could spend the rest of the day shopping. In connection with the trip our PR department was asked if they could arrange for the Lord Mayor-Elect to do a radio interview by phone. This was arranged. During the interview I mentioned that I had once lived in the Manchester area in Tyldesley. A couple of days later someone rang up to ask whether it was true that I had lived in Tyldesley. Apparently they were trying to find out if I was the same person as the captain of Tyldesley Rugby Club in the early fifties. Someone had been looking out old newspaper cuttings in which I was mentioned. The visit was duly arranged. The President of the Club was Jim Lewis who had played in the team that I had captained. We had a lunch attended by the Mayor of the Metropolitan Borough of Wigan and other local dignitaries. They had also managed to get hold of ten of the players from the team that I had captained. There was a match afterwards that we stayed to watch. Clearly, they had decided that I was a 'Tyldesley lad' and seemed to be quite proud of their former captain. It was a very happy occasion. Afterwards we paid a visit to Stonyhurst where Douglas and Michael had been educated.

There cannot have been many Lord Mayors who were able to look forward to welcoming an old friend as a visiting head of State.

The Yang DiPertuan Agong of Malaysia was still Raja Azlan Shah, the Sultan of the State of Perak. When I first met him in the early sixties he was a High Court Judge. At the time he had just bought a site and was building a house in Petaling Jaya. He still owns the house. From time to time we played golf together usually as part of HRH the Sultan of Selangor's team. Raja Azlan rose up the judicial ladder. He became the Lord President of the Council, that is the head of the Malaysian judicial system. The Sultan of Perak died. Raja Azlan was chosen as Sultan of Perak. Within a matter of months he was elected Timbalan Yang DiPertuan Agong (Deputy King). This meant that in another five years or so he would become King. The twist was that the King to whom he was Deputy was the Sultan of Johore. As a young man before he became Sultan of Johore, the King had been sentenced to three years in jail in connection with a shooting incident. The judge who sentenced him was Raja Azlan Shah.

When I was Sheriff Wyn took a phone-call at the Old Bailey. It was from a judge who was a Bencher at Lincoln's Inn who wanted to speak to me. As I was not available Wyn asked if she could help. He told her that they wished to propose a Malaysian Sultan who was a member of the Inn to become a Bencher but that they did not know too much about him. Wyn asked who it was. When she heard that it was Raja Azlan she said, 'He was Head of the Malaysian Judiciary, he is the Sultan of the State of Perak, he is the Deputy King and most important of all he is a friend of ours'. Wyn then asked the judge if he would like me to call him. He said that there was no need to do so as she had given him all the information that he needed. Wyn claims that she is probably the only person who has been asked to give a reference for a Sultan.

While he was Deputy King Raja Azlan and I had met at a party in London when he was on a visit. We worked out that if things went according to plan I would be Lord Mayor during the period when he was King. We decided that we would try to arrange things so that he could be invited to come on a State Visit during my Mayoralty. There were quite a number of hurdles to overcome but suddenly it all came to fruition. Tuesday 9th November found me with the two

294

new Sheriffs, Alderman John Chalstrey and Jeremy Gotch, at Victoria Station to meet the Yang DiPertuan Agong who was arriving from Malaysia. Before the train pulled in we were lined up. After Her Majesty and the other members of the royal family who were present, came the Prime Minister and two members of the Cabinet, then the Lord Mayor and the Sheriffs. The rest of the line comprised those who were going to accompany the Agong on his visit. Her Majesty brought the Agong along the line introducing everyone. When they reached me the Agong said, 'Hullo Frank, how are you getting on?' Her Majesty smiled and said, 'You know each other then?' That evening I took along with me to Buckingham Palace a draft of what I had written to start off my speech in the Malay language. I knew that I would meet some of the people from the Malaysian High Commission. During the reception I found one of the senior staff and showed him what I proposed to say. He read it carefully and suggested changing one of the words. I was quite happy until he added, 'The trouble is that you speak old-fashioned Malay.' I was suitably deflated.

Our banquet in the Guildhall was very colourful. All the Malaysians were in their National Dress and there were the usual collection of tiaras, stars and sashes. During the meal I showed the Agong what I proposed to say in Malay and told him what had been said about it. He said that what I proposed to say was fine and he added that the problem with many of the younger generation was that they did not speak 'proper' Malay. I was pleased with his endorsement. When I started my speech in the Malay language there was a buzz around the hall. To give the King and Queen of Malaysia their full titles involves saying, 'Duli Duli Yang Maha Mulia Seri Paduka Baginda Yang DiPertuan Agong dan Raja Permaisuri Agong.' When I got this out without stumbling the Malaysians applauded enthusiastically. I welcomed their Majesties on behalf of the citizens of London. I then said that as everyone in the hall spoke better English than I did the Malay language it would be better if I spoke in English. Not since Sir Alexander Graham welcomed the President of Poland Lech Walesa in what appeared to be perfect Polish, has a foreign language speech been greeted in the Guildhall with such enthusiasm. The Agong was delighted and delivered his speech in perfect English.

The following evening Wyn and I attended the Dinner given by the Yang DiPertuan Agong in honour of Her Majesty the Queen and the Duke of Edinburgh at the Dorchester Hotel.

On Friday 12th November 1993 in the Silent Ceremony at Guild-hall I handed over to my successor Alderman Paul Newall the symbols of the Office of Lord Mayor of London. After returning to the Mansion House to have a cup of tea and to say, 'Goodbye' to the staff, Wyn and I went off to Douglas and Ianthe's house in Regents Park. My Mayoralty, which had started so badly, had finished on a high note. That evening the Benchers of Lincoln's Inn were giving a Dinner in honour of the Yang DiPertuan Agong. So there we were dining with him for the fourth time in a week. In Lincoln's Inn if the Chaplain is not present the custom is that the Junior Bencher says the Graces before and after the meal and also proposes the toast to the Queen. On this occasion the Chaplain was absent. At lunchtime I had still been a Very Important Person. By dinnertime I was 'Junior'.

After the mayoralty

It is the custom in the City that after the Lord Mayor's Banquet which is given in his honour the Late Lord Mayor does not appear in the City until the Easter Banquet when he is welcomed back. The Easter Banquet is attended by the Secretary of State for Foreign Affairs and members of the Diplomatic Corps. Because they are in office for only one year it is difficult for Lord Mayors to make a great impact. When they come back to the City after five months absence they find that many people even in the City cannot remember who had been Lord Mayor the previous year.

Because the press had supported some of my initiatives and because of the publicity engendered by the bomb I had achieved a modicum of public recognition. Nevertheless about eight months after the end of my year I found out how fleeting such recognition can be. I was a guest at a Livery Dinner and was seated next to one of the senior Past Masters of the company. He knew that I was an Alderman. During the course of our conversation he asked me when I expected to be Lord Mayor and seemed surprised when I said that I had already been Lord Mayor. He did not ask when I had been in office and I hadn't the heart to tell him that it was only a matter of months since I had moved from Mansion House.

I did however have a balancing experience some eighteen months later. I was standing on the platform of Camden Town Underground Station waiting for a train and I was watching some mice playing between the rails. An Afro-Caribbean man standing next to me was watching them also and we fell into conversation. While we were chatting, he suddenly said, 'You were Lord Mayor of London weren't you?' I was astonished and admitted that I had been. I asked him whether he was connected with the City. He replied that he was not but that he had a good memory for faces. What a boost to my ego that I was remembered that day in Camden Town.

At the first meeting of the Common Council in the new Mayoralty, in accordance with custom, the Common Council passed a motion thanking the Late Lord Mayor for his year as Lord Mayor. A copy of the resolution was presented to me again in the form of an illuminated address written in beautiful script. The motion sums up my year in the following terms:

A Common Council holden in the Guildhall of the City of London on Thursday the second day of December 1993.

RESOLVED UNANIMOUSLY:

That this court takes the greatest possible pleasure in recording its appreciation of the valuable services rendered by

SIR FRANCIS McWILLIAMS G.B.E., B.Sc., F.Eng., D.C.L., **as Lord Mayor of the City of London**

Sir Francis McWilliams brought with him to office many years of practical experience as an engineer and arbitrator in this country and abroad, mostly in the Far East. That experience led him to adopt as his theme for the year 'The City and Industry in Partnership' and The Register of Engineers for Disaster Relief or 'RedR' as the subject of his Mayoral Appeal.

In the year when the Single European Market officially began, Sir Francis made it clear that co-operation between the financial expertise usually associated with the City and Britain's manufacturing should be maintained and strengthened if the country was to compete successfully in Europe and the wider international markets. On trips around the country, the Lord Mayor sought to strengthen that co-operation by reminding his listeners of the expertise available within the Square Mile and of the tremendous potential opportunities available when the City and Industry worked 'in partnership'.

Successful Mayoral trips to Islamabad, Karachi, Lahore and Nepal, to Rabat, Casablanca and Tangiers, to Warsaw and Poznan and to Buenos Aires were supported by teams of businessmen with a combined objective of extending the goodwill of the City and promoting business activity. In the summer, Sir Francis led a team, specialising in engineering and construction projects, to Kuala Lumpur, Pergau, Langkawi, Kuching Singapore, Brunei and Manila, where his and Lady McWilliams fluency in the Malay language and their personal knowledge of the area were to be particularly useful.

At home Sir Francis and Lady McWilliams were based at 11, Ironmonger Lane for most of the year but were able to appreciate the rather grander facilities of Mansion House for a couple of months when the House was re-opened in September, on schedule, following two years of major refurbishment works.

During the year, the late Lord Mayor had the honour of extending a welcome on behalf of this Ancient City to the President of the Portuguese Republic and Senhora Soares and to His Majesty the Yang DiPertuan Agong of Malaysia and Her Majesty the Raja Permaisuri Agong of Malaysia on their State visits to this country, and to His Excellency the President of the Ukraine and Mrs Kravchuk. Both on these occasions and at the memorable special luncheon in Guildhall to Her Majesty the Queen and HRH The Prince Philip, Duke of Edinburgh, to mark and celebrate the 40th Anniversary of Her Majesty's Accession, the Lord Mayor worthily upheld the great traditions of the Corporation of London as host to Royal and distinguished visitors.

On behalf of the very many people who live and work in or just visit the City, Sir Francis continued to press, with all vigour, for much needed improvements in the public transport infrastructure and against the threatened closure of vital medical facilities at St Bartholomew's Hospital, all of which are essential to the future welfare of the City.

In April the resolve of the City and the preparedness of its various services were again challenged by terrorists but the practical experience and leadership of the Lord Mayor did much to show the rest of the World that life in the City could not be brought to a halt by such mindless acts of violence.

In thanking Sir Francis, we acknowledge the tremendous support given by his wife WYN, who has won our heartfelt admiration for the way in which she refused to let the injuries, that she suffered in a motor accident just prior to the start of the Mayoral Year, interfere with her duties. We wish **Lady McWilliams** a full recovery and trust that she and Sir Francis will enjoy many years of good health and happiness during which they will look back with well-deserved pride at a job well done.

The motion is signed by Sam Jones who, at that time, was the Town Clerk. Between them, the motion and the Livery resolution pretty well summarise my year as seen by those involved in the City.

Wyn has said on occasions when we have subsequently attended a function at the Mansion House that it is difficult to think that we once lived there. Sometimes too I look back and think, 'Did all this really happen to me?'